REMAINS
Historical and Literary
CONNECTED WITH
THE PALATINE COUNTIES OF
Lancaster and Chester

VOLUME XXXVIII – THIRD SERIES

MANCHESTER
Printed for the Chetham Society
1994

The Letters of Thomas Langton, Flax Merchant of Kirkham, 1771–1788

Edited by

Joan Wilkinson, M.A., M.Phil., Ph.D.

General Editor: J. K. Walton

MANCHESTER
Printed for the Chetham Society
1994

To the memory of my mother and father
Constance and Leonard Wilkinson
with love

The Letters of Thomas Langton,
Flax Merchant of Kirkham, 1771–1788
by Dr Joan Wilkinson

Published for the Society by Carnegie Publishing Ltd,
18 Maynard Street, Preston
Typeset in Linotype Stempel Garamond by Carnegie Publishing
Printed and bound in the UK by Cambridge University Press

British Library Cataloguing-in-Publication Data
Wilkinson, Joan
  Letters of Thomas Langton, Flax Merchant of Kirkham
  1771–1788. — (Chetham Society Series; Vol. 38)
  I. Title II. Series
  941.006

ISBN 0-948789-91-3

Contents

Foreword

The Langton papers were deposited in the Lancashire Record Office in 1952 by Miss F. M. Langton, with the hope that they might be useful. Miss Langton died in 1963. Her grandfather, William Langton, the letter writer's grandson, was the founder treasurer of the Chetham Society, subsequently secretary, and the editor of three Chetham Miscellanies and several other volumes on one of which he was working at the time of his death in 1881. The Advertisement to the first Miscellany, in 1851, asking for further material, including letters, to be sent to him, took the opportunity

> of reminding the members of the Chetham Society, and others who have an interest in antiquarian pursuits, that good service may be rendered to the future labourers in the field of historical research by rescuing from oblivion materials hitherto buried in private collections. Nothing which tends to throw light on the habits, customs, and institutions of our race, can be uninteresting to those who make mankind their study.

How better to make the Langton letters 'useful' than by rescuing them from oblivion and placing them in their historical context?

I hope that William Langton would have approved this edition of his grandfather's letters, released, some 140 years after his own first excursion into editing for the Society, to 'labourers in the field of historical research' in which he himself laboured so valiantly for so long.

Great Eccleston
February 1991

Acknowledgements

My greatest debt is to Dr John Walton of Lancaster University, for his interest, encouragement and constructive criticism. I am grateful to Dr Bob Bliss, also of Lancaster, for enlarging for me the American dimension. I thank the staffs of the Lancaster City Reference Library; the National Maritime Museum, Greenwich; the Museum of Textile History, Helmshore; the Hull Central Library; the Northern Marine branch of the Royal Insurance (UK); Lloyds of London; the Manchester Local History Library; the Public Record Office, Kew; the British Library; and especially the staffs of the Lancaster University Library and the Lancashire Record Office, Preston. Mrs Doreen Moss and Mrs June Grove have made my visits to the London libraries an excuse for enjoying their hospitality. Mrs Sylvia Berry has nobly grappled with my manuscript and without Miss Mary Roberts's assiduous checking of transcripts and proofs the book would not have been possible. To all these, and to all the many other friends who have, willy-nilly, listened without complaint to the latest reports on the Langtons, my grateful thanks.

Abbreviations

LRO	Lancashire Record Office
PRO	Public Record Office
LC	Lancaster City Library
LU	Lancaster University Library
Cam. Soc.	Camden Society
Chet. Soc.	Chetham Society
Ec. Hist.	Economic History
Ec. Hist. Rev.	Economic History Review
HSLC	Historic Society of Lancashire and Cheshire

The Langton Family

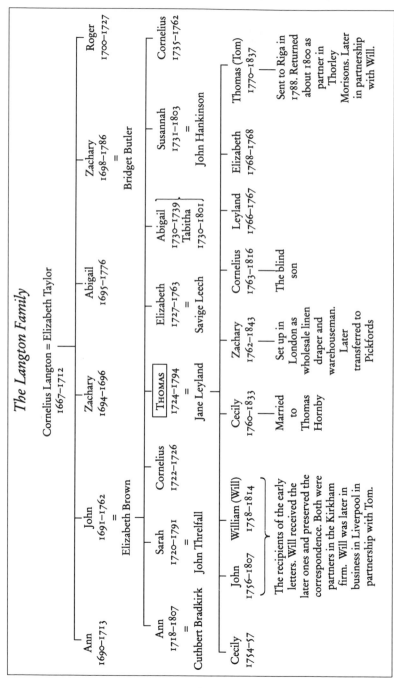

Cornelius Langton = Elizabeth Taylor
1667–1712

Ann 1690–1713

John 1691–1762 = Elizabeth Brown

Zachary 1694–1696

Abigail 1695–1776

Zachary 1698–1786 = Bridget Butler

Roger 1700–1727

Ann 1718–1807 = Cuthbert Bradkirk

Sarah 1720–1791 = John Threlfall

Cornelius 1722–1726

THOMAS 1724–1794 = Jane Leyland

Elizabeth 1727–1763 = Savige Leech

Abigail 1730–1739

Tabitha 1730–1801

Susannah 1731–1803 = John Hankinson

Cornelius 1735–1762

Cecily 1754–57

John 1756–1807

William (Will) 1758–1814

The recipients of the early letters. Will received the later ones and preserved the correspondence. Both were partners in the Kirkham firm. Will was later in business in Liverpool in partnership with Tom.

Cecily 1760–1833

Married to Thomas Hornby

Zachary 1762–1843

Set up in London as wholesale linen draper and warehouseman. Later transferred to Pickfords

Cornelius 1763–1816

The blind son

Leyland 1766–1767

Elizabeth 1768–1768

Thomas (Tom) 1770–1837

Sent to Riga in 1788. Returned about 1800 as partner in Thorley Morisons. Later in partnership with Will.

x

Introduction

SECTION I: PUBLIC LIFE

The Langton Letters

The Langton letters were written by Thomas Langton, flax merchant of Kirkham, to his two eldest sons, John, born 1756, and Will, born 1758. The first twenty-six letters were written to the boys at boarding school from 1771 to 1773. They form a reasonably continuous correspondence, at least one letter being written each month. The letters of the next fifteen years were written when either Thomas Langton or his second son was away from Kirkham. They do not form a continuous correspondence, and there are no letters covering seven of the fifteen years. Yet, in spite of this apparent paucity, they are an informative and seminal source. From the letters as a whole we may form an opinion about most of the facets of Thomas Langton's life, both business and personal.

A reading of the letters is reinforced by some valuable subsidiary material, both primary and secondary. Langtons of the two generations following Thomas wrote letters and memoirs which were privately printed.[1] Kirkham is rich in extant town records, and R. Cunliffe Shaw's monumental work on Kirkham in Amounderness,[2] published in 1949, is invaluable for reference. F. J. Singleton's article on 'The Flax Merchants of Kirkham'[3] was the pioneer work which brought the letters to public notice. From these, and some minor sources, it is possible to trace the evolution of the Langton firm, and to follow the fortunes of the family throughout the eighteenth century and, indeed, beyond, placing the period of the letters in historical context.

[1] Anne Langton, *The Story of Our Family*, privately printed, 1881. Thomas Langton, *Letters of Thomas Langton to Mrs Thomas Hornby 1815–1818*, privately printed, Manchester, 1900.
[2] R. Cunliffe Shaw, *Kirkham in Amounderness*, Preston, 1947.
[3] F. J. Singleton, 'The Flax Merchants of Kirkham', *Historic Society of Lancashire and Cheshire*, 1977, pp. 73–108.

We must, however, acknowledge that the source material, evocative as it is, is by no means comprehensive. There are no business documents of any kind relating to the Langton firm. There is much omitted from the letters as well as much included. There must remain much we do not know about Thomas Langton as well as much we do. But there is certainly sufficient for us to recognise him as an individual, and to understand something of his personality and of his approach to the business which occupied so much of his life, and to the family which sustained him emotionally.

The Fylde is not blessed with many records of this kind. Indeed, the diary of Thomas Tyldesley, the Catholic recusant of Myerscough Lodge, written between 1712 and 1714,[4] is the only one comparable with the Langton letters, and the letters contain a much greater variety of historical interest. From them, as we establish a perspective, we may measure the Langton experience against historians' perceptions of the late eighteenth century and come to an assessment of where this particular man stood in relation to his immediate forbears, his personal contacts and his immediate descendants, for, as Roy Porter reminds us, it can be highly misleading to isolate a man from his times.[5] We must endeavour to place Thomas Langton in as complete a context as we can if we are to appreciate the letters to the full.

The eighteenth century was the century of the merchants. The rich venturers of the main sea ports such as Bristol or Liverpool, the powerful city fathers of Leeds, the predominant influences on the Hull Aldermanic bench, were merchants, men of substance and the 'mainspring of the eighteenth-century economy'.[6] Merchant trading was an honourable and, if successful, lucrative way of life, but those in the top stratum of the merchant hierarchy did not have any hand in making what they sold. The Leeds merchants, for instance, who handled so much of Yorkshire's woollen cloth, supervised only the finishing of the fabric, acquiring it from a wide hinterland of producers, who sold it to them.[7] The merchants of the ports dealt with a variety of merchandise and traded with many parts of the world.

---

[4] Joseph Gillow and Anthony Hewitson, eds., *The Tyldesley Diary*, Preston, 1873.
[5] Roy Porter and W. F. Bynum, eds., *Medical Fringe and Medical Orthodoxy 1700-1850*, 1987, p. 56.
[6] Gordon Jackson, *Hull in the Eighteenth Century*, Oxford, 1972, p. 262.
[7] R. G. Wilson, *Gentlemen Merchants. The Merchant Community in Leeds 1700-1830*, Manchester, 1971, p. 59.

If they had any other interests, they were secondary to their activities as merchants.[8]

In lesser splendour were the merchant-manufacturers, who made and sold a single commodity. They put out work to workpeople (who executed it either in their own homes or were gathered into workshops) and sometimes gave work to hundreds of employees.[9] These merchant-manufacturers were also often wealthy and, though less elevated socially than the merchants proper, they had considerable influence and power in their neighbourhoods—Halifax, say, rather than Leeds[10]—and as the century progressed became increasingly numerous, even eventually penetrating the city enclaves. Merchants proper were seen in the eighteenth century as 'superior links of that chain which connects the various ranks of Society in the firm bonds of mutual necessities',[11] and were loath to undertake supervision of the manufacturing processes.

In the smaller towns, merchants and merchant-manufacturers, on equivalent scale, mirrored the experience of the more brilliant luminaries. They, too, formed oligarchies of civic influence, sometimes three or four families dominating the town through several generations, just as a score or more of families might do in the main commercial centres. Both the greater and lesser had often dynastic and social ambitions, aiming at emulating or, indeed, entering, the local landed society. Some, like the Milners of Leeds, acquired country seats and considerable estates.[12] Some, like the Wilberforces of Hull, chose to remain in the town.[13] All played an active part in civic and county affairs.

The commercial and civic superiority of the merchants was not to continue unchallenged into the next century. The captain of industry was to oust the merchant prince as the industrial revolution turned the workshop into the factory and as technical advance altered radically the methods of production. The very clichés which designate the two suggest the difference between them. The captain of industry was one who controlled his troops in the discipline of the

---

[8] Francois Crouzet, *The First Industrialists. The Problem of Origins*, Cambridge, 1985, p. 8.
[9] *Ibid.*, pp. 3 and 6.
[10] Wilson, *op. cit.*, p. 106.
[11] *Ibid.*, p. 59.
[12] *Ibid.*, p. 221.
[13] Jackson, *op. cit.*, p. 236.

factory, himself in charge, often physically present fifteen hours a day.[14] The merchant prince was the head of an empire, buying and selling from his headquarters as occasion arose, organising his minions who sailed his ships or his agents who acted for him, engaging in a variety of commercial transactions. His day was as he chose to spend it.[15]

The merchant prince seldom became a captain of industry as the technical advance altered the industrial scene. 'The world of the merchant prince [was] distinct from that of a factory owner.'[16] The merchant-manufacturers, however, especially in the textile industries, often made the transition. Power-driven machinery displaced domestic spinning and weaving and the constraints of factory production evolved in consequence.[17]

In the linen industry, technical advance was slower than in other textiles. Only in the 1770s was flax spun by power, for the nature of the fibre defeated earlier attempts to speed the process.[18] The processes required in the dressing of flax and the production of yarn were such that mechanisation was not able to make the rapid advance it made elsewhere, even when the flax-spinning machine arrived. Up to the 1930s the Belfast linen industry bleached the linen in open fields.[19]

Although fine yarn was imported by some manufacturers, there were also multi-purpose concerns which imported the raw material, processed, spun and wove it and then arranged the sale of the finished cloth. This was the usual case with the manufacturers of sailcloth, where the yarn was coarse and the finished product equally so, sometimes produced from hemp rather than flax. Finer linen demanded a finer yarn which was more frequently produced abroad.

As the century drew to a close, the factory system was proliferating in cotton and wool, as well as in the heavier industries. But there was, even here, considerable variety and the handloom was still in use, even in cotton and woollen production, until the 1840s and beyond. In the linen industry, with its slower march towards industrialisation, a manufacturer, throughout the eighteenth century,

[14] Crouzet, *op. cit.*, p. 106.
[15] Wilson, *op. cit.*, pp. 106–7.
[16] Crouzet, *op. cit.*, p. 102.
[17] *Ibid.*, p. 108.
[18] Patricia Baines, *Flax and Linen*, Shire Publications, 1985, p. 14.
[19] *Ibid.*, p. 28.

had good scope for success in developing the sailcloth business and at the same time engaging in some merchant venturing. Steam was no threat to sail until well into the nineteenth century and Eric Evans states that sail retained a substantial lead in the total tonnage until the 1870s.[20]

The firm of Langton, Shepherd and Birley, of Kirkham, was one such merchant-manufacturing concern, and Thomas Langton (1724–94) was its guiding light. It is possible to trace the development of this partnership, and to set the Langton family in a context of the town of Kirkham, while seeing their linen manufacture in relation to the linen industry in the country as a whole, with particular reference to Lancashire. Their overseas ventures and their inland markets, along with the communications making these practicable, all contribute to the overall picture of Thomas Langton's commercial enterprise.

But the Langtons were a family of human beings, not mere cyphers in the industrial game. The education of his children and the leisure pursuits of his family, as well as his attitudes to sickness and health, join his business concerns to give a rounded impression of Thomas Langton, the central figure, and allow us to link him to his immediate past, to his contemporary present, and to his immediate future.

R. G. Wilson wrote in 1971 in his introduction to his book on the gentlemen woollen merchants of Leeds that 'since the merchants have always had a dull press they have remained faceless men'.[21] The Langton letters enable us to redress the balance in the case of one flax merchant of Kirkham, and to give him not merely a local habitation and a name, nor merely a face. They reveal something of the man behind the face and, by suggesting something of his attitudes and standards, both in his public and private *persona*, enable us to relate his public and private interests to those of his time, and his business enterprise to the local and national economy.

The Langtons and Kirkham

There is no concrete evidence to suggest what brought the Langtons to Kirkham. The first Langton to settle there was Cornelius, the

---

[20] Eric Evans, *The Forging of the Modern State*, 1983, p. 118.
[21] Wilson, *op. cit.*, p. 1.

grandson of Roger Langton of Broughton Tower, near Preston. Cornelius came from Preston in about 1687. He had been apprenticed to a woollen draper, but could not have completed his apprenticeship, which began in 1683 and was for seven years.[22] In 1689 he married the daughter of the master of the free school and bought his freedom to trade as a woollen draper in 1690, the year of the death of his father, who was described in documents variously as 'salter' and 'yeoman', but in his will as 'gentleman'.[23]

Although the political instability of the 1680s, and the easier access to freedoms after the revolution, facilitated the migration of enterprising tradesmen into corporate towns previously closed to them, some of the more conservative boroughs clung to their ancient rights and influential gilds. Preston was one such, and although Kirkham was not a corporate town in the strict sense of the term, it had gild regulations imposed by ancient monastic charter. However, as there was scope for incomers to be accepted, once they had bought their freedom to trade, no doubt Cornelius chose to come to Kirkham because he would not be eligible for his freedom in Preston until he was out of his apprenticeship. Permanent shops began to appear in towns towards the end of the century, supplementing and complementing the open markets and fairs for the selling of consumer goods, and shopkeepers began to establish considerable businesses.[24]

The Kirkham to which Cornelius Langton came was a small market town with perhaps fewer than five hundred inhabitants. It existed, like similar market towns, 'principally to minister to the needs of the surrounding countryside'.[25] It was to retain this rural connection throughout the eighteenth century and, indeed, well beyond, even when manufacturing had added an important new dimension. Singleton has shown that, until 1750, the chief occupation of the town was agriculture and that, even later, there were farms and smallholdings within the boundaries. As late as 1840, 731 statute acres out of a total of 801 were used for agriculture.[26] Many deeds of the eighteenth

---

[22] LRO, DDX/190/90.

[23] LRO, DDX/190/3 87 90.

[24] Peter Clark, ed., *The Transformation of the English Provincial Town*, 1984, p. 26.

[25] Alan Everitt, 'The Market Towns' in Peter Clark, ed., *The Early Modern Town*, p. 156.

[26] F. G. Singleton, *Kirkham, A Short History*, Kirkham, 1980, p. 39.

century speak of gardens, orchards and fields in their conveyancing and, in 1775, Cornelius's descendants spoke of harvesting their hay.[27]

However, for Kirkham, as for provincial towns in general, the eighteenth century was a time of accelerating change. By 1801 the population had grown to 1,561, reflecting a buoyancy for which agriculture was not responsible. Well before 1800 the town was dominated by the families of the Langtons, Birleys and Hornbys, all of whom had come in from the neighbourhood and developed the flax industry; so much so that, in Tunnicliffe's *Survey* of 1787, after a note about the market day and principal inns, the Kirkham entry reads simply:

Hornby, Hugh and Sons, Merchants and Sailcloth Manufacturers
Langton, Birley and Co., ditto.[28]

Seven years later, John Aikin's *Description of the Country Thirty to Forty Miles Around Manchester* recognised the manufacturing importance in what was still ranked as a market town:

This is a market town situated eight miles westward of Preston, in the Field or Filde country … the chief trade in Kirkham is coarse linens and especially sail cloth, of which it makes a considerable quantity for the Navy.[29]

The Langton share in the preeminence reached its zenith in the third generation when it was finally consolidated. In Cornelius's early days he was not in a sound financial position, taking out a mortgage liability in 1693. Before this, he had to make the customary provision for his two sisters, as stipulated in his father's will, before he could inherit his father's Preston property. However, by 1694 the mortgage was discharged, and when he died in 1712 his inventory *post mortem* realised over £600.[30]

Cornelius Langton remained unequivocally a draper. His name appears in the town record as supplying cloth and tapes for the church, and he is designated 'draper' in his will.[31] By the time of his

---

[27] LRO, DDX/190/48.
[28] William Tunnicliffe, *The Survey of the County of Lancashire*, 1787, p. 95.
[29] John Aikin, *A Description of the Country Thirty to Forty Miles Around Manchester*, 1795, p. 288.
[30] LRO, DDX/190/92 90 107.
[31] MS records of the Thirtymen of the Parish of Kirkham, LRO, PR 2067: LRO, DDX/190/6.

death the maritime activity which was to lead to the development of the west coast ports was not fully under way and there is no suggestion that Cornelius had interests in overseas trade. As the century proceeded, the port of Lancaster knew its brief flowering, trading with the West Indies and the American colonies; Liverpool rose to such importance that by 1750 Dr Pococke supposed it 'the next town in trade to Bristol', which it was to overtake;[32] Poulton, nearer home, had by 1754 'a very good harbour' at Skippool and Wardleys.[33]

It was left to Cornelius Langton's son, John, to embark on the venture of overseas trading, very likely the better to provide for his two sons. John Langton's diversification enabled him to separate his drapery from his commercial enterprise so that, in his 1759 will, he could leave his business of 'mercer or woollen draper' to his second son and his interests with his 'co-partners in trade' to his elder son, Thomas, who was in the partnership with him.[34]

Thomas must, obviously, have been accepted into the partnership before this, joining the firm known as Langton Shepherd and Co. The other partner was William Shepherd, Mrs Thomas Langton's uncle, and when John Langton died, Shepherd's brother-in-law, John Birley, was brought in. It was characteristic of eighteenth-century enterprises, both great and small, to be sustained through a tissue of such kinship links. The common practice of forming partnerships spread the risks and enlarged the capital available.[35] The rival firm of Hornby and Hankinson had similar expansion and a similar kinship net; Hankinson was the first Hornby's brother-in-law.

Although the Langtons and Hornbys engaged in general trading, the principal concern of both firms was the production of coarse linen and sailcloth. The expansion of this manufacture during the second half of the century is reflected in the number of pauper apprentices put to the flax-dressers, some sixty-two, the greatest number allocated to any single trade and about 40 per cent of all such apprenticeships.[36] It is not difficult to imagine the change this manufacturing activity would cause in the town.

[32] Richard Pococke, *The Travels Through England of Dr Richard Pococke*, Vol. 1, Camden Society No. 42, 1888, p. 5.
[33] *Ibid.*, Vol. 2, Cam. Soc. No. 44, 1889, p. 6.
[34] LRO, DDX/190/16.
[35] Peter Mathias, *The First Industrial Nation*, 1983 edn, p. 146.
[36] LRO, PR 827/1–306.

In the Langton enterprise, the production was greatly expanded in John Langton's lifetime. At first the work was put out to the surrounding villages, cloth being collected from the cottage weavers and returned for sale to Kirkham, but after mid-century manufacture was more concentrated in Kirkham itself. In 1754 the firm bought land on which a bowkhouse (bleaching shed), weaving shed, starch house and spinning sheds were erected. In 1758 more land was added for further sailcloth factories.[37] The Langtons' small-scale multiple enterprise provided the base for growing diversity and specialisation.

As the Kirkham firms grew and prospered, increasing their work-force and adding to their commercial ventures, the chief protagonists became, not surprisingly, more and more prominent in town affairs. As the chief employers of labour, resident in the town and much in the public eye, they could hardly have escaped municipal commitment, especially in the structure of local government which obtained in Kirkham. Indeed, the Langtons did not have to wait until the firm was well established for this municipal recognition.

The pattern of local government in Kirkham was complicated by the smallness of the town in relation to its weighty legacy of ancient forms and traditions. At the Dissolution it was granted to Christ Church, Oxford, the Fellows holding the rectoral manor and eventually farming the manorial rights to the Cliftons of Lytham Hall, while retaining the advowson and the great tithes. Its charter had been granted by Vale Royal monastic house in 1296, the abbey holding the manor by gift of Edward I. The Charter was subsequently approved by both Henry IV and Edward IV.

In practice over time a fusion had occurred between the Common Council of Burgesses, the Jury of the Manorial Court and the Gild Merchant (granted by Charter to enable the men of Kirkham to control all who wished to trade in the town). This meant that what became established as the Jury of the Court Leet (elected each year and presided over by the Steward of the Lord of the Manor) was the operative organ of town government, appointing various town officials and hearing complaints both against those who broke the regulations governing manorial tenancies and those who did not keep the peace.[38]

---

[37] F. J. Singleton, 'The flax merchants of Kirkham', op. cit., p. 83.
[38] R. Cunliffe Shaw, 'The seigneurial borough', op. cit., passim.

The principal officers of the town were the two bailiffs, appointed by the Jury of the Court Leet. The bailiffs were important in both the municipal administration and the manorial estate. There were several lesser officials appointed by the Court Leet and the Jury received the accounts of the overseers of the poor, although the overseers were appointed by the churchwardens, themselves the appointees of the select vestry. This vestry, known as the thirtymen, consisted of two representatives from each of the fifteen townships forming the parish of Kirkham.

The thirtymen belonged to a completely different line of development from the Jury of the Court Leet. Thought to have originated in the fourteenth century, the thirtymen formed a standing council, representing the parish. Once elected they held office for life or until resignation, and their oath was administered by the civil, not the ecclesiastical, authority. The thirtymen were self-perpetuating, appointing new members when vacancies occurred. Above the churchwardens, whom they appointed, they acted as guardians of the parish property. These select bodies of sworn men were not uncommon in this part of Lancashire, existing in Preston, Lancaster, Goosnargh and Garstang. They had considerable powers, and they were frequently in contention with the incumbent. They levied all forms of taxation for the upkeep of the church, scrutinised the churchwardens' accounts, disbursed certain charitable funds and in Kirkham saw to the extermination of vermin. They contributed to the maintenance of the free school and appointed visitors to inspect it.[39]

Concerned though they were with the whole parish, the thirtymen met in the town itself and their records show a continuous activity throughout the century. Those of the Court Leet, on the other hand, suggest a falling off from the late 'twenties to the early 'thirties but, under a new steward, the Jury then became active again and remained so.

If the justices of the peace were the principal men of influence in eighteenth-century provincial England, as has been suggested,[40] this was not so in Kirkham, where there appears to have been no resident justice.[41] The channels of influence were the traditional ones of Court Leet and Vestry which, apart from some co-operation over poor relief, remained separate.

[39] R. Cunliffe Shaw, *op. cit.*, p. 138.
[40] Clark, ed., *Transformation*, *op. cit.*, p. 39.
[41] LRO, DDX/190/63.

If parish administration was an important pillar in governmental stability in the towns up to 1800, it was so in Kirkham largely because the same people dominated all branches of administration and influence. These same people also formed vigilante groups against criminals,[42] raised armed volunteers in time of crisis,[43] and administered, as trustees, various charitable trusts. They also sat, outside the town, on the Assize Jury.[44]

The Langton family served through four generations in the principal areas of public life, prominent in social service (and social control). Within two years of his freedom, Cornelius was a juryman and served on fifteen further occasions until his death twenty years later. He was churchwarden in 1693 and three times bailiff. Although an incomer, he was obviously assimilated quickly into the life of the town. His status as son-in-law of the master of the school and, indeed, in his own right as a woollen draper, would ensure a certain *entrée*, but there is no doubt of his comparative eminence. He appears to have been among the twenty names most frequently called for office.

His son, John, was juryman seven times between 1715 and 1726, in which year he was also bailiff. He was bailiff on four later occasions. After John's death, his son, Thomas, the letter writer, was seven times bailiff and both his sons in their turn, John and Will, served during their father's lifetime. The other names most frequently occurring are those of Shepherd and Birley (the Langton partners) and Hornby (the Langton rivals). It is significant that these families never held the less influential and more unpopular offices, such as that of constable. For thirty-six of the fifty-nine years from 1741 to 1800 at least one of the two bailiffs was from these families, and on twelve occasions both were. Not until 1780 did three consecutive years pass with none of them acting.

As for the Select Vestry, John Langton was appointed thirtyman in 1738, and from then until Will Langton's death in 1814 one of the two Kirkham nominees was a Langton. Langtons were visitors of the free school almost continuously for the same period,[45] and by 1802 no fewer then eight of the ten trustees of the principal charities in the town were Langtons, Birleys and Hornbys.[46] The trust of the

[42] Association for the Prosecution of Felons, 1754, LRO, DDX/194/54.
[43] Loyal Kirkham Volunteers, 1790, LRO, DDX/190/69–86.
[44] LRO, QDF/217/25 and LRO, DDX/190/36.
[45] Shaw, *op. cit.*, pp. 624–7.
[46] *Ibid.*, p. 622.

girls' charity school, of which John Langton senior was co-founder, was a Langton preserve, and Thomas Langton appears as trustee of village charities outside the parish of Kirkham, such as St Michaels.[47]

In common with his fellow flaxmen, Thomas Langton must have given a good deal of his time to civic and public affairs, and also a considerable amount of money. The Langtons would be expected to appear on all subscription lists, like that for the new organ in the parish church to which Thomas Langton gave ten guineas to Mr Shepherd's twenty pounds and Mr Birley's five guineas.[48]

Whatever reservations we may have about the long hours and low wages of the employees upon whose work they depended, we must, in the end, agree with Shaw that the prosperity of Kirkham from 1700 to the latter part of the nineteenth century was directly dependent on these families.

With the increase in economic prosperity and the accompanying elevation in status of those responsible, the town was, like many more, 'improved' in the latter half of the eighteenth century. The manufacturers built new houses or re-built old ones. The shambles was moved from the moot hall, which was eventually re-built.[49] As they became available, land and property were bought by the more affluent families and by the turn of the century a town of some pretension to gentility had emerged.[50]

Born in 1805, Shepherd Birley, grandson of Thomas Langton's partner, recorded in a manuscript notebook that 'the town of Kirkham in the day of [his] boyhood was inhabited by many well-to-do people'.[51] No fewer than nine or ten people kept their carriages at that time at the height of Kirkham's prosperity. He wrote that 'Houses of the better sort' were hard to come by when his father married, unless one built one's own; a statement which could be an ambiguous indicator of prosperity, but was meant to imply that the appropriate housing had not kept pace with the demands of young scions setting up their own establishments.

Eighteenth-century local government in towns was oligarchic, based not upon popular mandate but upon tradition and

[47] Records of St Anne's Church, Copp, Great Eccleston, PR 3238: Board in St Michaels on Wyre Church.
[48] Organ Book of Kirkham Parish Church, LRO, PR 2071.
[49] Singleton, *Short History*, op. cit., p. 20.
[50] Hornby Papers, *passim*.
[51] The Birley Papers, LRO, DDD (unclassified).

custom.[52] Certainly this was true of Kirkham. The rise and eventual domination of the flax merchants is an interesting, if less spectacular, parallel to the rise of merchants in cities like Leeds, Bristol and Hull who monopolised the corporations and were holders of all major offices. These were merchants on a much more sumptuous scale than the Langtons and their partners and rivals, and their influence longer-lasting and more widespread. But in the rural Fylde the flaxmen played an equivalent role. Just as some of the merchant princes eventually built fashionable residences outside the cities, so Joseph Hornby built Ribby Hall, and the Birleys Bartle Hall and Wrea Green Manor, combining the life of country gentlemen with their business dealings. Just as the mean streets of the cities rose on land which had been gardens and presentable dwellings, so the Birleys and Hornbys, in the early nineteenth century built cottages, not at all like 'houses of the better sort', for their workpeople. The greater merchants were influential in national politics and their empire more far-flung, their enterprises more ambitious and their monetary gain richer than in the case of their Kirkham counterparts. But they, too, were protected by a tissue of relationships and kinship ties, strengthened by intermarriage, and their sons were primed to succeed them.[53]

The social elevation of those merchants who, like the Kirkham families, rose from undistinguished origins through commercial success and civic influence to emulate the landed gentry, had been balanced for some time by the entry of younger gentry sons into business. This two-way movement led to a blurring of the dividing line between the gentry and the middle class and encouraged many merchants, from the more splendid city élites to the lesser fry of the provincial towns, to aspire to gentry status. Thomas Langton would have been gratified by the opening words of the entry concerning his great grandson, Charles, in Liverpool's Legion of Honour published in 1893, however inaccurate some of the details:

> Langton, Charles, J.P., D.L. for Lancashire of Barkhill, Aigburth, ranks among the landed gentry of Great Britain and comes from a family which has been wealthy and much respected in Liverpool from the commencement of this century.

[52] See Penelope Corfield, *The Impact of English Towns 1700–1800*, Oxford, Opus, 1982, p. 153.
[53] Wilson, op. cit., p. 212.

The entry, however, further relates that:

> During a long period the family have been intimately con-
> nected with the Hornbys and the Earles, and Mr Charles
> Langton, until he retired from active business was in the firm
> of T. and W. Earle, merchants, whose offices he still uses.[54]

These new 'landed gentry' did not, in fact, draw their principal
income from land but retained their business connections either
directly, like the Birleys, whose mill was not sold until the 1890s, or
by investment like John, Thomas Langton's eldest son, who kept
money in the Birley concern when he and his brother left the firm.
They remained connected to the commercial world, living in both
worlds, in fact, and modifying the composition of the gentry. All the
Langtons, after Cornelius, acquired the appellation 'gentleman' after
their names, but with Thomas began the aspiration to integrate with
the local landed society. His house guest hunted with Mr Clifton of
Lytham Hall;[55] he entertained Mr France of Little Eccleston Hall[56]
and cultivated the distant Langton relatives the Boltons, who moved
to their ancestral Askham Hall[57] (today the residence of Lord
Lonsdale), and whose son went to school with the elder Langton
boys. Yet, even so, he never for one moment lost sight of the
commercial world or considered himself above commercial matters.
Indeed, they were always, to the end, his prime concern. But for his
youngest son Tom, when the money ran out because of business
failure in the 1820s, emigration to Canada was the practical solu-
tion.[58] Money was in the last analysis more important than claims to
ancient lineage.

The social aspirations of the flax merchants and their descendants
reflected the rise in merchant status, on small as well as larger scale,
based on the security of non-landed investments and leading to the
emergence of a polite, but not exclusively landed, culture.

Kirkham cannot, of course, be compared with the great cities, nor
the members of the Court Leet and Vestry with the city aldermen,
but there is no doubt that the flax merchant families, the élite of the
town, eventually approximated to the older-established élite of the

[54] B. G. Orchard, *Liverpool's Legion of Honour*, Liverpool, 1893.
[55] LRO, DDX/190/37.
[56] LRO, DDX/190/61.
[57] LRO, DDX/190/60 et al.
[58] Anne Langton, *op. cit.*, p. 47.

county, while retaining commercial links. In the limited context of their small country town, the Langtons and their fellows reflected the characteristics of the grander urban merchants, predominant, like them, in their oligarchic civic influence throughout the eighteenth century, and like them, too, in their social aspirations and ambitions.

The rise of the Langtons, and especially of Thomas Langton, was contemporaneous with the zenith of the fortunes of the English linen industry, and it is necessary to understand something of the place of Kirkham in the wider context of that industry in the eighteenth century.

The Linen Industry in the Eighteenth Century

In contrast to the Scottish and Irish, there is no systematic study of the English linen industry. Apart from regional and local studies, reference to the linen industry usually occurs in discussion of cotton and wool. Linen was originally combined with cotton before a cotton thread was produced strong enough for the warp and the consequent expansion of cotton manufacture contributed in some areas to the eclipse of wool.

The main outline of the rise and fall of linen in England is, however, clear enough. Throughout the sixteenth and seventeenth centuries there was widespread domestic manufacture of linen from yarn spun by women in their homes. There were dealers in both flax and yarn who dealt with the distribution of surplus materials.

The period of the industry's greatest prosperity was between 1740 and 1790. After this, superseded by cotton, it declined but was not entirely eradicated.

Throughout the seventeenth century, England was a major importer of linens, as of all textiles except woollens. In 1700 15.6 per cent of all textile imports were linens, but by 1800 the percentage was only 5.6.[59] This fall in the percentage of imported linens coincided with the rise of the native English production to the rank of a major textile industry.[60]

This flowering was due to four main factors. The first was the competition with continental linens encouraged by protection. The second was the growth in the colonial trade, meetings the demands

[59] Peter Mathias, *The First Industrial Nation*, 1983 edn, p. 88.
[60] N. B. Harte, 'Protection and the English linen trade', in N. B. Harte and K. Ponting, eds., *Essays in Honour of Julia de Lacy Mann*, 1973, p. 103.

of the plantations and Africa, both direct to the West Indies and to the American seaboard, and also as part of the three-cornered slave trade.

The third boost resulted from the lifting of restrictions against the importation of raw flax and yarn; in 1731 the tax on imported raw flax was removed, and in 1753 and 1756 the taxes on imported yarn were first reduced and then abolished. This put the English producers on a sounder footing as they had previously paid heavily for imported flax and yarn.[61] The demand for linen steadily grew and the removal of these duties helped English manufacturers to go some considerable way towards satisfying it.

The fourth encouragement came from positive legislation. In 1746 it became obligatory for every vessel in Great Britain and America to be furnished at first sailing with one complete set of new sails of British manufacture, under penalty of ten pounds. Throughout the many wars of the eighteenth century, Navy contracts were valuable to the suppliers of sailcloth (poldavy) and, in peacetime, this 1746 Act guaranteed a regular outlet.

The increase in demand for linen goods naturally increased the demand for flax and hemp, but it is difficult to estimate the extent of flax cultivation in England.[62] It is obvious that cultivation was not to capacity. For most of the second half of the century inducements in the form of government subsidies known as 'bounties' were offered, but this did not have the desired effect of a considerably increased production. In contrast, crops were grown both in Scotland and Ireland where boards of trustees oversaw all aspects of the industry and where response to financial inducement was much keener than in England.[63]

As for Lancashire, it is impossible to tell how much flax was grown or how much of what was grown was marketed. Flax is not mentioned in the 1794 *General Survey* of the county for the Board of Agriculture, but the 1795 edition reported that the culture of both hemp and flax was never carried out to a great extent in the county. The 1815 edition added that they were once grown in small patches in many parts, especially the northern extremity.[64]

---

[61] Harte, *op. cit.*, p. 98.
[62] Harte, *op. cit.*, p. 105.
[63] Alastair J. Durie, *The Scottish Linen Industry in the Eighteenth Century*, Edinburgh, 1979, *passim*.
[64] R. W. Dickson, *General View of the Agriculture of Lancashire*, 1815, revised for publication by W. Stevenson, p. 388.

In spite of the *General Survey's* dismissal of flax-growing on any scale, Wadsworth and Mann unequivocally designate the Preston of the early seventeenth century as the natural centre of a flax-producing district with an expanding domestic industry in linen.[65] In Kirkham there is reference in the Bailiff's Book to penalties for drying or breaking flax in the 'forestones' of the houses, and there is evidence for the spinning of flax in several Fylde villages.[66]

The Lancashire linen industry began in the sixteenth century, alongside the manufacture of coarse woollens. It utilised such locally grown flax as there was, but was mainly dependent on imports of Irish yarn. The resultant linen was cheap and coarse and, as with the production of woollens, was mainly carried on by independent weavers also employed in agriculture.[67] By 1711 the linen trade was referred to as 'the most considerable in Lancashire' and, by 1808, many acres of land were said to be covered by yarn or cloth under various operations.[68] However, by then, linen was not the principal textile in production.

It has, however, probably been too easily accepted that cotton completely drove out the traditional linen manufacture in the Fylde before the end of the eighteenth century. In 1837 Baines put cambrics first among the principal articles produced in Preston and listed flax-spinning with cotton-spinning as among the prevailing manufactures of the town.[69]

By 1770 Kirkham's linen industry was principally involved in the production of sailcloth, with some coarse linen and seine twine (for netting). The organisation of this industry is impossible to reconstruct with accuracy. There are no letter books or account books extant, and the only direct reference to the workers in the letters merely says, 'Our fabrick will improve as greater attention will be paid to the weavers'.[70] Who or where these weavers were is not apparent, but it was obviously possible to oversee them. We may safely assume that, by the time of the letters, some were working in

---

[65] A. P. Wadsworth and L. de L. Mann, *The Cotton Trade and Industrial Lancashire*, Manchester, 1931, reprinted 1965, p. 57.
[66] LRO, DD CL 1097.
[67] D. C. Coleman, *The Economy of England 1450–1700*, Oxford, 1977, p. 81.
[68] Harte, *op. cit.*, p. 102; *William Marshall, Review and Abstract of the County Reports to the Board of Agriculture*, Vol. 1, 1808, reprinted 1818, York, p. 282.
[69] Edward Baines, *History of Lancashire*, Vol. 4, 1835, p. 331.
[70] LRO, DDX/190/63.

the firm's weaving sheds, but some may still have worked on their own looms, drawing part of their livelihood from husbandry, as had long been the tradition.

We may conclude that there was some kind of a linen industry in Kirkham before the eighteenth century. Flax is mentioned in many of the inventories of the Kirkham burgesses in the seventeenth century and figured in the small tithes of the church. Linen, coarse cloth and rope would be produced on a domestic scale, any surplus being taken to Preston for sale. It was in the eighteenth century, however, that the industry expanded beyond this domestic scope.

The records of apprenticeships bound by the overseers, the churchwardens and the two major charities give a good idea of the employment patterns in Kirkham during this century.[71] The lifting of restrictions on imported flax in 1731 made little apparent difference to flax-dressing in Kirkham. By 1746, however, the Act making British sails compulsory at first sailing, and the beginning of that period of rapid growth in the trade with the American colonies which was so important to both economies,[72] coupled with a general expansion of trade and the outbreak of the Seven Years War (1756–63) led to the taking on of more apprentices to the flax dressers than formerly, with no equivalent rise in the number of apprentices to the weavers. This would suggest that the weavers were either weaving in family units in their own homes, or were working on the looms in the shed, still responsible for providing, on the same basis as the domestic workers, their assistants from their own families. Imported flax was now removed from duty, so more dressers were required as importing became easier. The 1770s, even before the American War of Independence heralded thirty years of almost unbroken hostilities, saw an increase in both dressers and weavers.

The growth of the Langton firm marches with this pattern. John Langton (1691–1762) was designated 'draper' in his father-in-law's will of 1727; in his own wills of 1728/9 and 1748 he was 'gentleman', but 'merchant' in his four remaining wills.[73] In his 1759 will he made clear the division between his interests as 'a mercer or woollen draper' and those interests associated with his 'co-partners in trade', intending to leave, as noted above, one sector to each son. In his last

[71] Kirkham Apprentice Indentures, PR 827.
[72] Marc Egnal and Joseph A. Ernst, 'An Economic Interpretation of the American Revolution', in *William and Mary Quarterly*, 1972.
[73] LRO, DDX/190/10, 12, 15, 16, 17, 18.

will he appointed his 'good friend and partner in trade' William Shepherd as executor. This suggests that John Langton had diversified from linen drapery to merchant venturing and, as he intended his second son to inherit the drapery, had put his elder son Thomas (the letter writer) to learn the flax business with William Shepherd, who had diversified into merchant venturing from the flax-dressing which was his original trade. As a draper, John Langton would have experience of all kinds of cloth, not merely wool, and a draper's shop was considered a good training for young men.[74] No doubt Thomas, too, started in the drapery trade before joining William Shepherd.

Thomas bought his freedom in 1751 at the age of twenty-seven—too old to be out of any formal apprenticeship with his father—and he may have joined Shepherd then. He married Shepherd's niece two years later. He must have made a conscious choice to enter trade rather than attend university; his father's first will, made when Thomas was four years old, provided a sum of money towards university education or 'some laudable trade or employment' for him.

It may be assumed that Hugh Hornby, in like manner, went into an existing business, one owned by Hankinson, who became his brother-in-law. Both illustrate that diversification common in small businesses as they expanded to accommodate the employment of kin, and as they utilised kinship ties to assist them. After John Langton died, John Birley (Shepherd's brother-in-law) succeeded him, and the next apprentice taken, in 1769, was bound to Messrs Shepherd (spelt 'Sheppard' in the Apprentice Records) Langton and Birley.

It may be concluded that in John Langton's lifetime Shepherd ran the flax side of the business, and that Thomas Langton learned the trade from him and merchant venturing from his father. Certainly, later, both Thomas Langton and the Birley partners participated in both sides of the enterprise. In the indentures, only the Hornby and Langton firms aspired to merchant status, a status John Langton appeared to prefer to that of 'gentleman' once the firm began to expand.

The Langton firm shared in the trade boost afforded by the developments of the 1750s. In 1754 the partnership bought land in Kirkham, subsequently the site of spinning sheds, weaving and

[74] Francis Crouzet, *The First Industrialists. The Problems of Origins*, Cambridge, 1985, p. 144.

bleaching sheds and a starchhouse.[75] In 1749 the firm was selling deal to Gillows of Lancaster, suggesting that overseas ventures helped to finance the building at home.[76] The overseas trade continued to flourish, and in 1766 a warehouse, counting house and shops were added. In 1769 the widow of William Rawlinson, who had been in the partnership for a short time before his death, sold the firm stables, a warehouse and a heckling shop.[77] These property deals and building projects reflected increasing prosperity and enlargement of scope for the Langton enterprise.

Although it is suggested above that the manufacturing side of the partnership was carried initially by William Shepherd, with Thomas Langton learning from him, the first contract with the Navy Board for the sale of sailcloth, made as early as 1756 (the year of the outbreak of the Seven Years War) was in the name of John Langton, with a London agent acting for him.[78] The firm appeared in the list of successful contractors as 'Langton and Co.', and the contract was for 300 bolts, not the lowest amount.[79] Among the successful thirty, there were eight contractors supplying 1,000 bolts or more. This implies that the Langton firm had, by now, a reasonable volume of production, being in a moderate rather than a big way, and was among the firms with a middling but constant output.

The Langton contract was renewed in October 1756, this time for 340 bolts, but the first order was not completed until February 1757, the last eight bolts of No. 1 canvas being delayed from September 1756 when the rest of the order was settled. This suggests either that the Kirkham firm had found themselves stretched in the execution of the order, or that the dockyard inspector did not pass the cloth as up to standard. However, the firm held the contract again in March 1758, but no further contracts appear to have been held in John Langton's lifetime.[80]

The first order for the Hornby firm appeared in September 1770,[81] and the next entry for the Langton firm was in May 1772. There is no doubt that this is the Kirkham firm even though, once

---

[75] F. J. Singleton, 'Flax merchants', *op. cit.*, p. 83.
[76] Gillow Archive, Letter Book 1746–59, LU 4/361/87.
[77] Singleton, *op. cit.*, note 79.
[78] PRO, ADM 106/3634.
[79] *Ibid.*
[80] *Ibid.*, 3606.
[81] *Ibid.*, 3608.

more, it is entered merely as 'Langton' and not as the partnership. The entry reads:

✓ John
✓ ~~Thos~~. Langton and Co.[82]

Perhaps the firm had been a little ambitious in tendering earlier. It is significant that the next contracts for both Kirkham firms were in January 1776, five months after hostilities had officially begun against the American colonists and there was a considerable increase in the Navy Board's contracts for all kinds of naval stores.[83] The Kirkham firms held the contracts continuously until 1781 and after that frequently until at least 1793, the date of the last extant Navy Board Abstracts of Contracts in the Public Record Office.

The Langton firm had some moments of anxiety in their relations with the Navy Board. In 1780 Thomas Langton waited impatiently for news from the Board, probably about either the renewal of the contract or the settlement of payment due the previous year.[84] On another occasion the Board threatened the cessation of the contract if an overdue delivery were not made.[85] On the other hand, when the firm needed money before an order was completed, the Board allowed payment for what had already been delivered.[86] The Navy contracts were desirable because of their considerable monetary value; in 1780, for example, the contract was worth more than £2,400.

The thin edge of the cotton wedge was apparent in the Kirkham indenture records before Thomas Langton died. In 1785 an apprentice was taken by a 'cotton weaver' of Kirkham. The tentacles of the great Watson cotton enterprise in Preston, mentioned by contemporary observers, took four girls (one aged nine) and one boy between 1786 and 1789. But the inroads of cotton were slow to make a significant difference to Kirkham. Fifty years were to pass before Baines wrote that cotton manufacture had been 'introduced rather extensively *of late* in [the] town and neighbourhood'.[87] Cotton posed no threat to the Langtons. By the time Baines published, the

[82] *Ibid.*
[83] *Ibid.*, 3611.
[84] LRO, DDX/190/61.
[85] PRO, ADM/106/3621.
[86] *Ibid.*, 3616.
[87] Baines, *op. cit.*, p. 392.

Langtons had left Kirkham and the Hornby mill had closed in 1820 when the business moved to Bentham. The Birleys remained in linen production until 1895 when the former Langton concern was finally sold for conversion to cotton.

Locally-grown flax, whatever the amount, would obviously be inadequate for manufacture on the scale practised by the Kirkham flax merchants. The firms imported their flax and hemp and sold the surplus to chapmen, or dealers, for re-sale. Thomas Langton was anxious on one occasion to 'please the chaps'.[88] When production was plentiful they also sold their surplus 'navy canvas' through agents in London and Liverpool. As government standard the quality was guaranteed, as Thomas Langton was quick to point out.[89]

The supply of the raw material required by the flax merchants necessitated an interest in shipping. For the Langtons an extension of this was an interest in merchant venturing, both in their own products of sailcloth and seine twine, and in commodities unconnected with linen. If the early days of the partnership appeared to keep the two facets separate, by the time Thomas Langton inherited the firm in 1762 the two had become combined as the essential groundwork of the Langton enterprise. The term 'flax merchant' telescopes them and must not be taken to imply that the merchanting was solely in flax. It is impossible to separate the business from the merchant venturing, and their inter-relationship and characteristics emerge as Thomas Langton's letters throw light on his commercial practices.

Trade and Commercial Practices

As we have seen, Kirkham·was a small borough in the north-west of England, a satellite of Preston, itself a provincial town. Yet it operated in a context of a world economy which stretched from the far reaches of the Baltic to Barbados. To understand Kirkham's (and Thomas Langton's) success—and problems—we need to look first at this world economy.

From Elizabethan times the Baltic region had been an important source of naval supplies—hemp, flax, pitch, turpentine, tar and timber. By the early eighteenth century the Baltic was, to the British

---

[88] LRO, DDX/190/48.
[89] LRO, DDX/190/63.

government, so important for these naval stores that the freedom of the Baltic was essential to Britain.[90] In 1734, by the first commercial treaty to be made by Russia, Britain enjoyed favourable trading rights in Russia. The British were granted the status of most favoured nation and equality with the Russians themselves in duties paid on exports from Russia. Among other concessions they were allowed a discount on all duties by paying in muscovite coin instead of rixdollars (the currency of Amsterdam, the capital of European banking) like other nations. Resident British agents were accorded various legal privileges denied their foreign rivals. This agreement was renewed in 1766 but some of the most-favoured-nation position was undermined later by concessions to other powers.[91] By 1787, when the treaty was due for re-negotiation, Russia was strong enough to challenge British demands and sign a commercial treaty with France before the British terms were settled. Some British privileges were withdrawn and it was not until 1793, and the French Revolutionary Wars, that a new treaty was made with the 1766 terms practically reiterated.[92]

British trade proceeded against this diplomatic background and, on the whole, for the main part of the eighteenth century the British merchants settled in Russia enjoyed favourable conditions, although co-operation from the native Russians was not always certain.[93] Although the balance of trade was in Russia's favour, as far more was exported than was imported in return, many British firms were dependent on produce from the Eastland (as the Baltic region was known) for their continued existence. The importance of the Baltic trade to the British economy generally was widely recognised. When British negotiations for the trade treaty were hanging fire and the British diplomats appeared to be dragging their feet, pressure was exerted by pamphleteers who spelled out the significance to Britain of the various Russian exports.[94]

---

[90] Charles Wilson, *England's Apprenticeship 1663–1763*, 1965, p. 283.
[91] John Ehrmann, *The British Government and Commercial Negotiations with Europe 1783–1793*, Cambridge, 1962, p. 99.
[92] *Ibid.*, p. 13.
[93] Walter Kirchner, *Commercial Relations Between Russia and Europe 1400–1800*, Bloomington, 1906, p. 241 and *passim*.
[94] For example, Anthony Brough, *A View of the Importance of the Trade Between Great Britain and Russia*, 1787.

The Baltic trade was particularly vulnerable to international conflict and strained diplomatic relations.[95] Indeed, the need to break
the dependence of British shipping on the Baltic was one of the
reasons given for the encouragement of the colonisation of America.

By the eighteenth century the main naval contractors were importing timber from New England as well as from the Baltic, and
supplied the Jamaican and Antiguan dockyards as well as the English. British merchants, particularly from the western seaboard from
Whitehaven to Bristol, were led by attractions other than naval stores
to engage in vigorous trade with the mainland colonies and with the
West Indian islands.[96]

The initial impetus to the plantation trade was the provision of
African slaves to the colonists, necessitating a three-cornered run: to
Africa for the slaves, either in ballast or with textiles for the traders,
and homewards from the plantations with produce, chiefly rum,
sugar, tobacco, and timber such as mahogany to be used in furniture
and building. However, by no means all eighteenth-century traders
with North America were engaged in slaving. Many voyages went
direct with merchandise for colonists, but a great many merchants
had some connection at some time with the slave trade, and were
vocal in their opposition to Abolition.

As the century progressed, the colonial trade became vulnerable
to the worsening relations between the colonists and the British
government. When the War of Independence finally erupted in 1775,
and particularly when France entered the conflict in 1778 (the year
she had signed the trade agreement with Russia), British merchant
shipping was under severe threat. The war meant loss of markets to
the British on the American mainland and danger to shipping on the
high seas. The entry of Russia into an armed neutrality in 1780,
authorising the transport of material to hostile powers in neutral
ships, exacerbated the situation, for there was much dispute concerning the material carried. Although the merchandise was not to include armaments as such, the distinction between materials to be
used in war or for peaceful purposes was blurred. With France at
war with England, and a commercial ally of a Russia still not under
renewed treaty obligations to Britain, British merchant ships were
forced to sail in convoy, both to America and to the Baltic, under

[95] Wilson, *op. cit.*, p. 283.
[96] Ehrmann, *op. cit.*, p. 109.

the protection of the Navy. The hazards of the voyages caused a sharp increase in freight and insurance charges.

These two areas, the Baltic and the American colonies, were the main areas of the overseas trading of the Langton firm. From the Baltic they imported the major part of their raw material, as well as subsidiary merchandise such as iron, wheat and timber. With the colonies they engaged in ventures in part-ownership, and imported timber, rum, sugar and tobacco, exporting canvas and seine twine. They also had some dealing in slaves.

Throughout the eighteenth century there was a flourishing Baltic trade carried on from Wardleys on the River Wyre, where there was a large wharf 'and where as many as thirty master blacksmiths have frequently been known to sit down to dinner, come to buy iron when the ship was discharging'. The importation of flax constituted the 'staple trade of the Fylde country which when dressed, was given out to the country people to be spun and afterwards manufactured'. The making of sailcloth was thought to have begun during 'the long wars with France'. This account was given by a descendant of Thomas Langton in his preface to the published letters of Tom Langton to his sister, and gives a fair idea of the flourishing little port.[97]

By 1750 the Langton overseas trade was sufficiently under way for John Langton to have warehouses at Comley Pool, Staynall, with stock insured for £1,400,[98] and he was already supplying Gillows, the Lancaster cabinet-makers, with 'deal planks', a common import from the Baltic ports.[99] Some twenty years later Gillows were still acquiring 'oak billots' (thick pieces of wood cut to a suitable angle) from the Langton firm.[100] In September 1772 they purchased part of a consignment which was presumably that referred to by Thomas Langton the following month in his apology to his sons for his lateness in replying to their letters as he had been 'lately much abroad and otherwise engaged in the discharge of our Baltic ships'.[101]

As John Langton held the Navy contract in 1756, he was probably importing some flax along with the timber, though he may well have

[97] Thomas Langton, *Letters of Thomas Langton to Mrs Thomas Hornby 1815–1818*, Manchester, 1900, p. 1.
[98] Sun Fire Office Policy 123211, Guildhall Library, MS 11936/90/12324. I am indebted to Mrs Janet Nelson for this information.
[99] Gillow Archive, Letter Book 1769–72, LU 4/361/88.
[100] *Ibid.*, Letter Book 1746–59, LU 4/361/87.
[101] *Ibid.*, Cash Book 1769–75, LU 4/361/25; LRO, DDX/190/37.

been still importing it from Ireland, where he had business connections. Certainly, his son Thomas acquired the bulk of his raw material from the Baltic; Riga flax was considered the best in Russia, Königsberg hemp the best in the world.[102]

The first recorded venture of John Langton was, however, not with the Baltic but with America. In October 1746 the *Betty and Martha* (the Christian names of the partners' wives), a ship built in Boston and registered in Poulton in the name of Langton, Shepherd and Co., was in bond in London, bound for Lancaster laden with muscovado sugar and rum.[103] There is nothing to suggest it had been on the slave run. Indeed, it was common practice for ships built in New England to be freighted for the West Indies with foodstuffs and timber products, there to pick up a profitable cargo of sugar and sail for England where the ship and cargo were sold.

Ten years later, however, there is no doubt that the Kirkham firm had been dealing in slaves, among other commodities. The outbreak of the Seven Years War had affected the American market, as the firm of Austen Laurens of Charles Town (Charleston) were at pains to explain to the Langton partnership in August 1756. They wrote that the declaration of war had 'immediately reduced the price of slaves to a low ebb', and they formed the conclusion that 'Slaves will not do here during a war, which is a piece of intelligence may prove useful to you'.[104] A letter of October the same year confirms that the Langton slave ship had stopped in the West Indies and had not gone to South Carolina. Rum, indigo and rice are also mentioned.[105]

After John Langton's death, a further letter from the firm in 1763, at the end of the war, does not mention slaves but speaks of the sailcloth the Langtons had sent and the rice and indigo available in return. This letter seeks to dissuade the Langton firm from further ventures into 'this distant and precarious market' and to persuade them to concentrate on markets at home.[106] Thomas Langton was not deterred; the Liverpool Plantation Register makes it clear that, on the contrary, he expanded his enterprise to the colonies.[107]

[102] J. Jepson Oddy, *European Commerce*, 1805, p. 82.
[103] PRO, CUST/80 81.
[104] Philip K. Hamer, *The Papers of Henry Laurens*, Vol. 2, Columbia S.C., 1970, p. 290.
[105] *Ibid.*, p. 336.
[106] *Ibid.*, Vol. 4, p. 90.
[107] Liverpool Shipping Register Vol. R, Liverpool Record Office (Islington).

Throughout the 1770s Thomas Langton and William Shepherd were part-owners of several ships in conjunction with the Liverpool firm of Sparling and Bolden. Two were slavers on at least one of their voyages and the attempt to collect the debt on one of the slave transactions went on for years, as the Letter Book of the Liverpool firm reveals.[108]

They also traded from Lancaster, at the height of its importance as a colonial port. They co-operated with the Gillows in joint ventures, sharing the same ships for freight, like the *Nancy*, owned by Thomas Hinde of Lancaster and figuring in both the Gillow archive and the Langton letters.[109] As communications between the west and east coasts improved, the firm shipped Baltic produce through Hull, and it was from Hull that Tom, the youngest of Thomas Langton's five sons, embarked for Riga in 1787.

For the Langton firm, the procedures, problems and conditions in the two theatres of trade were vastly different. In the Baltic theatre the main problem, in addition to the international situation, was the shortness of the season. The navigation of the Baltic closed during the winter and became tempestuous as winter approached. Riga was open from March or April to October or November. Petersburg, served by Cronstadt, was closed until May. Thus Thomas Langton hoped Captain Williams' 'own prudence' would dictate to him to lose no time in the prosecution of his voyage to prevent a winter passage.[110] A winter passage would mean immobilisation in some Baltic harbour until spring. Thomas Langton waited 'with great impatience to hear of the sailing'.

Entering the Sound, all ships paid to Denmark the Sound dues, collected at Elsinore. Originally a payment to finance Denmark's defence of the Sound against pirates, the Sound dues had long ago become a toll. All the Lloyds lists marked Elsinore, some four or five days' sailing from Hull, as a compulsory port of call and carried details of all ships passing the Sound. These lists were used by owners to keep a watch on the progress of their ships. Thomas Langton was anxious to see a certain ship in the Sound list, and waited for the captain of another to pass the Sound.[111]

[108] MS Letter Book of Sparling Bolden, Liverpool Record Office (Picton), MN/219/1.
[109] Gillow Archive, Invoices 1782–9, LU 4/261/87.
[110] LRO, DDX/190/56.
[111] LRO, DDX/190/56; LRO, DDX/190/54.

In the American colonies the main problem was the increasing hostility to the British, and, in the West Indies, the strategic importance of the islands during any war. The mercantile interests of the colonists were particularly hostile to the English exporters who circumvented the established merchants by making contacts of their own and entering into direct dealing with shopkeepers and marginal importers in the urban centres. In the 1770s some of the larger colonial houses went bankrupt.[112] As matters worsened, resentment grew in many quarters. As the early skirmishes against the British forces moved towards open war, much anxiety was felt by the English merchants with American interests. The repressive legislation following the Boston Tea Party in 1773 led to civil unrest and military moves to quell it. In April 1775, skirmishes at Lexington Green led to open hostilities and the British forces moved back to Boston. In July 1776 the Declaration of Independence was issued.

Thomas Langton, taking the cure at the Hotwells in the summer of 1775, was anxious about 'the late affair at Boston' (the aftermath of the Lexington Green episode). He added that he had not heard any dependable news, but would be in Bristol the next day and 'if any North America accounts which might be interesting' arrived he would report in his next letter. The general opinion was that the situation was serious and the likely consequences threatening. He was aware that payments already owing from America were in jeopardy.[113] Like many another businessman in similar circumstances, Thomas Langton saw the American crisis as a crucial event in the fortunes of his own industry rather than in the fortunes of the country. Certainly the effects of the closure of the American markets, and the perils of crossing, came to a head in 1780 contributing to the pressures causing the firm's 'necessitous situation'. By December 1782 the Gillows noted that 'high freights ... insurance etc.' had discouraged trading with the islands for some time.[114]

The merchants of the Lancashire seaboard, much engaged in the American trade, were gravely concerned, and the Lancaster Chamber of Commerce joined the Liverpool Chamber in petitions to the Admiralty for the more effective protection of trade in St George's

[112] Marc Egnal and Joseph Ernst, 'An economic interpretation of the American Revolution', in *William and Mary Quarterly*, 1972, pp. 16–17.
[113] LRO, DDX/190/47.
[114] Gillow Archive, Letter Book 1782–6, LU 4/344/170.

Channel and the West Indies.[115] The privateers were proving a serious menace.

While to the merchants the war posed a series of practical problems, to the Admiralty the solving of these problems by protecting the traders proved insuperable. There were many privateers, some French and many American issued with Letters of Marque by the Continental Congress. These, with a sound knowledge of Caribbean waters, were able to use French ports to dispose of their prizes, and some combined privateering with trade with the French colonists. The Caribbean saw a number of naval actions and manoeuvres and some of the islands fell into enemy hands. In 1781, the year Yorktown fell, the British suffered several setbacks and the economy of the West Indies was severely damaged by the military and naval operations of the war.

The British firms on the islands which dealt with British business were in constant danger. In 1782 the Gillows commiserated with the Swarbrick firm in Jamaica, patronised also by the Langtons, on the severe military law they had been under, and added a wish that the French and Spaniards might not trouble them with a visit.[116]

The Navy did what it could to organise convoys to both the West Indies and the Baltic, for the French were striking at British ships wherever they traded. The American convoy sailed from Portsmouth, and the Baltic from Hull, with various assembly points *en route*. It was imperative to sail in convoy if insurance was to be valid, hence Thomas Langton's anxiety that Mr Swarbrick, returning to Jamaica, should catch the convoy at Portsmouth.[117] Hence, too, the production of a certificate to the insurers to prove that the Langton ships bearing damaged flax had sailed in convoy.[118] The escorting vessels were by no means always a deterrent. Thomas Langton feared that the firm might have to buy back ashes, shipped from Danzig for use in the bleaching process and confiscated when the ship was ransomed to a French privateer for more than it was worth.[119]

[115] Patrick Crowhurst, *The Defence of British Trade 1689–1815*, Folkestone, 1977, *passim*. Lancaster Trade Tax Account, LC.
[116] Gillow Archive, Letter Book 1782–6, LU 4/344/170.
[117] LRO, DDX/190/63.
[118] LRO, DDX/190/60.
[119] LRO, DDX/190/19/62.

After the war the islands were impoverished and depended for revival upon a re-opened commerce in provisions and lumber. Commerce was also re-opened with the independent United States. Exports from Britain rose as the planters became more prosperous.[120] The Langtons joined in this post-war enterprise. In 1784 they and their Birley partners became part-owners of two ships, and in 1785 invested in a further two.[121] The firm traded with the West Indies and America as long as Thomas Langton lived.

As noted above, one of the grievances against the British held by the American commercial interest before the war was that the British traded through their own contacts rather than utilising the American houses. These contacts were usually British merchants settled overseas who acted as middlemen in commercial transactions. They were common in both the Baltic ports and the American colonies. Much depended upon these agents. In Barbados, for example, where the Langtons traded through Thomson and Rowlandson, it was said that a person could not be too cautious how he connected himself with a Barbados merchant, as many of them kept no books and would bear 'dunning for years together without any marks of shame'.[122] The Langtons, however, were not let down by their Barbados agents, from whom they received their first transatlantic payments towards the end of the American war.[123] But the risk was open elsewhere, as the debt outstanding for many years on the Virginia slaves, mentioned above, bears witness.

In Jamaica the Langtons employed the firm of Swarbrick and Yate, and when Mr Swarbrick visited England, Thomas Langton had him as a house guest and made much of him. Will, in London, was to treat Mr Swarbrick with 'every civility' he could.[124] Good agents were to be cultivated. By making much of Swarbrick the Langtons were, in a sense, recognising the difficulty of finding men of trust in the islands.

It was no doubt with a view to making good the deficiency of Russian contacts that Thomas Langton sent his youngest son, Tom,

---

[120] Crowhurst, *op. cit.*, p. 200.
[121] British Register of Merchant Shipping, LC.
[122] Richard Pares, *Yankees and Creoles*, 1956, p. 145, quoted in M. M. Schofield, 'The Letter Book of Benjamin Satterthwaite of Lancaster 1737–1744', *HSCL*, Vol. 113.
[123] LRO, DDX/190/65.
[124] LRO, DDX/190/59.

to Riga at the age of seventeen, with the promise of a partnership in the firm of Messrs Thorley Morison and Co. on attaining his majority.[125] Seven years earlier he had complained that little attention had been paid to the firm's interests by the House at St Petersburg when an inferior cargo had been dispatched.[126] When Tom went, in 1787, at a time when the trade treaty was running out, about 750 ships a year arrived at Riga. In 1803, shortly after his return to England, 1,180 ships were recorded, of which 311 were British—the highest number of any of the fourteen countries listed. 'Wyrewater' and the 'River Weir' were listed among the destinations of Riga and Petersburg exports.[127]

In sending Tom to Riga, Thomas Langton was following two of the accepted practices of the day. He was deploying his sons to further the family interests as well as their own, and he was placing a relative as an overseas agent. He already had one son in London, to keep an eye on trade for his father as well as conducting his own business, and two sons were with him in the partnership.

The firm which Tom Langton joined was one of the three major Riga houses dealing in naval supplies from the Baltic.[128] Riga had been ceded to Russia in 1710 and by 1787 was second only to Petersburg in commercial importance. Riga was initially the exclusive province of British merchants but, during Tom's stay, the monopoly was broken. There were similar merchant colonies in all Russian trading ports; well over 200 foreign houses existed in Petersburg in 1804.[129]

The English merchants were protected by the Russian College of Commerce, established at St Petersburg, which controlled every department connected with commerce and acted in a judicial capacity in matters of dispute.[130] This gave stability to the British interest and lasted until the college was replaced by a tribunal to deal with foreign interests.[131] The English Factory (as the merchants were known) lived a life of comparative comfort and enjoyed a certain prestige, but business in Russia was hedged with restrictions, and

[125] Thomas Langton, *op. cit.*, p. 2.
[126] LRO, DDX/190/63.
[127] Oddy, *op. cit.*, p. 142.
[128] R. G. Albion, *Forests and Sea Power*, Cambridge, USA, 1926, p. 231.
[129] Oddy, *op. cit.*, p. 128.
[130] *Ibid.*, p. 194.
[131] Ehrmann, *op. cit.*, p. 59.

freedom of movement was limited. Russian trading was to buy from, not sell to, the Russians, so partners, like Tom Langton, in shipping companies were among those who benefited, earning substantial freight charges and percentages on their transactions.[132]

In the colonies the agents operated rather differently. Here they would collect the goods for export and receive the imported goods to sell to the colonists. In some cases the conditions were primitive. The Langton partner, John Birley, went as a young man to Jamaica to the firm of John Inman, an expatriate Lancaster merchant. There were other men with him, living in total discomfort. Only the ministrations of a fellow clerk saved John Birley from death from the fever which was a hazard of life in the islands. Life was hard, food poor, and there were no free days.[133] Of course, not all firms were like this, but the impression is that both living conditions and climate made the lot of some plantation agents much less pleasant than that of their Russian counterparts.

Engaged in overseas trade in both these major areas, often with several ships at sea at one time, Thomas Langton was principally concerned with the sale of the firm's surplus products and the various imported merchandise. Six years before his death, he wrote that they were 'near enough to Liverpool' to sell anything.[134] In addition to flax, sailcloth and twine, we know that the Langton firm sold iron, wheat, timber, tobacco and sugar. There is even one reference to 'sago powder' which, coming neither from Europe, nor America, nor the Baltic, and there being no evidence of trading with the East Indies, must have been acquired from some middleman.[135] As 1788 was a bad year for the firm, Thomas Langton's suggestions that his son, in France, should enquire into particulars of French imports and exports—especially the prices of cotton imported from the West Indies, and the identity of France's source of tallow—indicate a willingness to explore all possibilities. They also reveal a business eye open to the main chance—Will was on holiday. Thomas Langton was willing to offer a Canadian enquirer 'a fresh assortment more suited to his inclinations' if he did not want it immediately, suggesting a willingness to make whatever effort was necessary in order to obtain custom.[136]

---

[132] Kirchner, *op. cit.*, p. 232.
[133] LRO, DD, Shepherd Birley Notebook.
[134] LRO, DDX/190/67.
[135] *Ibid.*
[136] *Ibid.*

Agents were as important in internal trade as they were in over-seas transactions. They were more easily accessible, but it was still vital to deal through 'good men' and to be sure that they were 'sufficient'. One could not afford to take chances; the Gillows que-ried by letter a spurious Mr Shepherd,[137] and Zachary Langton, in London, held up a deal until he heard from his father that the client could be trusted.[138]

The usual channel from merchant to manufacturer or retailer was through 'the chaps', or chapmen, who distributed the commodities to those who did not ship direct. The chapmen usually dealt with the agents of the merchants and sometimes with the agents of the manufacturers. Thomas Langton would have preferred to dispense with agents altogether and shunned them whenever possible, to avoid the erosion of profits by commission payments. He instructed Will to by-pass them if he could to avoid the payment of 'their high prices and commissions'.[139] He advised his son to see some of the chaps himself and get to know them, 'which [might] seem to be of future use and save commission on sales'.[140]

It would appear that agents could be contentious as well as costly. As the Langtons were not near enough to London to supervise transactions themselves, and as Zachary had his own business to run, the London agents were particularly important. They were a con-stant concern to Thomas Langton. They were either dilatory, or they did not keep their clients informed, or they favoured other clients, or they were generally untrustworthy. Thus, he suspected Anderson and Davidson of making no progress in one transaction because 'their Scotch canvas prejudiced the sale'.[141] Another agent did not appear to have rendered sales of the last parcel.[142] Thomas was 'surprised' that another agent should have agreed with another client to sell at a reduced price without informing Will.[143] Will was to cultivate a certain agent with caution as 'he [was] agent for most of the Warrington makers'.[144] The Warrington makers, and the Liverpool

---

[137] Gillow Archive, Letter Book 1778–81, LU 4/311/89.
[138] LRO, DDX/190/67.
[139] LRO, DDX/190/62.
[140] LRO, DDX/190/60. Note: Letters 60 and 62 are wrongly numbered in the LRO catalogue; 60 comes later than 62 in the correspondence.
[141] LRO, DDX/190/48.
[142] LRO, DDX/190/62.
[143] LRO, DDX/190/60.
[144] LRO, DDX/190/48.

firm of Gaskell, also mentioned, held larger contracts with the Navy Board than those of the Langtons and Hornbys. The fluctuation of the market caused by their undercutting required watching.[145]

The Langtons appear to have had a London link in the person of Mr Threlfall of Turner and Threlfall, to whom Will was referred for advice. As he frequently came north to Kirkham, it may be assumed he was a relative of Uncle Threlfall, the schoolmaster. The firm of Birkbeck and Blake, and Mr Gale, working for himself, charged the more reasonable commission of 2½ per cent, in contrast to the 4½ per cent demanded by the other agents.[146]

John Langton had used a London agent named Stretland to negotiate the firm's first Navy Contract in 1766. The contracts were advertised when new ones were required, and were settled by a process of bargaining. The ledger of 1765 records how agreement was reached: all those tendering quoted the prices, the lowest was accepted and all those tendering above were asked to accept the lowest price. Not all of those tendering were accepted, perhaps because they would not accept the required terms.[147]

The Navy surveyors scrutinised each consignment and 'Navy canvas' was a guarantee of quality. The Langton canvas did not always pass muster; in 1788 Thomas Langton feared that 'they [would] have some objections to the carding'.[148] It was also difficult on this occasion to raise the quantity. The seven grades of canvas were usually specified in each contract and in this case only half of the contract had been honoured to date, and that 'chiefly No. 1 which [was] supposed most wanted'.[149]

Payment was usually deferred until the contract was complete, but a loose note in the ledger, dated December 1779, instructs payment to be made to Messrs Langton and Birley 'for such parts of the canvas they have delivered which has been surveyed'. It applied also to the Gaskells, and indicated a need for money on the part of the firms.[150] The year 1780 was a bad year for the Langton firm. Internationally, Spain had joined France in the American war, and in 1779 Ireland had raised volunteers. The Russian armed neutrality

[145] LRO, DDX/190/60.
[146] LRO, DDX/190/60.
[147] PRO, ADM 106 3604.
[148] LRO, DDX/190/67.
[149] Ibid.
[150] PRO, ADM 106 3616, loose sheet.

had restricted access to the Baltic and privateers threatened the passage to Barbados and Jamaica. The Navy Office did not settle their 1779 account until 1781,[151] and two cargoes of flax were damaged in transit, with subsequent drawn-out insurance procedures.[152] The cargo of ashes was lost in the ransom to the French, and the firm had outstanding debts owing them.[153] Property was bought in London, probably that intended for Zachary's business, and money was needed.[154] In addition, there was further trouble with the Navy Board in October, and it was in this month that Thomas Langton spoke of the firm's 'necessitous situation'.[155] The requirements of the London property deal led to the conclusion that they 'would be obliged to raise more money than [their] own resources would furnish [them] with'.[156]

1788 was also a difficult year. The cotton trade was in deep depression, and ramifications were wide.[157] Unlike the previous troubles of 1779–80 this international crisis was not affected by war. The American trade was uncertain and, because pre-Revolutionary France had ousted Britain from Russian preference, the Langtons found Russian hemp too dear.[158] Thomas Langton anxiously watched his cashflow, always the most serious problem facing merchants at this time.[159] Joseph Feilden, his brother-in-law, presumably riding the storm although a cotton manufacturer, lent one sum and promised another.[160] Thomas Langton was holding the balance in the Liverpool bank in reserve. He was trying hard to fulfil the Navy contract, fearful that the quality would not serve.[161]

Yet although money might be scarce, the firm's survival cannot have been seriously in doubt in either crisis. 1780 saw Thomas Langton take his only recorded holiday excursion, and 1788 saw Will

---

[151] PRO, ADM 106 3616. (The Hornby account was cleared in May 1780.)
[152] LRO, DDX/190/63, 64, 65.
[153] LRO, DDX/190/62, 63.
[154] LRO, DDX/190/60.
[155] LRO, DDX/190/59.
[156] *Ibid.*
[157] T. S. Ashton, *Economic Fluctuations in England 1700–1800*, Oxford, 1959, p. 136.
[158] LRO, DDX/190/67.
[159] Leonore Davidoff and Catherine Hall, *Family Fortunes. Men and Women of the English Middle Class 1780–1850*, 1987, p. 208.
[160] LRO, DDX/190/67.
[161] *Ibid.*

junketing in France. The London property purchase went through in 1780, and Thomas Langton was prepared to open new markets in France in 1788.

The firm's survival was partly due to the diversity of their interests but mainly to Thomas Langton's business acumen. His sound financial management and grasp of affairs steered them through the troubled waters. He must have established himself as a man of integrity in what was a 'face to face society',[162] showing that he could be trusted. The houses he dealt with were sound, and the mutual accommodation of the financial arrangements proved the mutual confidence not misplaced. No doubt aware of the necessity of the fluidity of credit which lay at the root of eighteenth-century business, Thomas Langton knew full well the desirability of cash. He insisted that it was advisable to give discount for payment rather than reduce the price: 'Don't scruple to allow 10 per cent discount for money,' he wrote, 'rather than reduce the price for Navy canvas'.[163] Again, 'If you can make an engagement for a quantity, I would allow 10 per cent for money'.[164]

If ready money was not forthcoming, short credit was the next best thing.[165] To Thomas Langton 'credit of two or three months [was] no object where there [was] a prospect of vending a quantity'[166] When short credit was a necessity, the price could even be reduced. This caution and foresight was characteristic of Thomas Langton. He vetted prospective clients and took pains to avoid the 'risque of making bad debts' while advocating selling 'for speedy payment' wherever possible.[167]

The ventures of the Langtons were covered by insurance negotiated, from the evidence of the letters, in London and not through a northern agent. From the Hotwells, Thomas Langton was glad that the 'insurance on the Betsey and Tindale [was] to be done so low'.[168] Again, Mr Anderson, the London agent, was to get the Riga insurance done by 'good men' and Mr Gale was given 'the needful to recover [the] insurance' on a certain voyage.[169]

---

[162] Peter Mathias, *The Transformation of England*, 1979, p. 101.
[163] LRO, DDX/190/63.
[164] LRO, DDX/190/60.
[165] Mathias, *op. cit.*, p. 88.
[166] LRO, DDX/190/67.
[167] LRO, DDX/190/59, 62; LRO, DDX/190/60.
[168] LRO, DDX/190/47.
[169] LRO, DDX/190/59, 62.

The two disasters reported in the letters illustrate both the man-made and the natural risks to which shipping was exposed. One ship was ransomed to a French privateer and another cargo suffered damage on the voyage from the Baltic. The ransoming might result in the firm having to buy back the ashes they had on board, as the captain had ransomed ship and cargo for more than it was worth, and the insurance claim on the damaged flax dragged on as such claims will. Thomas Langton commented that 'they [were] often tedious in pushing these matters forward'.[170]

To the end of the eighteenth century and into the earlier years of the next, many ships were still owned by a number of people in part-ownership, though some were already under the single owner-ship which was to become standard. Multiple ownership spread the risk, and manufacturer and part-owner were often one. Eventually shipping and manufacturing became separate. Part-ownership was also a means of investment for those not personally involved in the commercial aspect of the venture. In 1801, for example, Thomas's sister, Tabitha, bequeathed her share in the *Kirkham*.

The pattern of share holding changed, however, from the original equal sharing to the practice of one or two shareholders holding an appreciably larger share than the others, and from a random collec-tion of investing owners to a more cohesive group.[171] For example, in 1786 the *Young William* mentioned in the letters was entered in the shipping register with Thomas Langton and two others as 'sub-scribing owners' and John and William Langton and John and William Birley as part-owners. All the partners in the firm were thus involved and in this way their shares in the business were increased. On the other hand the *Nancy*, also mentioned in the letters, was already in the sole ownership of a single Lancaster merchant.[172]

Shareholding in ships provided an outlet for some of the merchants' capital and it was convenient to buy several ships, spreading the owner partnership while retaining the management. When the ships were carrying the goods of other merchants, high freight charges were made. When filled with the owners' merchandise there would be no freight charge, but the loss would be greater if the ship miscarried.

---

[170] *Ibid.*
[171] Ralph Davis, *The Rise of the English Shipping Industry in the Seventeenth and Eighteenth Centuries*, Newton Abbot, 1962, reprinted 1972, p. 83.
[172] British Register of Shipping, *op. cit.*

Reading the letters, one cannot escape the impression that Thomas Langton positively relished the management of affairs and the instruction of his sons in the ways of successful business, whatever the attendant anxieties. Thomas Langton was, himself, to the end of his life, effectively Langton Birley and Co.

Inland Transport and Communication

It may seem remarkable at first sight that the Langtons, situated in Kirkham in the south Fylde and away from the main traffic routes, were able to maintain the communications necessary for the success of their commercial ventures. A glance at Yates' 1786 map of Lancashire will reveal the apparent isolation of Kirkham even in regard to the rest of Lancashire, let alone the rest of the country. The turnpike road from Preston is shown as proceeding only as far as the town and no further. Kirkham was literally out on a limb. Off the direct road north, it had not the advantage of Garstang, which was a staging post, but was a little more fortunate than Poulton le Fylde, the third market town on the Fylde, which had no turnpiked road at all.

The road between Preston and Kirkham passed through the land of two owners, Thomas Clifton of Lytham and Sir Henry Hoghton of Hoghton Tower. The road was for a long time 'very ruinous and in bad repair' but in 1771 the two landowners agreed to make a new road at their own expense and the tolls on the new road were publicly auctioned.[173] Yates put the toll bar at Lea.

Although there was no turnpike to the west of Kirkham, William Hutton, travelling from Preston to the coast could write in 1788 that the approach to Blackpool was through good safe roads, easy for the traveller. The post-chaise fare was eighteen shillings for the eighteen miles. By 1783 coaches ran from Manchester to Blackpool.[174]

Although some eighteenth-century travellers, like Arthur Young, spoke almost despairingly of the state of the northern roads, finding the roads about Preston and Warrington particularly bad,[175] others,

---

[173] R. Sharpe France, 'The highway from Preston into the Fylde', *HSLC*, Vol. 97, 1945, pp. 35, 40 and *passim*.
[174] W. Hutton, *A Description of Blackpool in Lancashire*, 1788, reprinted Liverpool, 1944, pp. 11, 12.
[175] Arthur Young, *A Six Months Tour Through the North of England*, 1771, quoted in E. A. Pratt, *Inland Transport and Communication in England*, 1912, p. 70.

like the antiquary Pococke, writing some twenty years previously, appeared unconcerned about the conditions of travel.[176] Indeed, in the Langton circle there was much coming and going, on business to Lancaster, Liverpool and London; on family visits to Blackburn, to Preston, to Chester, to Fazakerley, to Ormskirk and to Oxford; for health reasons to Bristol, Bath and Lytham; for diversion to Blackpool, to Harrogate, and through the Lake District to Askham. In his youth Thomas Langton visited Ireland and returned via Scotland. The last letter is to Will Langton, on holiday in France, and the penultimate one came to the firm from Hull. There is no sense of a backwater existence. On the contrary, there is much movement and activity. Thomas Langton's statement in September 1772 that he had been 'almost continuously abroad' is no bad summing up.[177]

It is now considered that the roads must have been a great deal better than was thought until fairly recently, if only because the whole country was criss-crossed by a network of routes plied by a frequent carrier service.[178] Indeed, Pickfords, which eventually Zachary Langton was to help to run, started in the north in the seventeenth century. In the letters there are several references to Preston–London carriers, including one strong protest about the 'most exorbitant charge' of twenty-three shillings.[179]

The Manchester–London road was turnpiked in the early 1750s. It took until the '60s for the London–Warrington road to be continued as far as Liverpool, but by 1766 there was a London stage coach service from the port. By the 1770s the coach plied to London from Preston. By the time of the letters the journey from both Liverpool and Manchester took two days in summer and three in winter. The fare was in the region of two guineas for a night coach and £2 10s. for a day coach. Travelling inside from Preston to Liverpool cost 8s. 6d.[180] Thomas Langton does not appear to have owned his own carriage but his partner, William Shepherd, did.[181]

[176] Richard Pococke, *Dr Pococke's Journey into England from Dublin*, Cam. Soc., Vols. 42 and 44, 1887–8, 1889–90.
[177] LRO, DDX/190/36.
[178] J. A. Chartres, 'Road Carrying in England in the Seventeenth Century. Myth or reality?' *Ec. Hist.*, 2nd Series, 1977, p. 73.
[179] LRO, DDX/190/36.
[180] W. J. Jackman, *The Development of Transportation in Modern England*, Manchester, 1962 edn, Appendix 6, p. 704.
[181] LRO, DDD, Shepherd Birley Notebook.

When Thomas Langton wrote from Hull in June 1787 he commented on 'the pleasant journey' even though the roads, being cross country, would not all have been turnpiked.[182] (The summer weather might have helped, but Arthur Young did not find the summer a palliative to the discomfort of travel.) Even the difficult Langton journey to Oxford in March 1786 was difficult because of snow, not the roads *per se*.[183] Indeed, it must be said that Thomas Langton and his friends appear to have found the roads adequate for their needs. Even the mercenary Thomas Langton did not comment on the tolls.

The roads, however, were not the only means of transport open to the Langton firm for the dispatch of their merchandise. Although, situated as they were, they could not do without road transport completely, for longer journeys the Langtons sent most of their merchandise by sea or, later, canal. To the end of the century the coasting trade continued to be widely used even when the canals were developing, and there were many vessels plying to London and to northern ports.[184] Poulton-le-Fylde, for example, shipped corn, peas and beans to Liverpool, coal from Whitehaven, deals and iron from Grange.[185] Thomas Langton shipped canvas to London from Poulton via Liverpool, and to Whitehaven when a sloop was available.[186] From Lancaster he shipped direct to London.[187] Flax landed in Liverpool came on the coastal vessel to Poulton, and the Langton boys' desk was shipped 'by the first sloop' from Liverpool to the Ribble.[188]

By the time of the letters the canal system was not complete, but there were several routes available to the Langton firm. In 1780 flax landed in Hull would 'no doubt be speedily forwarded by canal', and in 1782 hemp was expected in Hull of which 'the conveyance from thence by Kildwick would be very speedy'.[189] The Leeds and Liverpool canal, to which this refers, was not yet cut across the country, the Pennines forming a more formidable barrier than expected. Cut from either end, it was to meet in 1816; by 1777 the Yorkshire cut had reached Gargrave, passing through Kildwick on

---

[182] LRO, DDX/190/68.
[183] LRO, DDX/190/66.
[184] Lancaster Trade Tax Account, LC.
[185] T. S. Willan, *The English Coasting Trade 1600–1750*, Manchester, 1938, p. 190.
[186] LRO, DDX/190/62.
[187] LRO, DDX/190/67.
[188] LRO, DDX/190/65, 33.
[189] LRO, DDX/190/61, 65.

the way from the Aire Navigation.[190] Road haulage would be required for part of the journey, which would nevertheless be speedier
than the sea journey round Scotland. The goods would no doubt be
eventually trans-shipped by the Rufford branch of the Liverpool end
to Freckleton across the Ribble estuary.

The remark in a letter of 1780 that, because of the absence of a
Whitehaven sloop, an order had to go by Liverpool and the firm was
therefore 'forced to send it by canal' implies that a coastal vessel would
have been preferred.[191] However, by 1782, Will was instructed to
ship the 'remains of the Petersburg' from Liverpool 'by the first canal
boat to Freckleton', a direct reference to the Ribble crossing at
Hesketh Bank.[192] The journey to London by the network of canals
then in operation was to be undertaken by the bales being 'shipped
pretty largely to Liverpool' by the coastal route then transferred 'on
board the Duke's flats' (the Duke of Bridgewater's barges) 'to take the
first conveyance by canal boats'.[193] They would be carried via the
Weaver Navigation to the Trent and Mersey for the first part of their
journey. As this was the Navy order, the quickest route was required.

The Ribble was as important for travellers as for merchandise. The
boys came home from Liverpool on horseback, crossing the river by
the ford, also at Hesketh Bank, which necessitated knowing the tides
so that they could arrive at the correct time.[194] A guide was essential;
Yates marks two guide houses at Freckleton. When Will was to
return from a business trip to Liverpool, Thomas instructed him to
go in the cart and let the guide carry the whiskey he was bringing.[195]

Thomas Langton, then, had various means of transport at his
disposal and made appropriate use of all of them. He had no difficulty in keeping in touch with his markets and in getting his raw
materials to his home base from the ports. Sea-going ships, coastal
vessels, barges and horse-drawn drays all served him in his commerce, and post-chaise and, later, possibly mail coach, in his travel.

[190] J. Langton, 'Liverpool and the hinterland in the late eighteenth century' in
B. N. Anderson and P. J. M. Stoney, eds., *Commerce Industry and Transport.
Studies in Economic Change in Merseyside*, 1983, map 6.
[191] LRO, DDX/190/62.
[192] LRO, DDX/190/65.
[193] LRO, DDX/190/65.
[194] LRO, DDX/190/33, 34.
[195] LRO, DDX/190/65.

The mail coach also carried his later letters, and he frequently referred to the postal service. Once the post waited outside until he had finished a letter;[196] on holiday, he intended to wait up till the post arrived at Askham at 11 p.m.;[197] he collected a letter at the Penrith office;[198] he had *poste restante* letters at Oxford;[199] when at the Hotwells he expected to hear from Kirkham 'by every post'.[200]

Until 1784 the rates fixed by the Post Office Act of 1711 still obtained: 1d. for one stage, 2d. for two stages, 3d. for up to eighty miles, and 4d. for over eighty.[201] In 1784 1d. was added across the board, these rates continuing until Thomas Langton's death. From the evidence of the letters the mail seemed to be reliable. There is no mention of lost letters. The service, nevertheless, was in some danger, manned until 1784 by unarmed postboys. In 1784 mail coaches were introduced, with passengers and with guards for protection.[202] No doubt with the uncertainty of delivery in mind, but more especially to spare his correspondents from paying the charges for which the recipient was liable, Thomas Langton used the postal services only when no personal contact offered. He preferred to send by the hand of someone travelling to the destination, but if this was not possible, it was an economical measure to send several letters under the same cover.[203] From Bristol, for example, he sent his letter to his children with one to a local resident, to save them the postage.[204]

We are left, then, with the conclusion that, however unpromising the contemporary map might appear, and however grimly some accounts paint the picture, the Kirkham of the Langtons was by no means cut off from the rest of the world. In fact, it appeared to be fully connected with a network of communications which stretched to Russia and America at the furthest and to London and many provincial centres nearer home. News of family and business doings was not seriously delayed and, in the letters, we have no hint of the roads causing accident or discomfort when travelling. London, the trading capital, was only two or three days away, and many of the

---

[196] LRO, DDX/190/63.
[197] LRO, DDX/190/58.
[198] LRO, DDX/190/61.
[199] LRO, DDX/190/49.
[200] LRO, DDX/190/47.
[201] Howard Robinson, *Britain's Post Office*, 1953, p. 100.
[202] Jackman, *op. cit.*, pp. 323, 327.
[203] See, for example, LRO, DDX/190/21.
[204] LRO, DDX/190/47.

family and their connections thought nothing of embarking on the journey.

In summary we may say that, during the latter half of the eighteenth century, especially in the last quarter, the linen industry was of paramount importance in Kirkham and the surrounding villages. The main manufacture was sailcloth, any surplus to Navy requirements being sold through agents. The Langton firm mirrored national developments from John Langton's diversification from woollen drapery into merchant venturing, around 1746, to Thomas Langton's control of the partnership up to the time of his death in 1794, his provision for his sons in positions to their own and the firm's advantage, and his expansion of the trading side of the business. Thomas Langton's own career, from his freedom in 1751 to his death, coincided with the height of the English linen industry's prosperity, and the fortunes of his firm reflected the national context, affected by national legislation and international affairs.

Thomas Langton died roughly 100 years after his grandfather came to Kirkham. During that century the Langtons came to form part of a respected commercial élite, of substance in their locality, and expected to assume responsibilities outside their commercial concerns. Their local prestige depended in large measure on their business prosperity, itself largely relying on their personal qualities and reputation. Carried from father to son as the century progressed, extending in scope as their enterprises prospered, their standing was assured.

Although provincial, the merchants of Kirkham were not parochial. Their horizons were not cramped and they were at home in a wide circle of business and personal contacts. If the most popular plays of the time depicted the provincial as raw, thinking only of his wenches and the alehouse, or coping unsuccessfully with fashionable society, he came from his ancestral acres, not his counting house.[205]

----

[205] Tony Lumpkin in Oliver Goldsmith's *She Stoops to Conquer*, produced 1773; Bob Acres in R. B. Sheridan's *The Rivals*, produced 1775.

Introduction

SECTION II: PRIVATE LIFE

Education

To prepare sons for their part in this far-reaching ambit, some thought had to be given to their education. Thomas Langton would have to consider what was the best preparation he could give them to fit them for their places in the family enterprise.

From the late seventeenth century onwards, children had come to be much more humanely treated than had been usual earlier in the century, when flogging and other severe punishments were commonplace. There was less emphasis upon driving out the old Adam and breaking the will, and more upon John Locke's advocacy of inculcating in them a 'love of credit and an apprehension of shame and disgust'. After Locke, the emphasis shifted towards social rather than religious principles in child rearing, and, for the middle and upper classes, this meant that the child must be equipped with the necessary accomplishments to fit him for gainful employment or for a respected place in society or, indeed, for both.[206]

The primacy of a classical education had been challenged by Locke as early as 1693. While admitting that Latin was necessary for a gentleman and Greek for a scholar, he questioned their value for a boy destined for trade.[207] In 1765 Joseph Priestley published an Essay on Liberal Education in which he stated that 'Formerly, none but the clergy were thought to have any occasion for learning', and that 'the whole plan of education from the Grammar School to the University' had been 'calculated for their use'. He advocated that a different and 'a better furniture of the mind' must be brought into the 'business of life'.[208]

---

[206] J. H. Plumb, 'The new world of children in eighteenth-century England', Past and Present, No. 67, 1975, pp. 65, 68, 69.
[207] Quoted in L. U. Clarke, Greek Studies in England 1711–1830, Cambridge, 1945, p. 11.
[208] Quoted in Irene Parker, Dissenting Academies in England, Cambridge, 1914, p. 115.

Classical education, on the other hand, had its advocates who agreed with William Pitt that Homer and Virgil contained the finest lessons for young men:

> lessons of honour, courage, disinterestedness, love of truth, command of temper, gentleness of behaviour, humanity, and, in a word, virtue in the true significance ... to the prodigious advantage ... to the heart and morals.[209]

This clash of the classical with the modern might seem on the surface to be a clash between the old grammar schools, originally endowed to teach the classics and providing free education, at least to those who could not afford to pay, and the new private sector which proliferated in the eighteenth century.[210] For the aristocracy there were still the private tutors, and the élite of the ancient foundations catered for those with money or the ability to win scholarships, but the bulk of the middle class still attended the local grammar schools and, as the century progressed, the private schools which offered a curriculum which seemed the better to answer their needs.

The standards of the best of the academies set up to provide higher education for those for whom dissent precluded attendance at Oxford or Cambridge were high, and the education they provided more liberal and much wider than that of the universities.[211] The thinking behind them influenced educational institutions of much less academic pretension and there were many such establishments offering practical advantage supplemented by sound moral principles. In the new ground they broke, the idea of a liberal education was no longer removed from everyday life and grounded on the classics. Their curricula were much more in touch with the contemporary world.

The endowed grammar schools were often in poor shape to compete with the new trends. They were bound in many cases by rigid foundation stipulations and by their mandate to provide free education. Inflation hit them hard. In practice, most had 'foreigners' (fee payers) as well as charity boys, and headmasters augmented their stipends by boarding pupils or teaching extra subjects. Fundamental change in the curriculum was not legally possible without alteration of the foundation deeds. Though most had a 'petties' department for

---

[209] *Ibid.*, p. 8.
[210] Nicholas Hans, *New Trends in Education in the Eighteenth Century*, 1951, *passim*.
[211] Parker, *op. cit.*, pp. 134–5.

young pupils to be taught their three Rs as well as rudimentary Latin grammar, the new subjects, increasing in popularity, could not always be introduced if charters were not to be violated. However, some did succeed in adopting something of the new curriculum and others managed to keep going with reduced numbers. Some became schools dealing exclusively with elementary education.[212]

The private schools, with their independent foundations, had virtually *carte blanche* to teach what they pleased. They attempted to provide an education contemporary in outlook and what would be called today more obviously 'relevant'. There were many of them, highly competitive and often precariously poised, with many failing. They taught a variety of subjects, each school compiling an independent curriculum, sometimes specialising in mathematics, sometimes in writing, sometimes offering a broader base including European languages, navigation, even fortification, along with the three Rs. The emphasis was overwhelmingly on commercial subjects, merchants' accounts (double entry book-keeping) being ubiquitous, with writing almost universally offered.[213] But many kept Latin among their subjects, as if to keep up their end with the ancient foundations and to show they were still able to cater for gentlemen.

There was much less provision for girls, far fewer of whom received education outside the home. There were middle-class boarding schools and charity foundations, while some of the grammar schools taught boys and girls together in the petties. In the middle-class establishments the emphasis was on social graces and suitable feminine accomplishments, in the charity schools on useful skills.[214] At dames' schools the very young were 'minded' and perhaps taught to read.

In Kirkham the public education was provided, from an unknown date but certainly before 1551, by a grammar school which probably originated as a chantry school run by a chantry priest, as was the practice at St Michaels on Wyre and other churches in Lancashire.[215] The school eventually passed under the direction of the thirtymen, who set up an endowment fund in the parish in 1604. Two subsequent seventeenth-century bequests added to the wealth of the endowment but caused confusion, as one bequest nominated a local

---

[212] Richard S. Tompson, *Classics or Charity*, Manchester, 1971, p. 126.
[213] Plumb, *op. cit.*, p. 72.
[214] Plumb, *op. cit.*, p. 72; MS notebook of John Langton, LRO, DDX/190/109, and R. Cunliffe Shaw, *Kirkham in Amounderness*, Preston, 1949, p. 540.
[215] Shaw, *op. cit.*, p. 147.

trust while the other appointed the Drapers' Company in London. Not until a chancery ruling in 1840 was an uneasy peace established between these contending interests.

Throughout the seventeenth century, however, the grammar, or free, school housed next to the church served the parish and sent some pupils to university. In 1670 a university scholarship for a poor scholar was endowed. Another chancery ruling of 1673 directed the third master to teach writing and arithmetic to about ten children 'whose parents [were] not able to pay', in addition to introducing the lower pupils to Latin grammar.[216] As all boys resident in the parish were to be taught free, either these boys must have resided outside the parish or writing and arithmetic must hitherto have been extra curricular. We may conclude, then, that a number of poor children were educated at the school in the rudiments. Girls were also accepted in the lower school until, in 1701, the masters refused to teach them.[217] There was no separate provision for girls until the girls' charity school was opened in 1760.

Shaw records no other eighteenth-century school in Kirkham, but we know from a list of schoolmasters who kept private schools and sent students to universities (appended by Nicholas Hans to his study of *New Trends in Education in the Eighteenth Century*) that a Thomas Taylor kept school in Kirkham from 1718 to 1738.[218] We know from the Langton letters that there was at least one dame's school, as John Hornby attended it;[219] and Shepherd Birley tells of another at the end of the century. By 1832 there were several day schools, including a Catholic one, catering for pupils who did not attend the grammar school.[220]

The Langton family was closely connected with the education provision in Kirkham. As noted above, Cornelius married the daughter of the master of the free school in 1689. His son, Zachary (the Uncle Langton of the letters), won the Barker Exhibition, the one endowed scholarship of the school, in 1714.[221] His granddaughter, the letter writer's sister, married a later master (the Uncle Threlfall of the

---

[216] *Ibid.*, p. 486.
[217] *Ibid.*, p. 493.
[218] Hans, *op. cit.*, p. 239.
[219] LRO, DDX/190/21.
[220] Shaw, *op. cit.*, p. 512.
[221] H. Fishwick, *The History of the Parish of Kirkham*, Chet. Soc., XCII, 1874, p. 152.

letters), a graduate of Wadham, who held the post from 1744 to 1801. John Langton was co-founder of the girls' charity school and, as noted above, the Langtons were trustees, governors and visitors well into the nineteenth century, closely connected with both schools.

Yet, although his Uncle Zachary had won his scholarship under Richard Taylor, who was master from 1701 to 1744, Thomas Langton, born in 1724, did not attend the local school. He was educated at Clitheroe Grammar School. The reason for this must remain a matter of conjecture. Perhaps Clitheroe was chosen on the recommendation of the Thomas Taylor (no apparent relation of the master) listed by Nicholas Hans as running a private school in Kirkham from 1718 to 1738 and sending pupils to University. Taylor was himself probably a former pupil, being a native of Waddington and curate of Clitheroe from 1701 to 1738.

In his will made when his son Thomas was four, John Langton made provision for the letter writer to be sent to University or put to some 'honest laudable vocation trade or employment'.[222] University education meant a classical curriculum in preparation, and Clitheroe certainly provided that. In the list of endowed grammar schools published by Carlisle in 1818, the school was said to be exclusively classical and 'free without limitation',[223] which it obviously was not in Thomas Langton's day, as accounts for books bought for 'poor scholars' prove. These include a formidable list: *The Whole Duty of Man* in Latin; Hool's *Accidence*; Clark's *Cornelius Nepos*; Bailey's Ovid's *Epistles and Metamorphoses*; Juvenal; Virgil; a lexicon; a Latin testament; Tully's *Orations*; Wilson Kennet's *Antiquities*. In 1740, when Thomas Langton would be sixteen and either a pupil or recently left, the governors funded a production of *The Tragedy of Cato* (presumably Addison's).[224]

This strong meat would have adequately fitted Thomas Langton, who must have boarded as he could not have travelled daily, for university entrance. It would seem, on the face of it, somewhat 'irrelevant' for the 'laudable vocation' of flax merchant which he espoused. Had he attended the Kirkham school he should have received something similar, if the Drapers' Company ruling of 1673 (that a strictly classical course was to be provided for the boys

[222] LRO, DDX/190/10.
[223] Nicholas Carlisle, *A Concise Description of the Endowed Grammar Schools in England and Wales*, Vol. 1, 1810 p. 652.
[224] Clitheroe Grammar School Accounts, LRO, DDX/22/5.

reaching the headmaster's class) was adhered to.[225] A long-serving headmaster was a common phenomenon of the eighteenth century, and a long incumbency meant that the well-entrenched holder of office could become something of a liability if he were not satisfactory.[226] At Kirkham, Richard Taylor was not assiduous in his duties, nor was the school well-disciplined.[227] Moreover, he was in fierce dispute with the vicar, refusing to teach girls in spite of the fact that there was nothing in the benefactor's will to preclude them.[228] John Langton sided with the vicar in the resultant dissension and dissatisfaction, eventually helping to provide for them in his own foundation by introducing reading, knitting, sewing and useful knowledge 'to poor girls only'.[229] His notebook shows his genuine concern that the endowment was being misinterpreted.[230] Although the girls' school came sixteen years after Taylor's death, John Langton would hardly have wanted to put his son in Taylor's care when he disagreed with him so profoundly, quite apart from the poor reputation of the grammar school.

By 1760 John Langton was in a position to put his stamp on the life of the town by way of this foundation. The charity school was a favourite form of charitable enterprise for the pious and philanthropic men of the eighteenth century.[231] The 'useful knowledge' and practical skills, suitably feminine and menial, dispensed to the girls were entirely in keeping with the contemporary insistence that children so provided for should be fitted for their station in the social structure. Whether or not John Langton was partially motivated by a desire to impress his neighbours by 'doing something for the poor'[232] as well as restoring something of the 'privilege' intended for them and subsequently revoked, the poor girls of Kirkham benefited from what would be an enhancement of status for the Langton family in the town.

[225] Shaw, *op. cit.*, p. 486.
[226] Derek Robson, *Some Aspects of Education in Cheshire in the Eighteenth Century*, Chet. Soc. 3rd Series, Vol. XLIII, 1966, p. 103 *et seq.*
[227] Shaw, *op. cit.*, p. 493.
[228] *Ibid.*, p. 494.
[229] *Ibid.*, p. 540.
[230] LRO, DDX/190/109.
[231] M. G. Jones, *The Charity School Movement in the Eighteenth Century*, Cambridge, 1938, p. 3.
[232] Robson, *op. cit.*, p. 162.

In spite of his classical education, Thomas Langton must have opted for a 'laudable vocation' rather than an academic calling. When the time came for him to educate his sons, the educational scene offered much more choice than when he was himself a boy. There is no doubt that their education was supremely important to him, but there is nothing to suggest that he offered them the option of the university education which his father had once offered him. In the light of his careful deployment of the human resources of his family, it is reasonable to assume he did not consider it. What is clear is his expectation of a due return on his investment in educating them. He looked for future 'advantage' to the Langton enterprise as well as to the Langton sons. In line with the progressive thought of the day, he required for them a 'liberal education' and, like Priestley, expected them to apply it to the 'business of life', or, in his words, it was to be 'of use'.[233]

For the foundation of this 'liberal education' the boys attended Kirkham free school under their uncle, the Revd John Threlfall, to whom Thomas Langton's sister, Sarah, was married. According to the ordinances of the Drapers' Company, the second master taught Latin grammar and 'such authors as the Headmaster appointed him, being such as are usual in schools'. The third master, or usher, was 'to enter the lower scholars into the Latin Grammar, or at least to teach the introduction commonly called the Accidence'. There was some overlap allowed in the two lowest classes.[234] Thus we read that the third Langton boy and the son of the Hornby rival were 'under the care' of the second master.[235]

Other boys as well as the Langtons left the school before completing the full course. When they were at school at Woolton, Mr Threlfall sent remembrances to the Langtons and to 'all the rest of the boys of his acquaintance'.[236] Some two months after Jack and Will had started at their new school, their father told them that Mr Threlfall might come to visit them 'as it [was] the season the scholars [were] instructed in writing', presumably not by Mr Threlfall.[237] Writing, then, did not feature in the regular timetable at Kirkham.

---

[233] LRO, DDX/190/35, 21.
[234] Shaw, *op. cit.*, p. 486.
[235] LRO, DDX/190/21.
[236] LRO, DDX/190/23.
[237] *Ibid.*

With his concern for his commercial prosperity, Thomas Langton needed a school which laid adequate stress on writing and accounts. Although more and more grammar schools managed to include these subjects, Kirkham was not among them. As late as 1831 the complaint was that:

> many boys [had] not the opportunity of being instructed in writing and accounts according to the present management of the school, so as to be materially benefited by the instruction given there, for when the boys [were] old enough, and so far instructed in English as to be considered competent to learn Latin and Greek, they [were] required to do so ... in all cases.[238]

The school chosen by Thomas Langton in 1771 had opened in Liverpool in 1765. The *Williamson's Advertiser* of 7 January carried the notice:

> On Monday, 7th instant, at a large and convenient room near the Old Church, Liverpool, will be opened an Academy for the instruction of Youth in the following useful and polite branches of learning viz. the English Grammar, the Latin, Greek, French and German languages, Geometry, Perspective, Arithmetic, the Italian method of Bookkeeping, Drawing, Music in the Spring and Summer and Autumn quarters. The Art of Fencing between the hours of twelve and one (during which time the Gentlemen will not be permitted to stay in the Rooms). Ladies may be taught Drawing, Writing, Arithmetic and Geography.
> Rev. Mr. Booth

It offered, then, the best of both worlds: the 'useful' and the 'polite'; the classics as well as modern subjects. As in all schools, much would depend upon the headmaster, and Thomas Langton was likely to know the Revd Mr Booth, who was one of the four curates attached to St Nicholas and St Peter's Church and lived at the time in the same street as Langton's brother-in-law, Savige Leech, a Liverpool broker.[239]

In 1766 Booth sold this school and moved to Woolton Hall. He must have hoped to attract sons of American colonists for, on 27 November 1766, he advertised his school in the *Virginia Gazette* with the terms. 'Young gentlemen' were educated 'At the Rev. B.

---

[238] Shaw, *op. cit.*, p. 512.
[239] Liverpool Directory, 1766.

Booth's Academy the seat of the late Lady Molyneux at Woolton Hall, five miles from Liverpool'. They were taught English, Latin, Greek, writing, arithmetic, merchants' accounts, geography, navigation, astronomy, surveying, mathematics in general, drawing and perspective, with music, dancing and fencing extra.[240] There is no mention of girls. No foreign languages were mentioned, though they were certainly taught.

There was no surveillance of the credentials of those who set up these private schools or of the conditions prevailing in them. The grammar schools had at least their trustees, contentious as some of them were. Some of the private schoolmasters were charlatans, with no qualifications but an eagerness to cash in on the demand of the manufacturers and merchants for a modern education for their sons. The expectations of some parents were not high, if Robert Southey reported accurately of his fellow pupils in the Bristol of the early 1780s: 'Writing and arithmetic, with at most a little French, were thought sufficient at that time for the sons of Bristol merchants.'[241] Many schools, but by no means all, were run by clergymen and this at least guaranteed an educated headmaster, albeit one educated in the classical tradition.

Thomas Langton made a fortunate choice in the Revd Bartholomew Booth and his school. Booth was the son of a schoolmaster, was educated at Manchester Grammar School, matriculated at the age of twenty-one at Brasenose and was incumbent of All Saints, Marple, from 1757 to 1761. In 1760 he was appointed master at Disley school, run on a charity basis.[242] An advertisement in the *Liverpool Chronicle* for 3 to 10 December 1767 suggests that he was a man of humanity and kindness:

Wanted at Woolton Academy
Near Liverpool
An Assistant in the English Language
Of Sober Character and Temper
That will bear with the little Foibles
Of Children.

[240] Information supplied to Maurice Whitehead by Professor Sheldon S. Cohen, Loyola University.
[241] Quoted in H. C. Brown and R. T. Harris, *Bristol England*, Bristol, 1964, p. 131.
[242] Information supplied by Maurice Whitehead.

Thomas Langton obviously thought well of him and desired his sons not to offend him.[243] He was sorry when the school was to move again, as he was 'well satisfied with the situation'.[244] When the Feilden brother-in-law visited the school he 'much approved' of Mr Booth's behaviour, and Thomas Langton appreciated the courtesy of Mr Booth's invitation to himself and his wife to visit the boys in Essex and stay in the school.[245]

At leat one member of his staff shared this golden opinion of Mr Booth. Mr Newby, who figures in the letters, was a Roman Catholic recusant, and his presence on the staff in itself suggested Mr Booth's broadmindedness. Newby was at the school for seven years, including the two-year residence of the Langton boys, which terminated when they left and Booth emigrated to America. So moved was Newby by the virtues of his headmaster that he celebrated them in verse 'with the surest confession of grateful regard for many kindnesses received'.[246] Nor did he forget his gratitude after Booth's death. In the prospectus of his own school near Preston he acknowledged that he was 'grounded in most of what he knew ... by the Attention and Goodness (almost parental) of the late Mr. Booth'.[247]

The Langton boys were fortunate in their teachers and they enjoyed the school so much that they begged their father, against his initial opposition, to let them accompany Mr Booth when the school moved to High Beach, in Essex.

Thomas Langton left the moral guidance of his sons to Mr Booth, whom he trusted, and instructed his sons to conduct themselves in the way Mr Booth approved.[248] He submitted their academic progress to a much more rigorous scrutiny, determined to get value for money. He asked to see the programme of work Mr Booth drew up for them, in itself suggesting that Mr Booth operated upon enlightened lines, suiting each programme to each boy.[249] Writing and accounts particularly engaged Thomas Langton's attention, with writing receiving constant comment no doubt because he had

[243] LRO, DDX/190/27.
[244] LRO, DDX/190/29.
[245] LRO, DDX/190/36.
[246] Maurice Whitehead, *Peter Newby. Eighteenth-Century Lancashire Recusant Poet*, Lancaster, 1980, p. 37.
[247] Josephine Malone, *Peter Newby*, Aylesford, 1964, p. 105.
[248] LRO, DDX/190/28, 38.
[249] LRO, DDX/190/21, 37.

obvious evidence in the boys' letters home. But the Langton background was not philistine. Books were sent from home as they were
requested—perhaps, where appropriate, Thomas Langton's own
from his schooldays—and they were sufficiently numerous for a list
to be drawn up, although the contents are not specified in the
letters.[250] At school the boys were told to acquire whatever books
their teachers recommended. As a young man Thomas Langton felt
at home among the dons at Trinity College, Dublin and, in later life,
seemed to relish consorting with his uncle's Oxford friends.[251] Yet
there is no mention of reading matter for himself, either newspaper,
periodical or book. With his business, his public commitments and
his correspondence he may have had little time for reading. The
boys, however, were to be ever ready to exploit events for the
possibility of some 'future use', as when a Dutch boy joined the
school from a Dutch academy. The newcomer's knowledge of Dutch
and French might be 'of use', even though all the Baltic contacts of
the firm were English. Thomas Langton bade his sons to prosecute
Dutch as well as the High Dutch (German) they were already
learning.[252] The Langton boys would have at least a superficial
acquaintance with several languages, including Latin.

If the poor were to be kept in their place by whatever education was
meted out to them, the merchant class was to be prepared for upward
social mobility by theirs, educated as gentlemen as well as tradesmen.
Some extra-curricular accomplishments were desirable. Towards this
end, Thomas Langton advocated dancing, as he thought it gave young
people 'a pretty easy manner and an agreeable behaviour'.[253] He did
not think of music in the same way, although he allowed Will to
learn the flute. He would have preferred the harpsichord, but there
was no instrument at High Beach. He thought 'wind music ... too
apt to prey on the constitution when too closely applied to' and
warned Will not to damage his health with it. On the other hand, if
he was to learn he should provide himself with a good instrument
and report progress to his father, who was paying. At all costs, the
flute was not to 'interfere too much with ... other studies'.[254]

---

[250] LRO, DDX/190/26.
[251] Thomas Langton, Manuscript Diary of a Tour of Ireland, undated, LRO,
DDX/190/111; LRO, DDX/190/50.
[252] LRO, DDX/190/39.
[253] LRO, DDX/190/38.
[254] LRO, DDX/190/36.

Dancing could be learnt earlier. Zachary, aged nine, and Cecily, at eleven, attended a local dancing school 'every day they [had] Mr. Bradley [there]' and Zachary was one of 'the finest dancers of the young ones in the school'.[255] At ten, Zachary was attending a writing school, whether instead of, or supplementary to, the grammar school is not clear, but probably the latter.[256] If the older boys had not gone to Essex, their father proposed to put Will, at fourteen, to a master where he would have had 'the opportunity of making a further proficiency in the French language, as well as writing and accounts, though these last [were] what was chiefly to be regarded'. The elder, John, would have been put to 'a master for writing and accounts for a few months at Liverpool, or some other place where he [might] incline to be fixed'.[257]

When Zachary, the third son, was fourteen, Thomas Langton took him to Hampstead Academy where he made him a parlour (full) boarder and again found a congenial headmaster.[258] Five years earlier Essex had seemed too far away and too expensive. Now a school near the capital seemed desirable. The firm already had London connections and Zachary was destined for settlement there, in his own business but as a family firm representative as well. Tom, the youngest, was also educated near London, very probably at the same school.[259] His intended posting to the Baltic no doubt required him to learn to be at ease socially. Cornelius, the fourth son, went blind in childhood and remained in Kirkham, at least learning to play the organ in the parish church.[260] It would seem that Cecily, the only girl, received no formal education away from home.

To Thomas Langton, if education was to be 'of service' it was to equip his sons to take their appointed places in the Langton enterprise and to enable them to develop into those reliable citizens whose good name would enhance the firm's reputation. It was to give them, essentially, commercial values and to inculcate in them the necessity of keeping accurate accounts of all expenditure.

It was also to furnish them with sufficient social grace to enable them to mix easily with other young people. It was not a drawing

[255] LRO, DDX/190/25.
[256] LRO, DDX/190/37.
[257] LRO, DDX/190/29, 30.
[258] LRO, DDX/190/52.
[259] Anne Langton, *The Story of our Family*, Manchester, 1881, p. 3.
[260] Organ Book of Accounts, Kirkham Parish Records, LRO, PR 207.

out of talent. It was a putting in of the acquisitions of learning appropriate for merchants. From his own point of view as the provider of the education, value for money was as important a criterion as it was in business. When the school moved to Essex, the fee of forty guineas a year he supposed to include all extras but wished to be informed. He feared the reduction of numbers to twenty boys indicated a restriction in the range of teaching.[261] Eventually he gave permission for his sons to move with the school, 'although it would be attended with a very heavy expense', which he hoped they would sufficiently repay 'by [their] diligent attention to [their] studies and utmost endeavours and improvements therein'.[262] He frequently reiterated this theme. He wished the boys to return to Kirkham 'improved' and ready to start their business training in the firm, but also with gentlemanly bearing and some social accomplishment.[263]

The Langton boys fared better than the sons of some of the more opulent city merchants. In Leeds, the majority of merchants sent their sons to the free grammar school, the private establishments in the city being 'very dubious places of learning'. Merchants used them only for the occasional special course in languages and accounts to supplement the classical fare of the grammar school.[264] Many of the Hull merchants are presumed to have sent their sons to the local grammar school, though by the 1780s excellent academies existed. In 1798 Tickell, the local historian, thought it necessary to defend the virtues of the classical curriculum, no doubt with men like Thomas Langton in mind, with their emphasis on 'usefulness':

> If it be asked what is its use in after life? it should be considered what is meant by use. If the idea be entirely mercantile the benefit of Grammar is not so evident. But how absurd to measure everything by money. The improvement of the mind, and the more solid feast of understanding, are ends surely worthy the attention of rational beings.[265]

The educational debate of the eighteenth century, like all such debates, was bound to be inconclusive. Certainly the classics were

---

[261] LRO, DDX/190/30.
[262] LRO, DDX/190/38.
[263] *Ibid.*
[264] R. G. Wilson, *Gentlemen Merchants. The Merchant Community of Leeds 1700–1830*, Manchester, 1971, p. 208.
[265] Gordon Jackson, *Hull in the Eighteenth Century*, Oxford, 1972, p. 276.

not entirely dispossessed. For some, the old curriculum was successful, particularly if supplemented by writing and arithmetic on an
extra-curricular basis. For some, the newer curriculum was preferable, particularly if supplemented by a knowledge of Latin to relate
it to the more traditional provision. A combination of the two no
doubt gave a sound balance. But basically, then as always, everything
depended upon the teachers and their attitude to their pupils. Many,
in all periods, have survived their formal schooling to flourish afterwards in ways unrelated to any obvious 'relevance' it may have had,
yet influenced for good or ill by the atmosphere and personnel of
their schools.

As for Thomas Langton's investment, what interest did it realise?
Socially, it made a sound return. His sons were able to take their
place with ease in their world and to aspire to something akin to
gentry status in later life. John, the eldest, retired in his late forties
to a life of leisure. Will, the second, was able from his mid forties to
spend most of his time in leisure in Kirkham, going but seldom to
Liverpool to his merchant firm.[266] Zachary, the London son, became
the master of the Skinners' Company,[267] a social rather than a
commercial distinction. Tom, the youngest, returned from Russia,
was appointed Deputy Lieutenant of Lancashire and elected president of the Liverpool Royal Institution.[268] On the commercial side
there is rather less to show. Educated though they might be in
writing and accounts, the two eldest boys opted out of the partnership ten years after their father's death. No dying in harness for
them. In the last extant letter, written six years before his death,
Thomas Langton was in absolute control, issuing orders, contemplating new ventures, critical alike of his son's gallivanting as of his
business oversights. Thomas Langton's associates were either likely
to be 'of service' to his business or to enhance his public standing.
To him, Will's travelling companions were something of a liability,
'not being conversant in trade'.[269] Ironically, equipped with a classical education and its irrelevancies, he was by far the most thorough-
going businessman of them all.

[266] Anne Langton, *op. cit.*, p. 6.
[267] Thomas Langton (Junior), *Letters to Mrs Thomas Hornby 1815–1818*,
Manchester, 1900, p. 9.
[268] *Ibid.*, p. 3.
[269] LRO, DDX/190/67.

John Langton died at fifty-one, Will at fifty-six, before the business he ostensibly partnered with Tom went into liquidation. When the crash came in 1821, Tom eventually emigrated to Canada and died soon after arrival.[270] Zachary abandoned his warehousing in 1817 for a large part in the resuscitation of Pickfords, hardly a move his father would have foreseen.[271] Perhaps the boys would have fared no worse if they, too, had been given a classical education, provided the schools had been as congenial to them as the ones they attended. Certainly, Will was something of an antiquarian; he copied out extracts from the Kirkham parish books, interpolating his comments and queries with a suitable sprinkling of Latin. It is to him we owe the preservation of the letters. Tom chose to spend several years on the continent of Europe, so that his own children could be taught by the staff of the Pestalozzi school at Yverdon in Switzerland.[272] His eldest son, however, subsequently attended public school in England, and then Cambridge, eventually becoming vice-chancellor of Toronto University.

But when Thomas Langton died in 1794 these developments were in the future. He left his sons a prosperous business, assured of a prominent place in the social oligarchy of Kirkham or settled, in some measure of prestigious eminence, elsewhere. He had enlarged their horizons beyond his own and ensured their material comfort. He could feel that, as far as he was concerned, he had made a sound investment in their education, and that the broad base of two good private academies had served his purpose well. It had been adequately 'of use'.

Sickness and Health

The society in which the Langtons lived was one in which, in Professor Holmes's words, 'disease was rampant and pain inseparable from everyday life'.[273] Many letters of the period showed a morbid preoccupation with health,[274] and satirists like Tobias

---

[270] Anne Langton, *op. cit.*, p. 74.
[271] George C. Turnbull, *Traffic and Transport. An Economic History of Pickfords*, 1979, p. 40.
[272] Anne Langton, *op. cit.*, p. 12 *et seq.*
[273] Geoffrey Holmes, *Augustan England. Professions State and Society 1688–1730*, 1983, p. 189.
[274] Elizabeth Hamilton, *The Mordants. An Eighteenth-Century Family*, 1965, p. 8.

Smollett, the novelist, and Thomas Rowlandson, the caricaturist, showed the credulous exploited by the unscrupulous in the pursuit of health. In 1817 Jane Austen poked fun at the hypochondriacal obsession of those who regulated their days by the demands of their various treatments and nostrums, and this was by no means the end of it.[275] Almost all of the Langton letters bear reference to the state of the health of the writer's immediate circle.

The profession of medicine in the eighteenth century was officially carried out by three separate branches: physicians, surgeons and apothecaries. The Royal College of Physicians was an exclusive body, officially with members who were graduates of Oxford, Cambridge or Dublin exclusively. The training was long—fourteen years in all—medical training of seven years following after the usual M.A. degree course.[276] Younger sons of gentry could be put to medicine without losing face, and, although by no means all who qualified were of gentle birth, it was socially acceptable to be admitted to the College.

The surgeons, of much more humble provenance, were until 1745 still joined to the barbers in the Company of Barbers, even though their work had long been more sophisticated than mere tooth-pulling and bone-setting. They were despised as mere craftsmen by the physicians.

The third branch, the apothecaries, once connected with the Grocers' Company, formed the Society of Apothecaries around 1680. Their origins and their official function as dispensers of drugs prescribed by the physicians put them in the ranks of the shopkeepers.

In the eighteenth century the profession was in a state of flux, but it also saw considerable improvement in standards of training in all three branches. It saw, too, an increased blurring in the lines of demarcation, even though the laws relating to the medical profession recognised the three orders as late as 1830.[277] Surgeons had often to act as physicians and, indeed, were sometimes even licensed by the College of Physicians to practise such medicine as was necessary in surgical treatment.[278] They were often more accessible than the

[275] Jane Austen, *Sanditon*, 1817, Folio Society edn, 1963, e.g. p. 166.
[276] Holmes, *op. cit.*, pp. 176–7.
[277] Ivan Waddington, *The Medical Profession in the Industrial Revolution*, Dublin, 1984, p. 1.
[278] Holmes, *op. cit.*, p. 195.

physicians, whose numbers were restricted by the licensing policy of the College. The apothecaries' training in the use of drugs was a practical advantage and as the century advanced they became more and more threatening to the physicians, increasing their rôle as advisers and practitioners of medicine as well as dispensers. By the end of the century the majority of town apothecaries, and practically all country ones, attended patients for slight, then increasingly serious, ailments, sometimes calling in a physician in dangerous cases.[279]

There are no records of the practices of Kirkham, but the manuscript account book of another Fylde doctor, Dr Loxham of Poulton le Fylde, for the years 1758 to 1772 throws light on their probable activities.[280] Visits were made for localised ailments, drugs and remedies were prescribed and, when necessary, operations performed. Apart from visits to women in childbirth, the most frequent cause of visiting was to patients 'in a fever'. There are few references to specific illness by name, but some are mentioned, such as nephritis, ophthalmia, pleurisy and chincough (whooping cough). Fractured and ulcerated limbs are numerous. Dr Loxham cut a cancerous lip, opened tumours, and once amputated a leg from a young woman suffering from 'a spina ventosa'.

As might be expected, his most frequent prescriptions were for purgatives, emetics, febrifuges and diaphoretics, with embrocation also common. A comparison of his remedies with those used on the crown prisoners in Lancaster Castle in 1775 and 1783,[281] or the 1784 account for the Preston House of Correction,[282] or the 1785 accounts for the Manchester House,[283] shows the usual medicaments of the period—gum arabic, tartar emetic, cinnamon, oil of vitriol and other well known substances, as well as less explicit 'aromatic drops' or 'Balsam traumatic'.

The practice of Dr Loxham, who emerges as a concerned and compassionate physician, probably marched with, and on occasion overlapped, that of the Kirkham practitioners to the south and that of the Garstang doctors beyond St Michaels.

---

[279] Bernice Hamilton, 'The medical profession in the eighteenth century', Econ. Hist. Rev., 2nd series, Vol. iv, No. 2, 1951, pp. 147–166.
[280] LRO, DDPR/41/27.
[281] LRO, QSP 294/13 and LRO, QSP 2196/5.
[282] LRO, QSP 2196/6.
[283] LRO, QSP 2202/11.

There were two practitioners in Kirkham at the time of the letters: Dr Clayton and Apothecary Parkinson. Both appear on the 1778 list of freeholders entitled to sit on the assize jury.[284] Mr Parkinson lived on into the nineteenth century to be remembered in the Birley notebook as 'Old Pothecary Parkinson', and it is obvious from the notebook that he worked as a general practitioner, riding out to patients, prescribing medicines as well as keeping his apothecary's shop. He is said to have been 'an honest and strictly honourable man, very modest in his charges'.[285] In spite of this modesty, however, he does not appear in the Langton letters. Perhaps he was not sufficiently socially elevated to qualify for attendance on the Langton household, as he lived in a simple way and was rather brusque in manner. Dr Clayton was the Langton medical adviser.

However, the three branches of the medical establishment did not by any means have a monopoly in treating the sick. The eighteenth century was a period prolific in what we should call 'folk medicine', from the mountebank peddling spurious nostrums to the wise woman with a useful knowledge of the curative properties of herbs. Advertisements for panaceas and wonder remedies were common in newspapers. *The British Courant* or *Preston Journal* of August 1750, for example, advertised Mr Davis's 'never failing itch water' and 'Mr Jackson's tincture published by His Majesty's royal patent'.[286] Lady Mary Wortley Montague had complained in the early years of the century that the English were 'more easily infatuated than any other people by the hope of a panacea', and the search for wonder remedies was by no means over by the end of the century.[287]

From whatever source he heard of its efficacious properties, Thomas Langton asked his son to bring from London half a dozen bottles of the 'Universal Balsam', the name speaking clearly of the claims made for it.[288] A small manuscript notebook among the Birley papers, written in the nineteenth century but undated, notes patent medicines and recipes for home cures, such as the balsam of Peru for

[284] LRO, QSP 217/25.
[285] Shepherd Birley Notebook, LRO, DDD/Birley Papers.
[286] Preston Reference Library.
[287] Quoted in Jane Lane, 'The diaries and correspondence of patients in eighteenth-century England' in Roy Porter, ed., *Patients and Practitioners. Lay perceptions of Medicine in Pre-industrial Society*, Cambridge, 1985, p. 98.
[288] LRO, DDX/190/59.

mortification, to be obtained from Dr Ainslie, M.D., Bath, and cures for toothache.[289]

Orthodox medicine attracted a good deal of criticism quite apart from the frequent complaint about the cost. In 1790 Dr Graham of Newcastle upon Tyne considered the 'general manner of living and conducting oneself' of much greater value than 'loads of harsh, nauseous, and unnatural medicines from doctors and apothecaries'.[290] Many books of medical advice for the general reader were in circulation and much self-help resulted. John Wesley's *Primitive Physic*, published in 1747 and a book of dubious practical advantage in some of its more esoteric remedies, was constantly reprinted into the nineteenth century;[291] but in 1727 another best-seller, *Domestic Medicine* by William Buchan, complained that 'the generality of people lay too much stress upon medicine and too little trust to their own endeavours'. He took issue with physicians for ignoring the part of medicine found in nature and common sense: 'Had men been more attentive to it, and less solicitous in hunting after secret remedies, medicine had never become an object of ridicule.'[292]

In the Langton household the doctor was called, when Thomas Langton was away, with some trepidation as to whether the absent head of the household would approve, even though Tom had smallpox. Thomas Langton's approval in his response to the information is so couched as to put their minds at rest.[293] Again in his absence Thomas Langton advocated that the doctor be called if John's cough persisted,[294] and when a friend of Cecily's was taken fatally ill on a visit to Kirkham a doctor was summoned, this time apparently from outside Kirkham, though the girl died before he came.[295] The first instance reveals uncertainty whether Thomas Langton would consider a doctor necessary; the second shows that the doctor is not the first line of approach, as John is to try bleeding first; the third shows the understandable anxiety of responsibility for someone else's child. This does not suggest a constant recourse to the doctor. Thomas

---

[289] LRO, Birley Papers.
[290] Quoted in Ginnie Smith, 'Self-help and advice in the late eighteenth century' in Roy Porter, ed., *op. cit.*, p. 209.
[291] Robert Southey, *Life of John Wesley*, Vol. 1, London, 1820, p. 346.
[292] Quoted in Ginnie Smith, *op. cit.*, p. 276.
[293] LRO, DDX/190/52.
[294] *Ibid.*
[295] LRO, DDX/190/64.

Langton's advice to his sons at school did not go further than telling them not to get their feet wet or skate on thin ice. His commiserations upon a cold did not include a suggested remedy.[296] His most pressing concern was shown over Will's desire to learn the flute, as over-assiduous practice on a wind instrument was 'injurious to growing boys'.[297] He had a commonsense faith in the beneficial properties of country air, weighing his guests on the warehouse scales to see what improvement was to be shown.[298]

There was in the letters something of Buchan's insistence on the patient's 'own endeavours', for the phrase Thomas Langton most frequently used in this connection was 'getting the better' of the 'disorder'.[299] This is also an interesting reflection of the medical orthodoxy of the century for, although the doctrine of the Humours—the fluids of blood, phlegm, black and yellow bile—had been modified from its ancient and medieval form, the state of the body's health was still considered to be an equilibrium of the various humours within it. Boerhaave, the Dutch professor of physic, whose writings had much influence on the medical schools of the eighteenth century, dismissed the four classes of humours as merely aspects of the one humour, the blood. But he held that many more humours were contained in it and that, combined with the solids of the body, they made up human physiology.[300] So an illness was indeed a 'disorder' of the component parts of the body. The humoral theory in some form dominated medicine and most medical practice was based on it. When Tom Langton had smallpox in 1776, Thomas Langton said that it was 'such a disorder which often leaves bad humours lurking in the blood after if proper precautions are not taken'.[301] No doubt no physician would have accepted such a vague diagnosis, but the word 'humours' was obviously familiar to Thomas Langton, with a suggestion of its application in illness.

Occasionally Thomas Langton used the word 'complaint' in this connection.[302] This, too, was in keeping with the times. The patient

---

[296] LRO, DDX/190/41.
[297] LRO, DDX/190/37, 38.
[298] LRO, DDX/190/62.
[299] For example, LRO, DDX/190/38.
[300] Lester S. King, *The Medical World of the Eighteenth Century*, Huntingdon N.Y., 1971 reprint, p. 103.
[301] LRO, DDX/190/52.
[302] LRO, DDX/190/48.

was supposed to specify his complaint that something was disordered, that is, that the harmony of the body was jarred.

Some 'disorders' were, of course, more common than others. 'Fever' was the greatest killer of the eighteenth century;[303] as we saw, it was the most frequent complaint in Dr Loxham's accounts. There were many manifestations of fever and many disputes as to its treatment, but its lethal potential was not disputed. The form of fever to which most people were at risk was smallpox, some writers of the time believing it was virtually inevitable.[304]

The most satisfactory way of dealing with smallpox was to prevent it. As inoculation became more and more used, the disease declined dramatically, especially during the last third of the century.[305] Inoculation had been known in England since the early 1700s, but some members of the College of Physicians had opposed it, approving it only in 1754.[306] William Buchan, on the other hand, recommended that parents should inoculate their own children and think nothing more of it than giving a dose of physic.[307] It does not appear, however, that Tom Langton had been inoculated, even though a Langton baby had earlier died from smallpox. None of the others caught it from Tom, perhaps because they had already had it. Nor do they seem to have been unduly alarmed; Cecily took the child away with her, as planned, before they informed their father of the illness. Thomas Langton himself would have been 'very unhappy' if he had not heard of the recovery before hearing of the illness. He hoped Cecily had not acted 'too precipitately' in taking Tom away and asked if they had taken proper care to give Tom some physic, 'which is certainly necessary after such a disorder' to dispel the bad humours.[308] His advice was sound: gentle purging and a light diet with diluting drinks were the nursing treatment for smallpox.

If smallpox was the most common fever, the most common remedy for most disorders was bleeding. This arose directly from the humoral interpretation of the human physiology, but the practice varied considerably. Buchan wrote that 'physicians themselves have been so much the dupes of theory in this article as to render it the

[303] King, *op. cit.*, p. 103.
[304] Quoted in Peter Razzell, *The Conquest of Smallpox*, Firle, 1977, p. 113.
[305] Razzell, *op. cit.*, p. 149.
[306] King, *op. cit.*, p. 322.
[307] *Ibid.*, p. 234.
[308] LRO, DDX/190/52.

subject of ridicule', but he nevertheless asserted that 'no operation of surgery is so frequently necessary as bleeding'. It was the usual treatment for all fevers and topical inflammations, as for the great majority of illnesses; 'But though practised by midwives, gardeners, blacksmiths, etc., very few [knew] when it was proper.'[309]

Although it does occur from time to time, Dr Loxham's accounts do not contain frequent entries of phlebotomy. This may support the view that it was carried out by people other than physicians, or it may show that he did not often prescribe it. When Thomas Langton recommended bleeding as a measure for John to take before the doctor was called, someone other than the doctor was obviously to operate. Not always authorised by a doctor, it would seem that bleeding was something of a folk remedy.

Bleeding was not new to the eighteenth century, but two 'cures' of a very different nature were to become fashionable as the century proceeded: 'taking the waters' at a spa, and bathing in the sea. Spas had been in sporadic existence before the eighteenth century, but they were to rise to the zenith of popularity during it and to sink somewhat at the end, declining as sea-bathing resorts took over.

The spas had been honoured by royal patronage as early as 1702 when Queen Anne took the waters at Bath. Bath was at the height of its fame, under Beau Nash, from 1705 until almost mid century, but other spas, like Tunbridge Wells and the Bristol Hotwells at Clifton, were well patronised by the quality in search of health and amusement. As the century progressed the personnel frequenting the watering places became more and more heterogeneous, from the dubious hangers-on looking for ill-gotten gains from card-sharping or procuring, to the socially ambitious anxious to improve their social status.[310] In 1771 Smollett gave a merciless picture of the 'vile mob' at Bath. Yet the same spectacle called forth a different reaction from another beholder who saw nothing but 'gayety, good humour and diversion' as 'the highest quality and the lower tradesfolk [jost-led] with each other without ceremony, hail-fellow well-met'.[311]

The Hotwells at Bristol seems to have attracted a less repellent crowd, Bath being the apogee towards which social aspirations turned. By the 1760s there were some two hundred houses at Clifton,

[309] King, op. cit., p. 319.
[310] J. A. R. Pimlott, The Englishman's Holiday, 1977 reprint, p. 47.
[311] Tobias Smollett, The Expedition of Humphry Clinker, New American Library of World Literature, N.Y., 1960 edn, pp. 58, 48.

most offering accommodation, and the Pump Room and the Assembly Rooms offered the same kind of service as at Bath. It was considered a summer spa, complementary to Bath's winter season. Bathing was regarded here as of little importance, but the curious white water issuing through the Avon mud was drunk warm twice a day, and prescribed for a variety of disorders.[312] It was widely sold, bottled, in London and the provinces and enjoyed a national, even an international, reputation for its properties.[313]

In 1745 George Randolph, M.D., sometime Fellow of All Souls, wrote an enquiry into the properties of the Bristol water and the cures it offered. He summed up in truly humoral fashion that, while Bath water invigorated the phlegmatic, Bristol attemporated the choleric constitution. It was 'serviceable in all hot dry constitutions, moistening and cooling the body ... prejudicial in all watery phlegmatic constitutions, griping the stomach'.[314] Smollett, a doctor as well as a novelist, spoke through Matthew Bramble his own views on Bristol water:

> I have read all that has been written on the Hot Wells, and what I can collect from the whole, is that the water contains nothing but a little salt and calcareous earth, mixed in such inconsiderable proportions as can have very little, if any, effect on the animal economy. This being the case, I think, the man deserves to be fitted with a cap and bells, who for such paltry advantage as this spring affords, sacrifices his precious time, which might be employed in taking more effectual remedies, and exposes himself to the dirt, the stench, the chilling blasts, and perpetual rains, that render this place ... intolerable.[315]

Some five years after this broadside, in 1775, Thomas Langton was prepared to 'sacrifice his precious time' to go to the Hotwells with a 'complaint at [his] breast'.[316] As ailments of the lungs were among the disorders said to benefit from Bristol water, he might have

[312] Bryan Little, 'The Gloucestershire spas: an eighteenth-century parallel' in *Essays in Bristol and Gloucestershire History*, Bristol, 1976, p. 174.
[313] Sylvia McIntyre, 'The mineral water trade in the eighteenth century, *Journal of Transport History*, Vol. 2, No. 1, 1973, p. 5.
[314] George Randolph, M.D., *An Enquiry into the Medicinal Virtues of Bristol Water and the Indicatives of Cure which it Answers*, Oxford, 1745, pp. 26, 31.
[315] Smollett, *op. cit.*, p. 33.
[316] LRO, DDX/190/48.

been suffering from pleurisy or bronchitis, but no particulars are given. It is obvious from the letters home that he resented the time spent away from business, about which he continued to issue orders and ask questions. For him to be prepared for the considerable expense attendant upon his visit, he must have been initially persuaded that a fair return was likely.

About this time, the Hotwells clientele included some eminent persons, if arrivals notices for the following year are to be believed. They list eight peers, several baronets and knights, a judge, and many clergymen.[317] Thomas Langton's name-dropping apothecary was keen to establish that he had just left Lord Strathmore.[318] The Hornbys were at Bath at the same time that Thomas Langton was at Bristol, and the Shepherds went to Bristol the following year.[319] The flax merchants of Kirkham could now assume something of the pretensions of the upper middle class. It is not likely that John Langton senior could have done so.

The situation of the Hotwells near the Downs was part of the attraction. Thomas Langton thought Bath, where he visited the Hornbys, a 'sweet place' where 'improvements [were] making every year, but the country about the Hotwells [was] much pleasanter and more agreeable rides'. He found the Downs 'very pleasant' with 'fine extensive prospects over a whole county well inhabited and interspersed with a number of fine houses chiefly belonging to the Bristol merchants'.[320] Evelina, in Fanny Burney's novel (1778), would have agreed. She found Clifton 'situated upon a most delightful spot; the prospect ... beautiful, the air pure ... and the weather very favourable to invalids'.[321] Neither would have agreed with Matthew Bramble that the place was 'unbearable'.[322]

Thomas Langton outlined the routine of his days. He took two half pints of water in the Pump Room every morning before breakfast. He then rode, in fine weather, on the Downs for an hour or two, returning to drink two more glasses before taking a walk, often to Bristol, about a mile away. In the evening he went to the Long Room for about an hour, supping about eight, of water gruel, before

[317] Bryan Little, *op. cit.*, p. 175.
[318] LRO, DDX/190/49.
[319] LRO, DDX/190/52.
[320] LRO, DDX/190/47.
[321] Fanny Burney, *Evelina*, Everyman Library, 1951 edn, p. 250.
[322] Smollett, *op. cit.*, p. 58.

retiring about ten.[323] Not for him the public breakfast with cotillions and country dances, or the river trips with music to Avonmouth or Portishead, or the gardens at Long Ashton, advertised as attractions.[324] Not for him, either, the evening assemblies.

There was 'a good deal of company' but most of it must have been dispiriting, 'mostly invalid and many of them in the last stages of life'. To compensate, there were many accounts of 'surprising' cures for encouragement.[325] Thomas Langton, whose physician, Dr Rigge, appears by name in *Humphry Clinker*, was glad to be told he could return home, even though 'everything tended to make [the] place agreeable', and he expedited as much as he could the obligatory bleeding prior to discharge.[326] His dandified apothecary, arriving hotfoot from Lord Strathmore, complete with 'his large gold-headed cane and umbrella', took a 'large basin of blood'.[327]

About the efficacy of the cure Thomas Langton had his doubts. He felt better for his six weeks' stay, but he did not know whether to attribute his recovery to the Bristol water, the 'temperate fine air … or the gentle and healthful exercise of riding with regularity and sobriety'.[328] So too commented Richard Sulivan after his Bristol visit in 1785, when one of the physicians had said to him that 'it was of no consequence whether the benefit to the invalids [proceeded] from the water or the downs' as 'they [were] both great restoratives and that it was more than probable that the downs [might] be entitled to the merit of a moiety of the cure at least'.[329] About the cost, however, Thomas Langton had no doubt. After the apothecary left him he observed wryly: 'I fancy I shall have a large bill to pay him, and I fancy I have paid a good many.'[330]

We cannot add Thomas Langton's cure to the testimonials for the water. Certainly he lived another nineteen years. To his own and Sulivan's remarks we may add that a six weeks' rest from his usually busy life of business responsibility and public work might have been in itself a sufficient restorative.

---

[323] LRO, DDX/190/48.
[324] Bryan Little, *op. cit.*, p. 175.
[325] LRO, DDX/190/47.
[326] LRO, DDX/190/48.
[327] LRO, DDX/190/49.
[328] LRO, DDX/190/48.
[329] Richard Joseph Sulivan, *A Tour Through Parts of England Scotland and Wales in 1778*, 1785, p. 217.
[330] LRO, DDX/190/48.

He did on at least one occasion take a shorter break. We have evidence in the letters of an excursion to Blackpool with his wife, sister and friends. The Langtons were well placed for the second great nostrum of the century, sea-bathing, for Blackpool, still little more than a straggling village on the shoreline, was already known for its salubrious situation and health-giving sea. By 1788 William Hutton could speak of it as 'frequented for sea bathing' when he wrote his descriptive booklet. [331] 'This abode of health and amusements' served a less elevated clientele than even the lesser spas, but in the catholicity of its visitors like could find like.

The curative properties of sea water had been in the folk consciousness long before they were advocated by the medical profession. Immersion in the sea as treatment was practised in south Lancashire in the early eighteenth century, a continuation of an older tradition.[332] The mystique of the powers of sea water persisted throughout the century and beyond. As late as 1831 bathers came to Lytham to wash away 'all the collected stains and impurities of the year'.[333] In Lancashire, sea-bathing was rooted in custom and not confined to the wealthy. Pursued for benefit as well as pleasure, it was an extension of the many home and patent remedies popularly resorted to both by those who could afford no other and by the better off who saw a medical practitioner as by no means the first line of defence.

The seal of medical approval for sea-bathing came with Dr Richard Russell's *Dissertation* in mid century. It gave an impetus to the growing interest in the sea, and took the practice out of the domain of folk medicine into that of medical orthodoxy. It advocated the internal as well as the external use of sea water for much the same purposes as spa water. Russell claimed the sea had been provided by God as a 'common defence against the corruption and putrefaction of bodies, particularly efficacious against consumption'.[334]

The resorts, following the spas, provided amusements to while away the greater part of the day when neither immersion nor drinking was taking place.[335] As sea water was plentiful and accessible to all, a wide

[331] William Hutton, *A Description of Blackpool in Lancashire Frequented for Sea-Bathing*, 1788 ed. R. Sharpe France, 1944.
[332] John K. Walton, *The English Seaside Resort: A Social History 1750–1914*, 1983, p. 10.
[333] Quoted in Walton, *op. cit., ibid.*
[334] Pimlott, *op. cit.*, p. 52.
[335] Walton, *op. cit.*, e.g. p. 19.

social spectrum could share in its offerings. William Hutton claimed that, in the 1760s, people frequenting Blackpool were chiefly of the lower class,[336] but by 1788 his daughter wrote that manufacturers, gentry, merchants and merchant-manufacturers from all parts of Lancashire congregated there, accommodated according to their social level.[337]

There are several references in the letters to seaside visits to Lytham and to Blackpool. Mrs Langton went for her health, relatives for health or a day's outing.[338] Thomas Langton's sister took her ailing baby, and when the baby died Thomas Langton and his wife took the grief-stricken mother for consoling diversion.[339] The delicate Mrs Langton actually bathed, a sure sign that the therapeutic powers of the sea had been given laudatory publicity, for she seldom went anywhere. Even Mr Booth visited the Fylde coast and in 1773 Thomas Langton told Will that he hoped the health of a friend had greatly improved by his journey into Lancashire.[340]

Mrs Langton bathed at Lytham, said by Thornber in 1837 to have a mild and warm climate rendered 'particularly conducive to the health of the weak and consumptive invalid'.[341] The climate was of importance at the resorts, as was the environment generally, credited by some, as at the spas, with the lion's share of the cures. Blackpool had air 'probably as pure as air can be'.[342]

Living so near to such a salubrious spot, the inhabitants of Kirkham should have been particularly healthy, but by no means all those figuring in the letters enjoyed the longevity said by Hutton to characterise the inhabitants of Blackpool.[343] The early letters were written in the shadow of Mrs Langton's chronic invalidism. She was aged about thirty-eight when the correspondence opened and, though her disorder is not specified, every letter bears some reference to her health: 'She [was] of a very tender constitution and [could] not stir much abroad without catching cold.'[344] She died in December 1774,

[336] Hutton, op. cit., p. 19
[337] Quoted in Keith Parry, The Resorts of the Lancashire Coast, Newton Abbot, 1983, p. 18.
[338] LRO, DDX/190/21, 27; LRO, DDX/190/35, 56.
[339] LRO, DDX/190/35, 52; LRO, DDX/190/37.
[340] LRO, DDX/190/31, 42.
[341] William Thornber, A Historical and Descriptive Account of Blackpool and its Neighbourhood, Poulton le Fylde, 1837, p. 336.
[342] Hutton, op. cit., p. 13.
[343] Ibid., p.13.
[344] LRO, DDX/190/23.

a few months after John and Will left school. The fourth son, Cornelius, had an eye condition which blinded him at the age of seven or eight, and he, too, appears in almost every letter. There is a recipe for an eye salve among the Langton papers which might have been intended for him.

At no point in the letters is the doctor said to have attended these two chronic invalids. Relatives came to stay to cheer Mrs Langton, and an attendant was hired to accompany Cornelius out of doors.[345] There is no reference to doctors' opinions, prognosis or diagnosis. It was hoped for each that they would 'get the better of' their respective disorders. This absence of medical attention might be because the chronic conditions were known not to lend themselves to permanent improvement or medical prescription and so would not justify a doctor's fee. No chronic cases appear in Dr Loxham's books, either. In the Langton case, however, it might be a reflection of Thomas Langton's attitude to illness.

He was fully aware of the state of health of his friends and relatives. He was concerned, sympathetic, and in no way indifferent to their sufferings, but there was no preoccupation with health. There is a sense of the omnipresence of indisposition and of the general insecurity of life, and of crises of life and death arising unexpectedly to be faced with fortitude. Death took the six-months-old baby of his sister (even though he had been to Lytham), and his daughter's friend died under his roof.[346] His undated letter on this occasion shows his genuine distress both for the girl's mother and for his daughter. Death threatened two more nephews, the one in a teething fever, the other, a doctor himself, suddenly taken ill. Three Langton children had died in early infancy from smallpox, chincough (whooping cough) and convulsions.[347] Unspecified complaints and disorders are frequently mentioned and concern for health is never far below the surface. Yet there is no hint of hypochondria, no morbid scrutiny of the physical condition.

There was a strongly fatalistic strand running through much of the eighteenth-century attitude to death, as well as a degree of resignation towards personal suffering.[348] Some patients still sought a spiritual interpretation of illness and saw an epidemic as God's

[345] LRO, DDX/190/28, 38.
[346] LRO, DDX/190/36, 64.
[347] LRO, DDX/190/103.
[348] Joan Lane, op. cit., p. 217.

judgement.[349] There was a polarity between those of a philosophical frame of mind who adopted the enlightenment ethic of stoicism, and those of pious introspection who acknowledged frailty and illness as symptomatic of spiritual progress.[350]

As for Thomas Langton, he had something of both these attitudes in his approach to sickness and health. He had a stoical acceptance, but he saw the outcome as determined by God's providence. He did not suggest divine judgement or retribution, but he saw the stoicism as submitting to the will of God rather than mere endurance to a physical end. He wrote:

> I am sorry to say your brother Nely is no better, he continues much as usual. His eye sight is very bad and the violent pain in his head occasionally troubles him, but as it is an affliction under the hands of Providence, we must submit to it, and poor lad, he bears his illness with the greatest patience and resignation.[351]

His wife '[had] all [their] most earnest prayers for the restoration of her health, and [they] must rely upon Providence for the event'.[352] The boys were told they must remember the bounteous hand of Providence and 'must earnestly implore his aid and assurance with whom are the issues of life and death'.[353] When the boys were told of their duty, it was to their 'Maker' that they owed it.[354] 'Providence' was reserved for the ways of God to men for, although in neither case did Thomas Langton use the word 'God', the Godhead was clearly intended.

Thomas Langton did not appear to expect much from the medical profession as such. Sceptical of the Hotwells cure, aware of the high fees, calling in the doctor only when absolutely necessary, he commiserated in suffering and sympathised in grief. But there was acceptance, not complaining. There was not the slightest questioning as to why those concerned should be afflicted. While prepared for meas-

---

[349] Jonathan Barry, 'Medicine and Religion in Bristol' in Porter, ed., *op. cit.*, p. 172.
[350] Johanna Geyer-Kordisch, 'The enlightenment and the pious in eighteenth-century Germany' in Porter, ed., *op. cit.*, pp. 194, 203.
[351] LRO, DDX/190/28.
[352] LRO, DDX/190/36.
[353] LRO, DDX/190/37.
[354] LRO, DDX/190/20, 35.

ures to be taken within the human capability to regulate disorder and prolong life, he believed that, in the end, the outcome lay outside man's domain.

As far as evidence goes, Thomas Langton was not especially devout. There is no mention of church attendance, though he certainly did attend. There are no questions about Mr Booth's sermons, though he must have preached to the school. There are no biblical allusions in his correspondence, although Thomas Langton had an uncle and a brother-in-law in the Church. Yet his attitude to illness and death is very like that of Richard Kay, doctor and devout nonconformist, who recorded in his diary in November 1744:

> Lord, we are subject to the Disposals of Thy Providence and must submit to them yet may we be not too much surprized by these changes for may we be daily expecting them ...

Unlike Kay, however, Thomas Langton did not speculate upon what happened after death. Kay continued:

> ... and constantly be preparing for them and by the grace of God and through the merits and mediation of our Lord and Saviour Jesus Christ may we all be prepared for Heaven and eternal glory and happiness.[355]

Thomas Langton was content to accept the inevitability of death in the midst of life. Illness and disability were an integral part of the human condition, and the Maker's intentions, not the ministrations of the medical men, were the deciding factor in getting the better of, or succumbing to, the disorder. The rest was silence.

Leisure

The eighteenth century saw the commercialisation of leisure and the commercialisation was in itself one of the social signs of the increasing affluence of the growing middle class.[356] Thomas Langton's patronage of the Hotwells Spa illustrated that middle-class intrusion into the spas which some think marked the beginning of the development of holiday resorts. As long as the spas were the province of

[355] W. Brookbank and F. Kennedy, eds., *The Diary of Richard Kay of Baldingstone near Bury*, Chet. Soc., No. 16, 1908, p. 91.
[356] J. H. Plumb, *The Commercialisation of Leisure in Eighteenth Century England*, 1974, p. 3.

the wealthy leisured, the diversions offered merely provided a variation of the social round. When merchants and professionals were able to afford them, in a break from business or professional commitments, the spas became something like embryo resorts.[357] Even when anxious to get home, Thomas Langton found the Hotwells very pleasant. Well before the end of the century the seaside watering places, visited initially for the health-giving properties of their sea water and fresh air, were also providing entertainment which was to become a powerful additional attraction.

When the letters were written, the ritual of the family holiday, with a sea-bathing component, was still in the future for the Langtons but, within twenty years of Thomas Langton's death, his youngest son was taking his children on annual migration, *en famille*, to Southport.[358] Thomas Langton recorded one visit of ten days' duration to Blackpool, undertaken for his grieving sister's sake and therefore not solely for pleasure. He does, however, refer to guests who went to Blackpool for the day, with no mention of their intention to bathe.

In the 1770s Blackpool was already offering some of the diversions Hutton was to mention in 1788. Horse-riding, card-playing, bowling, archery, sailing and dancing were to become popular, and a theatre was set up in a barn. There would certainly be the daily promenading on the parade, 'a pretty grass walk on the verge of the sea bank divided from the road with white rails', by those who considered themselves worth seeing.[359] In Preston, the Avenham walk on the bank of the Ribble was well established by the beginning of the eighteenth century,[360] and Thomas Langton mentioned the interest his party aroused in the inhabitants of Kendal when, in 1780, they stayed a night and duly 'took a view' of the town the following morning. He wrote: 'I assure you we made a handsome parade, many enquiries made after us, and not a little gazing, but we gave them liberty to feast their eyes.'[361] There seems to have been a certain art in promenading, the 'company' being propelled into contact with each other, 'to gossip and flirt, to see and be seen'.[362]

---

[357] Pimlott, *op. cit.*, p. 46.
[358] Anne Langton, *op. cit.*, p. 6.
[359] William Hutton, *op. cit.*, pp. 22, 19.
[360] P. N. Borsay, 'The English Urban Renaissance 1661–1770', unpublished Ph.D. thesis, Lancaster, 1981, p. 331.
[361] LRO, DDX/190/58.
[362] Borsay, *op. cit.*, p. 276.

Thomas Langton did not seem to participate, himself, in leisure activities as a regular practice. In those in which he did take part, the activity was usually secondary to a more serious overall purpose. His letters, however, refer to various pursuits which reflect the admixture of traditional, fashionable and status-enhancing entertainments available to his circle. His family certainly displayed to leisure an attitude different from his.

At the traditional level come the fairs held in local centres, providing entertainment as well as trading opportunities. They had become general holidays, with their attractions open to all classes.[363] For example, Lancaster had three fairs a year for cattle, cheese, wool and pedlary.[364] In October 1780 Thomas Langton reported that his partner, Mr Birley, accompanied by Mr Yate, a relative and business connection from Liverpool, 'set out to attend the fair at Lancaster', obviously not on business.[365] On another occasion a young friend was said to request a 'Chester fairing', or memento of Chester Fair.[366] Traditional, as well as on a more elevated level, was fishing, and two Langton guests went on fishing excursions on the River Wyre.[367]

An interesting omission from the Christmas letters is any mention of the traditional football match which, according to Shepherd Birley, took place in the streets of Kirkham on Christmas Day. Such town matches could become 'more like battles than sport', and the Birley description certainly makes the Kirkham match a rough affair.[368] It must have been visible from the Langton windows, but the Langtons probably considered themselves too genteel for such diversions.

Also patronised by a social mixture was racing, but the widest heterogeneous attendance at race meetings, now become a major recreation of the ruling élite, had been somewhat refined by legislation.[369] Meetings were better organised and the races were under the jurisdiction of the Jockey Club by the time of the letters. From the Hotwells, Thomas Langton hoped that those at home would

---

[363] Stella Margetson, *Leisure and Pleasure in the Eighteenth Century*, 1970, p. 126.
[364] G. A. Cooke, *Topographical Description of the County of Lancashire*, n.d., p. 18.
[365] LRO, DDX/190/62.
[366] LRO, DDX/190/37.
[367] LRO, DDX/190/56.
[368] J. M. Selby and A. W. Purdue, *The Civilisation of the Crowd. Popular Culture in England 1750–1800*, p. 23.
[369] Borsay, *op. cit.*, p. 347.

have 'great diversion at the races'.[370] There were races at both Preston and Liverpool, and in a later letter he referred to the Oxford races and the 'great diversion' they effected.[371] Again, he did not patronise the events himself.

Fashionable visits to the seaside and to the amusements afforded at the spas were enhanced by the socially useful accomplishments of music and dancing, useful also in a local social circle. We saw above Thomas Langton's championing of dancing and his care that his children be taught to dance. With this skill young people were given 'a pretty easy manner and an agreeable behaviour'.[372]

Some leisure activities, like hunting, were status-enhancing. Some aristocrats might share Lord Chesterfield's contempt for the 'illiberal sport of guns, dogs, and horses which [characterised] our English Bumpkin country gentlemen'.[373] but the Game Laws precluded those of no substance from killing or trapping game. The Kirkham Dogs would not be followed by any Tom, Dick or Harry. They coursed the hare in company with Cecily Langton and, on at least one occasion, Mr Clifton, squire and lord of the manor, accompanied Thomas Langton's guest 'a-hunting'.[374] This shows the social thrust of the Langtons in their environment. Again, Thomas Langton does not appear to have gone coursing.

For the local leisured, Preston was the social centre of the county. It held a winter season. Although the Langtons were not of the set to migrate to the attractions of the Preston season, their distant relations, the Boltons, were. They were moneyed and rather higher in the social scale, and there is a somewhat reverential tone in Thomas Langton's references to them. They went to Preston for the winter, and on at least one occasion had Cecily Langton staying with them there.[375] Cecily was aged twelve, and it suggests that the Preston visit was something in the order of a 'finishing'. Already able to dance, she would have ample opportunity to try her skill.[376] The town hall had been used for assemblies since the 1720s,[377] and we

[370] LRO, DDX/190/48.
[371] LRO, DDX/190/50.
[372] LRO, DDX/190/38.
[373] Quoted in Margetson, *op. cit.*, p. 118.
[374] LRO, DDX/190/59, 35.
[375] LRO, DDX/190/35, 40.
[376] LRO, DDX/190/25.
[377] Borsay, *op. cit.*, p. 328.

may be sure that diversions such as plays (there was a theatre in Woodcock's yard),[378] card parties and private 'routs' were offered. The holding of a Preston season continued into the nineteenth century.

If Cecily was to be polished in Preston, her brothers were to have their horizons widened in London by sightseeing. Jack and Will, on their way to the new location of their school, were met in London and shown the sights.[379] Later Zachary, *en route* for his school in Hampstead, was 'very much surprised with London' and had a week to see 'the amusements and variety of the place' before school began.[380]

This London was the London of Dr Johnson, for whom to be tired of London was to be tired of life. It overlapped with the London of Charles Lamb, who felt lost anywhere but in the hurly-burly of the capital. Behind the coffee-house society and the elegant haunts of Vauxhall and Ranelagh were 'rookeries', or criminal quarters, no-go areas for the timorous or squeamish, some close to the respectable West End. When Jack and Will knew London well enough to pride themselves that they could find their way anywhere with their map, it is not surprising that their father counselled caution.[381] When they allowed a stranger to depart with money, under pretext of getting change for them, Thomas Langton's rebuke was comparatively mild: it would teach 'better caution in future'.[382] It was obvious that they enjoyed London, and in later years Will visited it on business and Zachary lived there for most of his life.

London was the centre of fashion. By the time of the letters the Langtons, *pace* their drapery origins, obviously thought themselves superior to the provisions of the local outfitters. The letters are sprinkled with commissions for varying items for the family: handkerchiefs for Cecily, a hat and habit for Cecily, a hat and other items for Thomas Langton.[383] Cotton items were made up for Aunt Tabitha, and the boys were fitted with new suits before they returned north.[384]

---

[378] P. Whittle, *History of the Borough of Preston*, Preston 1837 (dedication 1821), p. 95.
[379] LRO, DDX/190/35.
[380] LRO, DDX/190/51.
[381] LRO, DDX/190/43.
[382] LRO, DDX/190/41.
[383] LRO, DDX/190/59, 52, 54.
[384] LRO, DDX/190/52, 46.

The social assumptions of the family are clearly mirrored in these requests. Of course, the London commissions enumerated here would form only a small part of the Langton wardrobe, but it is obvious that no opportunity was lost to acquire London clothes.

The Langtons had quite a number of London connections, both business and personal. The boys, on school holiday in London, were asked by their father to make a considerable number of social calls on these connections. They were instructed in this vein: 'I would have you call upon Mrs. Loxham with our compliments and to enquire after Mrs. Whitehouse of this town who is now with her brother.'[385] In their free time the Langton boys were expected to discharge social obligations, useful to the family and business, and their enforced stay in Essex over Christmas was to be enlivened by seeing the countryside and engaging in a copious correspondence.[386]

Indeed, for the Langton circle the main source of entertainment was the giving and receiving of hospitality. The letters are full of visits to and from relatives and friends. There were visits to connections in Newark and Chester at some distance, as well as in nearby towns like Blackburn, Fazakerley, Ormskirk and Preston, and to family and business connections in London and Liverpool. Maiden aunts came to stay for months at a time, no doubt earning their keep by domestic help. Cecily departed on visits, also for months at a time. Thomas Langton, away from home, was anxious that an adequately sumptuous meal be provided for a visiting relative and suggested some flookings (a local mussel).[387] In Askham he remembered that a fellow thirtyman was due for his customary meal on the day of the vestry, and issued instructions.[388] He obviously prided himself on his 'Christmas entertainment', and Shepherd Birley remembered the Christmas of his youth as a 'great gay time'.[389] To compensate the boys on their first Christmas away from home, a box of Christmas delicacies was dispatched.[390]

A malicious vignette in the Shepherd Birley notebook suggests that Thomas Langton regarded certain aspects of entertaining as a

[385] LRO, DDX/190/44.
[386] LRO, DDX/190/39.
[387] LRO, DDX/190/53; Shepherd Birley: 'A very fine species of mussel taken from the banks of the Wyre.'
[388] LRO, DDX/190/61.
[389] LRO, DDX/190/40; LRO, DDX/190/27; DDD, Shepherd Birley Notebook.
[390] LRO, DDX/190/27.

means of social climbing. An anecdote, obviously in the Birley canon, tells of an evening party at the Langtons when 'an awkward man-servant who was most probably oftener employed in the garden or the stables than as a waiter indoors' broke some china when 'the company were all assembled'. Thomas Langton severely berated his erring minion and his social pretension is tacitly exposed by his giving such parties without the correct staff to field them.

After visiting, travel itself provided a major diversion. For Thomas Langton the travel was usually with some practical purpose—business, health, family duty. Any additional activity was not only a bonus, but also a means of making the most of the possibilities of the journey, extracting the utmost from the occasion and getting full value for money. Thus, returning from the Hotwells he paid a visit to his uncle in Oxford, and on his way north his intention was to see Blenheim, Ditchley and Heythrop, all houses open to the public.[391] He was denied the pleasure of the Oxford 'Grand Encoemia' (or commemoration ceremony) but he spoke of it with relish.[392]

Travel on an extended scale with an improving purpose was the aristocratic way of combining an extension of experience with the culmination of the educational process for the young noblemen about to enter, on their return, various spheres of public life. The Grand Tour had from the seventeenth century formed part of the education of the young aristocrat and, in the eighteenth, additionally of those of the middle class who could afford it. The Grand Tour often deteriorated into the mere pursuit of pleasure although ostensibly intended for the learning of foreign languages and the study of antiquity, yet some still thought it preferable to the university as a means of preparing a young nobleman for responsibility.

For the prospective merchant, a tour abroad was often taken with different expectations. When just out of his time, he would tour Europe with samples of his wares and to study his industry in the various countries through which he passed. A year would be spent abroad during which the young man would make comments on general trade, list bankers and dealers in the sizeable towns and make useful contacts.

[391] LRO, DDX/190/50.
[392] LRO, DDX/190/47.

Neither the Grand Tour nor the finishing of the apprentice took full shape for Thomas Langton, but in his young manhood he made an Irish visit which had something of both in it. It would seem he was sent to Ireland to combine the social pleasures of a family visit with some investigation into the trade which was to be his life's work and with a certain amount of sightseeing. He stayed at first with his uncle (the Uncle Langton of the letters) who then had an incumbency outside Dublin, and he visited linen manufactories and warehouses in Dublin, Drogheda and Newry. It is virtually certain that the firm's early supply of flax came from Ireland and there were business connections in most places he visited. The greater part of the visit, however, was taken up with social visiting and sightseeing.[393] At the end of the month he had added new perspectives socially, intellectually and commercially, as was expected both of the Grand Tourist and the finished apprentice.

His son Will, however, went abroad with no idea but enjoyment. The Grand Tour had passed through a period of transition and eventually gave way to the continental holiday taken for its own sake. By the time of the French Revolution, continental travel was an established institution among the upper classes and those with leisure and means. Like going to Bath, it was considered '*bon ton*', and the original educational purpose was lost.[394] Between 1763 and 1765 it was estimated that 40,000 Englishmen travelled through Calais alone.[395] Gibbon was told that in the 1780s some 40,000 English, including servants, were in Europe.[396] Though the numbers must be conjectural, there is enough evidence to establish that continental travel was by no means confined to an aristocratic handful.

Among the travellers abroad before the French Revolution (indeed just before, in 1788) was Will Langton, taking french leave in France and only writing to apprise his father of his continental intentions when he had already arrived in Paris. Thomas Langton deplored the fact that Will was travelling with friends purely for pleasure. He urged his son to investigate wherever he went matters 'of use' to the firm in an attempt to turn his foreign trip to some

---

[393] Thomas Langton MS Journal, LRO, DDX/190/11.
[394] Pimlott, *op. cit.*, p. 73.
[395] *Ibid.*, p. 68.
[396] *Ibid.*

sound purpose. Thomas Langton was in line with those who lamented that:

> the majority of our travellers run over to France from no other motives than those which lead them to Tonbridge or Scarborough. Amusement and dissipation are their principal, and often their only, views.[397]

Though Will showed no sign of dissipation, he was obviously out solely for amusement. His father had seldom, if ever, been that. He had no doubt that Will might make it 'a very pleasant tour' but he was fearful that it would prove a very expensive one, which could 'have little prospect of its turning to any advantage in Trade in [their] line of commerce'. No doubt remembering his own youthful excursion and mindful of merchant practice elsewhere, he would have preferred a more practical purpose in the foreign travel, and he asked detailed particulars of French commerce which the firm could utilise to their advantage. If this could be accomplished he reassured himself that all might not be lost. Yet he did not hold out much hope, as Will's companions were 'not ... conversant in trade and [would] not give him opportunity of attending to anything that [looked] like business'. Even so, abroad so uselessly, Will was not spared a detailed report of the current trading situation until, at last cutting his losses, Thomas Langton finally asked him to ship some 'good burgundy cheap' to Liverpool, but he had to be sure it was the best quality. He appended a postscript in which he left the date of Will's return to him, hoping he would not stay too long and urging him at the end to do what he could in business if opportunity offered.[398]

We do not know how Will fared on his holiday in pre-revolutionary France. That he took a French holiday showed that the custom of journeying for pleasure to the continent had reached the lesser merchants of the new generation. If it was indeed considered '*bon ton*' then the Langton family was high enough in the social scale to echo the tone.

The father had combined his youthful excursion to family and friends in Ireland with meetings with business connections and a weather eye open for the expanding trade of the 1740s. To him it was reasonable to expect some commercial return as interest on the investment in the journey. It is unlikely that his exhortation to his

[397] *Ibid.*, p. 59.
[398] Wilson, *op. cit.*, p. 64.

son to go and do likewise bore the required fruit, even in a year of financial difficulty for the firm.

If Thomas Langton had lived to see it, he would no doubt have found his youngest son's residence in Europe quite incomprehensible. Tom in Riga as a partner in Thorley Morisons was there for sound commercial reasons. Tom in Switzerland for the education of his children would have been quite another matter.

There is just one occasion recorded in the letters on which Thomas Langton might be said to have been almost (but even here not entirely) free from ulterior motive in pleasure seeking, and which in itself is in keeping with the climate of the time. On this occasion he was doing the fashionable thing, not looking for material benefit, unless, perhaps, the subsequent enhancement of status when he could boast of having done it. In 1780 he made a picturesque journey through the Lake District.

Although the Thomas Langton of 1748 travelled through some of the most beautiful country of Ireland and crossed to Scotland, there is not one remark in his journal about the scenery. He might not have gone to the lengths of Lord Chesterfield, who is said to have pulled down the carriage blinds when in sight of the Alps, but he certainly did not approach Gray's fervid transports at the wild scenery of the Grand Chartreuse some few years earlier than the Irish tour.[399] It would seem that he just did not consider the scenery worthy of note.

By his journey of 1780, however, things had changed. Travellers had been taught to look with differing eyes, especially at mountains, lakes and wild scenery. To Celia Fiennes, that practised traveller, Windermere 'seemed to be a standing lake encompassed with vast high hills that [were] perfect rocks and barren ground of a vast height' from which many little springs flowed down to the water.[400] Her favourite adjective for hills was 'barren' and she did not respond to scenic beauty. By 1750 Bishop Pococke, travelling with the main purpose of viewing antiquities, commented that, fine as the country was about Ambleside, 'the Lake of Windermere, and the ground above it exceeded it in beauty' but he did not elaborate, though he went so far as to describe Ullswater as 'romantick'.[401] Some twenty

[399] Alex Notan, ed., *Silver Renaissance. Essays in Eighteenth-Century History*, 1961, p. 133.
[400] Celia Fiennes, *Journeys*, Christopher Morris, ed., 1945, p. 193.
[401] Richard Pococke, *Dr. Pococke's Journey into England from Dublin*, Vol. 1, Cam. Soc., Vol. 42, 1887/8, p. 42.

years later Arthur Young, in his tour to record the condition of agriculture, was moved by the Lodore Falls to the extent that he dubbed the setting 'romantick and sublime' as it set off this touch of 'rural elegance',[402] but about the same time the timorous Gray was afraid to proceed to Borrowdale past Grange. For him 'the crags named Lodore Banks [began] to impend terribly over the way' and 'more terribly' when he was 'told of a recent landslide and was afraid to speak for fear of starting another'.[403] But by then the Lake District had begun to attract tourists for the mere pleasure and thrill of the scenic spectacle and when in 1772 William Gilpin made an extensive tour of the Lakes, the pursuit of the 'picturesque' had already begun even though his book elucidating it was not published until 1786. That is to say, the tourists who visited the Lake District came in order to look at their surroundings, not for information, but for aesthetic sensation.

To assist the visitors in making the most of their visit, Thomas West, a local antiquarian, published in 1778 neither a description of a place nor an account of a tour, such as the literate visitors up to this time had done, but a guide book, the first of its kind. He quoted liberally from previous writers, but he directed specifically what to see and, to a large extent, how to see it. He designated certain positions as 'stations', or viewpoints, with appropriate details of what should be seen from them, to

> heighten the pleasure of the tour and relieve the traveller from the burthen of dull and tedious information on the road or at the inn, that frequently embarrasses and often misguides.[404]

There is no direct evidence to suggest that Thomas Langton saw West's *Guide*. It was very popular and a second edition was published in 1780. It is more than likely that some of the Langton party knew it. Indeed, Wordsworth himself was to pay tribute to West as having been 'eminently serviceable to the tourist for nearly fifty years'.[405]

---

[402] Arthur Young, *A Six Months Tour Through the North of England*, 1771, reprinted N.Y., 1967, p. 118.
[403] Quoted in Norman Nicholson, *The Lakers*, 1958, pp. 57–8.
[404] The Author of 'The Antiquities of Furness' (Thomas West), *A Guide to the Lakes*, 1778.
[405] Peter Bicknell, ed., *The Illustrated Wordsworth's Guide to the Lakes*, 1984, p. 154.

In September 1780 there was a Parliamentary election at Lancaster. It was feared that Mr Stanley, a scion of the Derbys, would be opposed, so the freeholders who supported him were called to Lancaster and Thomas Langton duly went. In the event, the election of Mr Stanley went ahead 'without the least thought of opposition', so the call to freeholders had been 'quite unnecessary'.[406] Thomas Langton, never one to miss an opportunity of killing two birds, had not left Kirkham merely to support Mr Stanley. The Boltons had moved to Askham Hall and had invited the Langton party to visit them. So, having attended the election, Thomas Langton extended his absence from home to proceed to Askham, taking in the Lakes on the way.

Whether or not the party was served by West's *Guide*, they certainly knew what was expected of them on the picturesque tourist route. They expected to be impressed and they appointed one of their number to keep a diary to record their impressions. This was to be printed upon their return, a move which Thomas Langton saw as partly defraying the expenses of the journey. There is no trace of any such publication, but Thomas Langton gave enough pointers to Will in his letters home to suggest their reactions to what they saw.

From Lancaster they made a late start to Kendal, passing Levens and Sizergh 'too late to partake of any pleasure in the views'. After parading in Kendal the next morning, they went on to Bowness and ordered a boat to Mr English's island, now Belle Isle, one of the expected ports of call. In a fashionable contemporary imitation of the landscape of Claude Lorraine, an artist much favoured by the seekers after scenic beauty, the circular house was placed in a landscaped garden. Thomas Langton did not expatiate on the 'beauties of the place', leaving that for the diary.[407]

After 'tolerable' accommodation at Ambleside, they took a detour from their route to Keswick to view the lakes of Coniston and Esthwaite, a change of plan 'amply repaid by the agreeable prospects which were varied from every hill [they] ascended'.[408]

West began his Lakes tour with Coniston, reached over the sands of Morecambe Bay, and waxed more lyrical than Thomas Langton:

The change of scenes is from what is pleasing to what is surprising, from the delicate and elegant touches of Claude to

[406] LRO, DDX/190/57.
[407] LRO, DDX/190/58.
[408] LRO, DDX/190/58.

the noble scenes of Poussin ... to the stupendous romantic
ideas of Salvator Rosa.[409]

The basic sentiment is, however, the same. With the rest of the day's
excursion the party was duly impressed: 'Nothing [transpired] from
the ladies but heavenly and glorious epithets and astonishment at the
tremendous and romantic scenes [they] viewed.'[410]

They ended their day as they had begun, with waterfalls: at
Ambleside in the morning, the 'highly picturesque' and 'noble cata-
ract' of West's effusive enthusiasm, and those 'at Sir Michael le
Flemings' (at Rydal Hall) in the evening.[411] These Rydal falls drew
from West a truly purple passage, and from Wordsworth the dismis-
sive statement that they were 'pointed out to everyone'.[412]

The next day they arrived in Keswick and hoped to take their
expected way to Vicar's Island, then known as 'Mr Pocklington's
Island', Mr Pocklington, a native of Nottinghamshire, having, as
Wordsworth saw it, 'played strange pranks by his buildings and
plantations'.[413] Frustrated because Mr Pocklington was entertaining, they took a boat and sailed around the lake, in keeping with
West's dictum that 'every dimension of the lake appears more
extended from its bosom than from its banks or other elevated
position'.[414]

Whether or not West was literally their guide, the party did not
approach their excursions unprepared. The ascent of Skiddaw was
to be followed by a sail to the head of Borrowdale, 'another favourite
excursion for all parties of pleasure who visit these rural and romantic mountains'. Cecily's postscript that they were 'all astonished and
delighted beyond description' witnessed to their appropriate reaction.
Thomas Langton was also obviously impressed by the 'stupendous
rocks where the eagle builds his nest', echoing West's sentiments that
the 'rocky scenes in Borrowdale are most fantastic, the entrance
rugged'.[415]

We do not know how far the party proceeded when they left the
Boltons at Askham, whether their plans for Carlisle and Gretna

[409] West, *op. cit.*, p. 13–14.
[410] LRO, DDX/190/58.
[411] West, *op. cit.*, pp. 78–9.
[412] West, *op. cit.*, pp. 80–1, and Bicknell, ed., *op. cit.*, p. 47.
[413] Bicknell, ed., *op. cit.*, p. 188.
[414] West, *op. cit.*, p. 89.
[415] West, *op. cit.*, p. 100.

materialised. What we have of their excursion is sufficiently revealing of their complete conformity to the typical lakers of their day. They, 'like all parties of pleasure' visiting the Lakes, knew it would be 'romantic' and knew what were the essential items on their itinerary. The party would be of a certain social status, sufficiently moneyed and sufficiently leisured. They would also be of a certain aesthetic expectation, directed by the fashionable mentors of taste to an appreciation of the picturesque, whether by West himself, by references in magazines, or by personal recommendation on the spot. It is in keeping with Thomas Langton's cast of mind that he welcomed the projected publication of the diary as a means of defraying some of the cost.

As there are no other letters referring to holidays we may assume this was the only one Thomas Langton took. His youthful Irish tour had practical application to his work; his Hotwells stay had repaired his health; his journey to Hull to see Tom off to Riga was enjoyable but undertaken for a practical purpose. He may well have taken no other excursions but to family and business connections. This Lakes journey was probably the only time he allowed himself to travel primarily for pleasure, and even then he carried his business concerns with him, as his letters bear witness.

For Thomas Langton, then, there was to be virtually no leisure apart from entertaining, often with a further fetch. His daughter, however, was allowed a good deal of freedom of movement even though, her mother dead, she had home responsibilities. His sons were allowed the occasional fling at the races and were encouraged to acquire certain social accomplishments. We may assume that his children had a greater interest in leisure than their father, leisure made possible by their father's money and position. At least three of the four sons in business opted for a life of comparative leisure when it was possible. Their father died still working, really only approving of any activity which could be 'of use'. Leisure, pursued for its own sake, was seldom 'of use'.

Nevertheless, the elegancies of entertaining, hunting, fishing, travelling, which the Langton children enjoyed even before their father died, were a minor reflection of the more splendid enjoyments of the aristocracy. As first the landed gentry and then the merchants aspired to their version of aristocratic pleasures and refinements, so the lesser merchants emulated them as far as circumstances and money permitted.

Thomas Langton could not hope to 'vie with the nobility in their magnificence',[416] but he could give careful thought to a Christmas entertainment which would be worthy of his position in Kirkham.[417] Thomas Langton and at least one of his sons (Zachary, the erstwhile master of the Skinners' Company) had their portraits painted, for Cecily left them to specific beneficiaries in her will of 1832, along with those of her father-in-law (Hugh Hornby) and her late husband, Thomas Hornby. The portrait of Cecily's brother-in-law, Joseph Hornby, the builder of Ribby Hall and a solid country gentleman, still hangs in St Michaels Hall. The Kirkham merchants did not employ the great portrait painters, but local talent served them well enough. Thomas Langton did not keep a butler and footmen, like his grander city brethren,[418] but he at least attempted to train a homespun menial to perform their tasks. The Langton circle hunted with the Kirkham Dogs, attended races and fished the Wyre. Although Hambleton flookings might not have classed as a city delicacy, Thomas Langton wanted his guest to be well provided for.[419] The Langtons, like many provincial social aspirants, sought London's help in dressing as befitted their station, and Thomas Langton devoted time and care to looking for a suitable stock buckle for Will to go with the 'very handsome knee buckles' he had acquired in Bristol.[420] Cecily had wintered in Preston, the social hub of the county, and Thomas Langton had his Gillow card table in fashionable mahogany.[421] The young Langtons danced, and Will played the flute, a conveniently portable instrument.

The Langton experience, then, suggests an increasing pretension to elegant standards. It also suggests a change of attitude in the generation following Thomas Langton. If the father left no record of books read, at least one son was bookish and his daughter bequeathed three bookcases of books. If he did not travel abroad, his youngest son was to reside for three years on the continent. If the father did not miss any opportunity for commercial advantage, his second son took a French holiday purely for pleasure. All in all,

[416] Wilson, *op. cit.*, p. 213.
[417] LRO, DDX/190/40.
[418] Wilson, *op. cit.*, p. 215.
[419] LRO, DDX/190/53.
[420] LRO, DDX/190/49.
[421] Gillow Archive, Waste Book 1778–80, LU 4/344/7.

⊦hanks to the success of the Langton enterprise, at the end of Thomas Langton's life the family was able to mingle with the socially desirable on more or less equal terms. On their small scale they represented the merchant class which could enjoy a share in the pleasures of those whose status and material advantage rested on their birth and financial independence.

There is no mausoleum to mark their social standing even in death, as was sometimes the case. But the Birleys are buried in a vault with a superstructure unique in Kirkham churchyard, and the Langton names are writ, certainly not in water, but in Latin.

The Family

It may be confidently asserted that the main purpose of the Langton commercial activity, the education of the sons and their placing in appropriate positions, was to stabilise and enhance the social as well as the commercial standing of the Langton family, identified as it was with the Langton enterprise. When Thomas Langton died in 1794 his two eldest sons were in the partnership, there was a son in London in business and another in an important Riga firm with whom the Langtons dealt. Eighteenth-century trade, though usually conducted through risk-spreading partnerships, was uninstitutionalised and decisions about the deployment of property and the conduct of the business remained largely within the family.[422]

The progress of the Langton concern through the eighteenth century shows a development from a family business centred on a shop, in which the wife participated (Mrs Langton was paid two shillings for making a surplice in 1729)[423] to an enterprise which was widespread and from the profits of which a household was supported, with the female members taking no part in the business except for the occasional investment.[424] This meant an upward social mobility leading to the partial or total emancipation of the male members from active participation and their withdrawal into leisured, or partially-leisured, retirement comparatively early.

---

[422] Leonore Davidoff and Catherine Hall, *Family Fortunes: Men and Women of the English Middle Class 1780–1850*, 1987, p. 195.
[423] R. Cunliffe Shaw and Helen G. Shaw, *The Records of the Thirtymen of the Parish of Kirkham*, Kendal, 1930, p. 80.
[424] Will of Tabitha Langton, dated 1796. Tabitha died in 1801.

It is virtually certain that Cornelius, the first Langton to come to Kirkham, lived over the shop and that John, his son and the letter writer's father, who inherited, did the same. Workplace and domicile were still one. John's father-in-law, however, left his grandson Thomas (the letter writer), still a minor, his Kirkham property including Ash Tree Hall, and John took over the lease. Whether John ever lived there is uncertain, but Thomas did and, in line with the growing prosperity of the family, rebuilt it, probably in the 1760s.[425] Three-storeyed, with Georgian symmetry, it emphasised his social pretension through such detail as the pillared doorway and corniced windows on the outside, and a fine mahogany staircase indoors. The workplace—by now for flax-dressing and sailcloth production—was no longer the domicile and Thomas was a merchant-manufacturer expanding his capitalist ventures. He did not himself dress flax or weave sailcloth as his father had sold cloth. His method of production was to utilise a labour force who worked for him and from whom he lived separately, in a much more sumptuous style, and to whom he was socially superior.

The world of the family, to a large extent the milieu in which the emerging middle class moved, imposed responsibilities upon the head of the household/business to make careful provision for his dependants. In the Langton experience it is interesting to note how succeeding generations achieved this. When Cornelius died in 1712 he left three sons and two daughters. He had already set up his daughter Anne, the eldest, in the millinery trade, and his other daughter received a legacy to the same value as her two younger brothers. These two, aged fourteen and twelve, were to have their legacies used, the one to make him a scholar, the other for his 'preferment'. The residue was to go to the eldest son, John, who therefore inherited the business. But among Cornelius's inventoried goods *post mortem* were grocery 'appurtenances' to the value of £81 6s. 9¼d. as well as drapery goods valued at £209 19s. 1¼d.[426] As the elder of the two cadets (the Uncle Langton of the letters) had obviously already been marked as bookish, it would seem that Cornelius intended to build up the grocery business for his youngest son, as John was to will in 1759 his drapery business to his second

[425] Shaw, *Kirkham in Amounderness, op. cit.*, p. 693.
[426] LRO, DDX/190/107.

son and the residue of his estate to his elder son, the letter writer, already in partnership with him as a merchant.[427]

John's previous wills (he made six in all) had left the residue 'share and share alike' to all his children, with no special mention of Thomas, the eldest. It was not until the younger son was twenty-four that John finally established Thomas as his undoubted heir, having provided for the younger in an independent line. The age of twenty-four is significant. The Statute of Apprentices, still not repealed, put twenty-four as the age for ending apprenticeships in corporate towns, as against twenty-one in the country (though many urban apprenticeships ended at twenty-one also). As the will specifically states that his son had been 'trained to that trade' we may conclude he had served a formal apprenticeship. Only when the younger was adequately provided for did the father make the elder son his heir. The daughters lost their share in the residue and had legacies in lieu.

The provisions of John Langton's will of 1759 suggest the stirrings of dynastic intent. By 1759 the Langton firm had some way to go before its flowering under Thomas, but there is an indication that a business house was in the making when the elder son was so much advantaged over the others.

Thomas Langton's will does not survive, but his granddaughter told in her book how he arranged his legacies. She recorded that he

left his property to his sons according to seniority, in diminishing ratio, and [her] father being the youngest of them came in for the least share, the one daughter being equal with him.

She appends a note about Thomas Langton:

He inherited property in Preston from his ancestors, and Ash Hall in Kirkham through his mother ... He also had land through his wife. All this went to his eldest son.[428]

She presumably meant all assets, including property in the restricted sense, though Thomas Langton's estate would, indeed, consist substantially of property and his share in the business.

This notion of an undoubted heir was well-established in the Langton family by the end of the century. In 1799 William Langton, the second son, spoke of his elder brother as continuing the 'line'

[427] LRO, DDX/190/16.
[428] Anne Langton, op. cit., p. 1.

and he resuscitated the Langton coat of arms from the Broughton Tower connection, thus combining the commercial with a hereditary lineage.[429] With five sons Thomas Langton, the letter writer, was faced with a problem spared his father, John, and his grandfather, Cornelius. The question of establishing a 'line' through the eldest son had, in the two preceding generations, solved itself by the death of the younger sons and by the wish of Thomas Langton's uncle (the Uncle Langton of the letters) to become a scholar rather than enter business. Thomas Langton's own brother had died a little before their father, leaving Thomas as the sole surviving son.

Anne Langton, Tom's daughter, might have thought her father hard done by as the youngest of the family but, in fact, Thomas Langton had made careful provision for all his children. Another descendant stated that Anne's father returned from Russia quite affluent, having been sent to Russia 'for his portion'.[430] Zachary, the London warehouseman, became sufficiently prosperous to become a burgess of the City of London, and whatever the source of his income, the blind son had enough to live on in the care of a housekeeper. Will was in the partnership and Cecily was comfortably married. There was, then, a move away from the equitable inheritance of the early wills of Thomas Langton's father, John, to the modified primogeniture of Thomas Langton's own provisions. He obviously aimed to establish his eldest son as a man of property and substance and as the senior partner, whilst establishing his other sons in good openings for advancement.

Thomas Langton's strong personality quite obviously dominated the family, but it also provided a bond holding the family in affectionate friendship. Will Langton's addendum to the mention of his father's death in the family's genealogical details, 'deeply lamented by his children', has a ring of truth rather than the hollowness of mere convention, and it is apparent in the letters that, exacting and demanding as he was, Thomas Langton was deeply attached to all his children.[431] There is abundant evidence that he took his paternal rôle seriously, as guide, adviser, corrector and provider. His aim was to prepare his sons for the part they were to play in adult life. His statement, 'I am willing to allow you anything you want in reason' might suggest an over-indulgent father were it

[429] LRO, DDX/190/103.
[430] William Langton, ed., *Early Days in Upper Canada*, Toronto, 1926, p. xiii.
[431] LRO, DDX/190/103.

not for the qualification 'in reason'.[432] It could, of course, be a let-out, but it is true at its face value. He was open to persuasion and did not exercise a tyrannous hold upon his offspring. Although initially opposed to the boys' moving with the school to Essex, he yielded to their entreaties.[433] If his sons chose to have green suits, he let them; if John wished to have silk stockings, so be it; if Will wished to play the flute, he might do so, in spite of his father's reservations— although his studies might suffer, he should be the judge.[434] There was just once a hint that the sons were 'vehicles of social emulation'[435] when he told them that Thomas Hornby (Cecily's future husband and the son of his business rival) had improved in his writing and, in Thomas Langton's own words, 'I would not have him surpass you therein'.[436]

Whether consciously or subconsciously, he projected his own social attitudes and moral imperatives: the boys were to visit their relatives and the firm's business connections and engage in a copious correspondence;[437] they were to master the groundskills of business (apart from languages, also useful in business, no other subject was mentioned);[438] they were not to displease Mr Booth;[439] they were not to frequent a public house;[440] they were to go decently clad to stay with friends in London;[441] above all, they were to keep accurate accounts of their expenditure.[442]

This careful evaluation of cash was very much a part of the middle-class mercantile ethic, with its emphasis upon the importance of an awareness of the value of money and the avoidance of debt. This contrasted with the lavish display of some aristocrats, who disdained sordid money matters, amassing huge debts through gambling and extravagance.[443] Credit-worthiness and sound financial management were essential to those of the emerging middle class

---

[432] LRO, DDX/190/43.
[433] LRO, DDX/190/31.
[434] LRO, DDX/190/32, 43, 36.
[435] Plumb, *op. cit.*, p. 70.
[436] LRO, DDX/190/36.
[437] LRO, DDX/190/44, 45, *et al*; LRO DDX/190/early letters *passim*.
[438] *Ibid.*
[439] LRO, DDX/190/27, 28 *et al.*
[440] LRO, DDX/190/27.
[441] LRO, DDX/190/27, 41.
[442] LRO, DDX/190/41 *et al.*
[443] Davidoff and Hall, *op. cit.*, p. 21.

who were to stand a chance of upward social mobility. Without credit your business collapsed.

However, Thomas Langton gave no pointers to the middle-class virtues of dignity, piety, honesty and love of a proper family life which were 'increasingly adopted by the middling sort'.[444] He counselled business, rather than domestic or personal, virtues, perhaps because he believed these latter would take care of themselves by the example of the Langton household, whereas the others had to be acquired like professional skills.

The only exhortation to piety was the reiteration of the necessity of acknowledging one's duty to one's maker and a trust in divine providence. The Langtons attended Kirkham parish church, where they had their own pew, a necessary status symbol.[445] Such attendance would be obligatory for a family of their prominence. Although many successful merchants were non-conformist, moved by the evangelical revival or encouraged to shun the follies of mankind with the Quakers, the Langtons were people of the Establishment. In the small community of Kirkham, with the vestry such an organ of influence, nothing else would have served, quite apart from the family's clerical connections.

Although evangelicalism could be found in the Church, there is no hint of religious fervour in the letters. Religion was part of their experience but did not play a prominent part. This would in itself affect the attitude to children. The will was not to be broken at all costs as the Puritan ethic of the seventeenth century and the extreme evangelicalism of the eighteenth taught. It was to be moulded into acceptable domestic and social practice. The time of children being seen and not heard was yet to come.

A warm affection for all his children permeated Thomas Langton's letters. The baby Tom was 'a charming boy' and later a 'fine chattering lad'.[446] His tenth birthday celebrations were reported to his elder brother away in London.[447] His concern for the son with the weak eyes was apparent.[448] When his daughter's friend died suddenly he was 'almost distracted for fear of [his] dear Cecily'.[449]

[444] *Ibid.*, p. 152.
[445] Kirkham Parish Church Organ Accounts, PR 2071.
[446] Davidoff and Hall, *op. cit.*, p. 189; LRO, DDX/190/39.
[447] LRO, DDX/190/62.
[448] LRO, DDX/190/early letters *passim*.
[449] LRO, DDX/190/64.

He felt for his sons away from home at Christmas.[450] He made Zachary a parlour boarder as it would be 'more eligible' for him.[451]

The family did not consist merely of parents and their children. Thomas Langton's concern and affection extended to his sisters. He reported their state of health and was troubled by the effect of excessive grief upon the one who lost her baby.[452] His wife's relations were similarly included under the family umbrella, her half-sister spending the winter with the Langtons. His Blackburn brother-in-law, the prosperous cotton manufacturer, was frequently mentioned and much visiting took place between the two families. When the firm experienced a cash-flow crisis, kinship ties held and the Feilden brother-in-law offered financial help. This was common practice and the kinship arrangement led to greater stability than when money was borrowed through trade credit or mortgage.[453]

Eighteenth-century society was male-orientated and the domestic rôles for women were unquestioned by all but the progressive few. No Mary Woolstonecraft resided in the Langton circle. But the Langton women were cherished and provided for and given a good deal of freedom. There is a sense of camaraderie, of people enjoying each other's company, and of the female members not by any means ignored by the male members of the family.

Thomas Langton was obviously fond of his wife. She wrote seldom, no doubt because of her health, so the correspondence to the boys at school was almost entirely in the father's hands. However, it is more than likely that he would have written the same letters and concerned himself with the same minutiae had his wife been well. Boys' education and training was very much a father's affair. It is unlikely that Lord Chesterfield warned his son not to get his feet wet, but Thomas Langton was no less anxious than the noble lord that his progeny should be prepared for their intended station. Responsibility and affection characterised Thomas Langton's parenthood. He was fair and evenhanded; even the boys at school often received separate letters. His provision for all his children shows his wish to be just while still establishing a dynasty. His displeasure at Will's unauthorised holiday abroad did not lead him to order his son home. He was both unable and unwilling to do so, not only because

---

[450] LRO, DDX/190/26, 27.
[451] LRO, DDX/190/52.
[452] LRO, DDX/190/36, 37.
[453] LRO, DDX/190/68; Davidoff and Hall, *op. cit.*, p. 215.

of the financial waste but also because he wanted his son to make the most of the venture.[454] As in his early letters to his sons, affection broke in to soften a blow which was not really such a hard knock in the first place, and his tone of rebuke was always more in sorrow than in anger. He was not to be taken lightly, but we may well believe that the loss of his commanding, but fundamentally benevolent, presence would indeed be lamented by his children.

There was a lifelong close relationship between the Langton siblings and some of their cousins. When Cornelius died in 1816 Tom, in Switzerland, wrote to Cecily in Kirkham:

> A few years, my dear sister, have reduced our family to half the number at which it had stood for forty years before the death of poor John [in 1807] and the remainder of us are going downhill fast. Yet a few years and the reunion for which we hope will have taken place and left the stage for the next generation.[455]

Only the previous year he had enquired of his sister how Cornelius was taking the death of their cousin Henry Feilden. He wrote: 'I fear no-one will more need consolation for the loss of poor H. Feilden, who was deservedly a great favourite with him.'[456]

In spite of the marks of the Langtons' undoubtedly later gentility, there is in the early letters the suggestion that they were not entirely, or indeed largely, always removed from the lesser fry of Kirkham. Cornelius was 'very fond of being out of doors among his playfellows' in the company of his attendant, the brother of a Langton servant.[457] Mr Booth objected to a certain visitor who called on the boys at Woolton, Thomas Langton felt, because it was thought the visitor might draw them to a public house, and he promised Mr Booth that the man would call in the future only to receive messages for Kirkham.[458] As time went on there seems to have been a conscious attempt to woo genteel recognition. It would appear that such recognition did not come as a matter of course. The same malice which led Shepherd Birley to relate the anecdote of the broken crockery led him to relate that of Thomas Langton's encounter with

[454] LRO, DDX/190/68.
[455] Thomas Langton Junior, *op. cit.*, p. 96.
[456] *Ibid.*, p. 76.
[457] LRO, DDX/190/38.
[458] LRO, DDX/190/28.

the yokel leading a calf. Shepherd Birley described Thomas Langton as 'a proud man of very passionate temper', which is how the Birley memory must have perpetuated him, as Shepherd Birley never knew him personally. He related that one day Thomas Langton met a countryman leading a frisky calf which was hard to restrain. Thomas Langton, ignored by the man, asked him why he did not touch his cap to a gentleman. The man replied that, if Thomas Langton would hold the calf he would 'pull [his] hat off'.[459] This anecdote is revealing in what it tells of both the subject and the narrator. There seems to have been some needle in the Birley attitudes to the Langtons, although they intermarried in the nineteenth century, and in the letters references to the Birley partner were restrained and impersonal, unlike those to Mr Shepherd. (The Birleys were kin to the Shepherds and not to the Langtons in Thomas Langton's lifetime.)

Does this leave an ambivalent impression of Thomas Langton, so much more laudable in his letters to his sons than when his social pretensions were thwarted? The Birley anecdotes show that Thomas Langton was not universally revered or held in the respect the local quality might expect. Would the same attitudes have been shown to Mr Clifton of Lytham Hall, the lord of the manor? John Langton senior might have designated himself 'gentleman' in two of his wills and be commemorated in Latin on his gravestone, but this did not mean that his son was automatically accorded gentle status. The anecdotes refer to no specific dates, but they were obviously considered worth much re-telling. This suggests that Thomas Langton shared in what has been called 'the precariousness of middle class life', to which a well-ordered, well-appointed home acted as an antidote.[460] If indeed the family mediated between the public and the private, connecting the market with the domestic, it also gave the *pater familias* a sense of purpose and importance quite separate from that in the public domain. At home, in the bosom of his family, he found his identity. Monarch of all he surveyed, at heart despotic, because he loved his family he was enlightened in his despotism.

[459] LRO, DDD, Shepherd Birley Notebook.
[460] Davidoff and Hall, *op. cit.*, p. 397.

Mutatis Mutandis

When Zachary Langton (the Uncle Langton of the letters) published his treatise on the human rational soul in 1753, he showed a scholar's concern for the dying phases of a theological discourse which presented man as a rational soul in search of virtue, as distinct from an immortal soul in search of salvation. When Will Langton, in 1793, copied the records of the Kirkham Thirtymen, interspersed with a sprinkling of Latin and with any mention of his family particularly noted, and six years later endeavoured to trace his family's genealogy and revive the Langton coat of arms, he coupled the antiquarian's interest in his town with the gentleman's pride in lineage.

Uncle Langton's *magnum opus* was somewhat anachronistic, reflecting the paradox of the early eighteen century. As Basil Willey puts it:

> During the seventeenth century the acquisitive urges still hid behind religious and political outworks but by now it was too clear that what both individuals and states were really after was the material spoils of the world, now lying readier for exploitation than they had ever been ... Yet the old standards lived on in ghostly fashion, sitting crowned upon the graves of Christianity and Humanism; it was to them one instinctively turned and by them one was still, in theory, supposed to be living.[461]

By the end of the century Will Langton's antiquarian researches were by no means anachronistic, however much they delved into the past. By then the 'acquisitive urges' had led to the emergence of the towns as the 'pacesetters for rural England' and their dynamic expansion brought increased confidence and self-consciousness to urban society.[462] This led the urban middle ranks to show much interest in the history and tradition of their towns. Many town histories were written between 1781 and 1800, and not only by learned clergymen in their rectories, but often by professional men or tradesmen above a shop or a stone's throw from a counting house, reflecting civic pride and a sense of achievement.[463] Those who now

[461] Basil Willey, *The Eighteenth-Century Background*, 1946, p. 101.
[462] P. J. Corfield, *The Impact of English Towns 1700–1800*, Oxford, 1982, p. 186.
[463] Peter Clark, ed., *The Transformation of English Provincial Towns*, 1984, p. 45.

felt confident in their personal social superiority showed an equivalent interest in their family's past.[464]

Yet, however much Thomas Langton might have wished to be
equated with the gentry, he remained, to the end, a representative of
the urban middle class, hard-working, shrewd, hard-headed (but not,
in his case, hard-hearted). He was no Mr Gradgrind, either, and the
mechanisation of the linen industry did not take place in his lifetime.
Not only was flax not spun mechanically until Marshall's machine
(developing the patent taken out in 1787 by Kendrew and Back-
house) was utilised in the 'nineties, but even then hand-spinning died
hard.[465] Kirkham was no Coketown. Shepherd Birley's genteel town
at the turn of the century had not yet known the serious threat of
cotton, and when Thomas Langton died the Horrocks brothers had
only just arrived in Preston. Nevertheless, the Langtons were part of
the early years of the industrial revolution. Some of their workpeople,
perhaps most, spun and wove in the Langton sheds, and the firm was
a capitalist enterprise run for the benefit of the partners. The expansion of their linen production led to the employment of many
workpeople, and many families in Kirkham and south Fylde must
have depended on the Langton and Hornby firms for the major part,
if not all, of their livelihood. Thomas Langton left the town much
more prosperous than his grandfather found it and his family's
success had helped to alter the character, even though it had not
changed the fundamental nature, of Kirkham. It was still a market
town. The Langtons helped to make Kirkham just as Kirkham
helped to make the Langtons. In this they were of their time. The
merchants on a grander scale knew the same inter-relation with their
cities.[466]

The transition from the cloistered learning of Uncle Zachary to
the urbane antiquarianism of Will was reflected in the development
of the fortunes of the Langton family. By the time of the letters, trade
and commerce were justified in their own right. Thomas Langton
believed in straight and honest dealing, but left religious considera-
tions of virtue for personal, not business, life, without any scruple.[467]

[464] Wilson, *op. cit.*, p. 216.
[465] Patricia Baines, *Flax and Linen*, Shire Publications, 1985, p. 14; François
Crouzet, *The First Industrialists. The Problem of Origins*, Cambridge, 1985,
p. 14.
[466] Jackson, *op. cit.*; Wilson, *op. cit.*
[467] LRO, DDX/190/59.

The young Will had to be reminded that mercy was not one of the commercial virtues.[468] Thomas Langton was not likely to consider the ethics of business in a philosophical way. His ships occasionally dealt with slaves. Like many another pillar of society he considered the cargo merely another commodity, as many once viewed the question of trading with South Africa. He adopted the mercantile standards of his day, seeing no contradiction between striking a hard bargain and loving his neighbour as himself.

Among the oligarchic leaders of the small town of Kirkham, increasingly prosperous as the business expanded, the Langtons were able to provide for their progeny and enjoy their position in a widening social circle. In touch with distant places like Russia and America, they were in constant contact with much of the north of England and with London. Educated on a broad base, the Langton sons learned the business by participation in it. Their future was decided by their father's provision, younger sons dealt with as fairly as circumstances allowed. Their religious background was the Church of England; they were not stirred by evangelicalism nor shaken by enlightenment. Politically they were also of the established Whig tradition. While taking whatever prudent measures offered, in matters of health they trusted to Providence. For recreation, when not meeting in family conviviality, they followed their version of the genteel pastimes of the day, heading in the same direction as the gentry. In their family life they were bound by genuine affection under a strict, but loving, father. Their business world was criss-crossed by a tissue of kinship ties.

In much of this they were typical of the merchant class of their time, reflecting in their lesser orbit the lifestyle of more glowing luminaries. City oligarchies were the more imposing models for the Langton–Birley–Hornby côterie in Kirkham. But the Langtons and their rivals were not truly parallel to the great city merchants. They would be classed as merchant-manufacturers, looked down on by their city exemplars who strove to keep the merchant-manufacturers in their place. Thomas Langton would not have cut much ice with these merchant aristocrats.

Nevertheless, the Kirkham flaxmen contributed to the development of regional trade. The prosperity of the ports of Poulton and Lancaster, and the rise of the port of Liverpool, coincided with their

[468] LRO, DDX/190/63.

own development and was part of the same economic advance. The development of the inland waterways facilitated internal trade, and the Kirkham merchants took advantage of it. Thomas Langton's working life exactly spanned the years of the linen industry's most fruitful period. Success was not automatically guaranteed. The national and international influences which helped to mould the firm were balanced by the internal influence of the personal qualities and business acumen of Thomas Langton who steered its survival course.

The marriages of the Langton sons did not forward the fortunes of the firm as those of the older partners of the firm had done. John married his first cousin; Will, the friend of his sister; Tom, the daughter of a clergyman and his sister-in-law's first cousin. Only Zachary married into a merchant family, but to no advantage to the Kirkham firm. By the end of the century kinship ties in commerce were no longer of such paramount importance, for the mercantile world was beginning to change. The day of the merchant was over. He was no longer the leader and prime mover in a booming economy, but merely one of many factors.[469] As the nineteenth century approached there came a certain revulsion against trade and industry. As early as 1793 Jane Austen could write that a heroine's fortune made her of some consequence but her birth gave her no other claim to the hero's attention, 'for her father had been a merchant'.[470]

If merchant and gentleman could be synonymous in the latter half of the eighteenth century, they were not necessarily to be so during the nineteenth. Certainly a mere manufacturer would have difficulty in qualifying, as the status of many families which produced industrialists was rather low, and even when they became rich, industrialists were thought by the traditional ruling class to be despicable for their low birth and uncultivated manners—and their necessary attachment to really hard bargaining.

The Langton family, however, had not been solely allied to the mercantile interest in their family relationships. One of Thomas Langton's sisters married a lawyer, another a schoolmaster in orders who officiated in a church in the parish as well as ran the free school. The learned uncle was a scholarly cleric. Will's father-in-law was a doctor. These three professions of medicine, law and the Church proliferated during the eighteenth century and enjoyed considerable

[469] Jackson, op. cit., p. 263; Wilson, op. cit., p. 215.
[470] Jane Austen, Catharine (1790–3), Folio Society, 1963, p. 202.

prestige. Kinship threads, then, bound the Langtons to the learned professions as well as to the mercantile world. After Thomas Langton's death they could be upwardly mobile within the middle class even if they could not break out of it.

The Langtons' social advancement was not to take them fully into the ranks of the landed gentry. As we saw above, even Thomas's great grandson, living in style as a Liverpool gentleman, still attended his office. But it was to take them out of the ranks of the manufacturers altogether and into more cerebral and therefore, in the climate of the time, more acceptable areas of influence. The first signs were visible when John and Will opted out of the flax concern in 1804, ten years after their father's death, by which time the shadow was already cast. Although steam power came to the firm only in 1807, changes were obviously inevitable and the neighbouring cotton mills pointed to the future. The brothers may have disliked the implications. They withdrew from manufacturing and settled to more leisured occupations. Their brother, Tom, after his continental sojourn, became President of the Liverpool Royal Institution as well as Deputy Lieutenant of Lancashire. The next generation took the cerebral still further. Will's son, Joseph, became Secretary of the Bank of Liverpool, and his grandson, Chairman of the Dock Board (the Langton Dock is called after him) and Treasurer of the Blue Coat Hospital—still nominally a merchant, but a cultivated man. Tom's younger son became Vice-Chancellor of Toronto University and auditor of the public accounts for the Dominion of Canada; his elder son, William, also a banker, was active in the founding of Manchester University, serving on the College Seal Committee following the Owens College Act of 1871, and himself designing the coat of arms still used by the university today.[471] He was a long-serving member of the committee of the Chetham Society and concerned with many cultural projects in the city.

This was not what Thomas Langton could have foreseen. He had worked so that his firm would pass down from generation to generation—as indeed it did, but in the Birley, not the Langton, family. The social changes and the new demands generated by the industrial revolution in the nineteenth century brought a more varied choice of openings than the merchants of the previous century knew. The

[471] Joseph Thompson, *The Owens College: its Foundation and Growth*, Manchester, 1886, p. 446.

provincial middle class, finally emerged from its chrysalis as the eighteenth century closed, flourished in an urban environment, taking new prestigious appointments and living among an urban culture of learned societies, scientific interests, new universities and civic orchestras. This was particularly true of the northern cities and it was to those cities that the Langtons gravitated, playing a prominent part in civic and intellectual life. They had outgrown Kirkham.

They had also outgrown the family concern, ready for a change of direction which would take them away from the sphere of the new industrialists. If, in the early eighteenth century, their expensive apprenticeship had set merchants apart from the rest of the community, by 1800 it was their superior education that gave them an enhanced status *vis à vis* the manufacturing class.[472] The Langtons' education which had cost their father dear in money and anxiety, though intended to be 'of use' in business, was superior to that of many of the rising industrialists who came from families not socially acceptable. The day of the ideal of the self-made man was dawning. Those families in the higher echelons who also chose to turn their backs on the brave new world of industry also sent their sons into the professions instead of trade.[473]

Thomas Langton displayed many of the qualities necessary for the successful industrialist who was to supersede the merchant at the head of the industrial world. He was a leader and a disciplinarian, seeing to all branches of the enterprise with a total and personal commitment. But he had never to face the challenge which a mechanised industry would have given him: the need to understand technical problems, to remain aware of technical developments. Had he been thirty years younger he might well have tried to become one of those instruments of continuity between the merchant-manufacturer and the industrialist (as his Birley associates became) which operated side by side with the various 'new men' who, with no commercial background, took their chance in the factory-orientated world.[474] Even before he died he was something of an anachronism. The very versatility of his business pursuits, which had contributed so substantially to the firm's survival through the hard times, was soon to be an 'archaic trait'.[475]

---

[472] Wilson, *op. cit.*, p. 211.
[473] *Ibid.*, p. 132.
[474] Crouzet, *op. cit.*, p. 8.
[475] *Ibid.*, p. 7.

The Langtons, then, were part of a process of change. Their status was undoubtedly enhanced in their home town, to whose prosperity they handsomely contributed, even if the prophet was not always honoured in his own country, but their mobility was geographical and intellectual as much as social. Unlike the Birleys—who kept a local base, living as pseudo country gentlemen in the vicinity while continuing to manufacture, perpetuating the ideal of 'country life in business' so cherished in the eighteenth century[476]—the Langtons became diffused and dispersed. They had no focal point of family identity except Cecily, married into the rival Hornby family and living in Kirkham until her death in 1833. With many varied pockets of influence, they became involved in the peripheral activities of the industrial revolution. So much men of their time in the eighteenth century, the Langtons were no less so in the nineteenth. Although Thomas Langton would have found it hard to believe, there had been development and progress, not stasis or diminution. Times changed and the Langtons changed with them. The virtues of the education and training to which Thomas Langton submitted his sons furnished them with sufficient resilience to adapt even if they did not give them the persistence to keep the old ways together.

A reading of Thomas Langton's letters, against a background of the relevant situation of their times, enables us to realise a perspective as we see established practices of the day in the specific terms of a particular place at a particular time. It allows us to understand something of the late-eighteenth-century experience, crystallised in terms of the personal experience of an authentic voice.

[476] Wilson, *op. cit.*, p. 220.

The Letters

NOTES

Transcription and Annotation

The abbreviations used by Thomas Langton have been extended to complete words and spelling modernised. Where the manuscript is damaged or totally illegible, that has been noted, as have occasions when a word has been conjectured or completed. Although all the principal figures mentioned in the letters have been identified, it has not been possible to identify everyone referred to. Where a person or firm is not identified in a note, no clear identification has been established. Notes are appended to each letter, together with the Lancashire Record Office classification number. The location of the recipient is given when it is other than Kirkham, and when a covering direction is extant. Names of ships have not been italicised.

Classification Numbers of the Letters

The letters in the Langton deposit in the Lancashire Record Office are numbered DDX/190/21 to DDX/190/68. The chronology is not strictly adhered to in the numbering of six of the letters and adjustment has accordingly been made: DDX/190/64 written 7 February 1780, follows DDX/190/56 dated 23 July 1778; DDX/190/61 dated 25 September 1780 follows DDX/190/58 dated 21 September 1780; DDX/190/62 follows, dated 10 October 1780; DDX/190/63 follows, dated 22 October 1780. Next comes DDX/190/59 dated 24 October 1780, to be followed by DDX/190/60; DDX/190/60 is followed by DDX/190/65 and /66 dated 13 August 1782 and 2 March 1786 respectively. Chronologically, DDX/190/68 now follows, dated 10 June 1787, addressed to 'Dear Sirs' rather than to Will, apparently to the business partners. DDX/190/67 dated 23 April 1788 is the last letter of the collection.

(DDX/190/21)
Kirkham   August 2nd, 1771

My dear lads,

It has been with pleasure that I have heard by several of my friends that you were very well and pleased with your situation at Woolton.[1] Mr Yates advised me that your desk was duly forwarded to you by Mr Booth's[2] servant and I hope you found everything therein agreeable to the account given you. I should have wrote to you sooner in answer to Will's letter by Mr Shepherd,[3] but that I expected to have the opportunity of sending it by a private hand,[4] and was at last disappointed, so that you will have this by post. I did not return from Liverpool before Tuesday after I left you, and at my coming home, I found your mother was gone to Lytham with your Aunts Feilden[5] and Rigby,[6] and had taken your sister[7] and two brothers[8] with her. She bathed every day during the time she stayed there,[9] and your sister and brothers bathed 3 or 4 times, which I think has been of service to them all, and particularly to your mother, who, I hope, is much better. She was extremely pleased to see your kind enquiries after her, and I trust in Providence that in a little time her health will be perfectly restored and then she may perhaps take a journey to see you at Woolton, which might be of service to her, but her desire to see you and the place you live in would be her sole inducement. Your brother Cornelius is got clever[10] and hearty again. He says he is quite well, and is playing and rambling about the streets from morning to night. He went to school[11] last Monday and is under Mr Cockin's care.[12] He took his Accidence with him in great spirits, but he has not yet made a beginning in it. Hugh Hornby[13] goes along with him to Mr Cockin, and John Hornby[14] is sent to Dame Coup's.

Your Uncle and Aunt Shepherd and all the Miss Shepherds set out last Monday to go to Harrogate,[15] where they propose to stay 3 weeks. I hope the journey will be of service to Mrs Shepherd, who is at present in a bad state of health. They have bought a new single horse chair which they have taken with them. Your Aunt Tabitha[16] has got two ladies, strangers, with her from Prescot, say Mrs Chapman and Miss Topping, and Captain Threlfall and his lady from Liverpool are now at your Uncle Threlfall's.[17] How long they propose to stay here I cannot say. Your Uncle Threlfall frequently enquires after you, and was well pleased that you remembered him when you wrote. Mr and Mrs Bolton[18] are come to live at Wesham for a few months this summer at the house he bought of Mr Loxham.

He was here a few days ago and told me he had received a letter from Will giving him a very pleasing account of his son James. It gave him signal pleasure and says he is much obliged to you for writing to him. William Whiteside wrote me a letter the other day by Samuel Salisbury who was at Liverpool to let me know that he had been to see you at Woolton and that you were both well. He said you wanted some trifling things which he had bought you and would send them to you which was well and I would have you to pay him for them, when you see him again, and I can order Mr Yates to send you a little money at any time you may want. I was well pleased with the scheme Mr Booth had laid out for William but you do not tell me how John employs his time. I expect to hear that in your next letter. I will not perplex you with pressing your attention to the studies you are engaged in, as, I hope your own good dispositions will sufficiently prompt you to a due care and diligent application by which you will gain the esteem and approbation of Mr Booth and the other masters, and I shall have the pleasure in reflecting that the care and expense I am at in giving you a liberal education will be greatly productive of turning to your future advantage. All your friends here are very well. Mrs Bolton who is now here upon a visit to your mother desires to be particularly remembered to her son James, and she begs her compliments to you both and Richard Bradkirk,[19] and thanks you for writing to them and hopes you will continue to do so. Mr Bradkirk's[20] family are all well and beg to be remembered to Richard and you, so does Mr Threlfall and your Aunt Tabitha. I have wrote you a long letter, which I hope will make amends for my long silence. I shall hope to hear from you very soon. Your mother joins me in proper respects to Mr Booth and the two ladies and with our most sanguine good wishes for you both I remain,

Your affectionate father,
Thomas Langton

Notes to DDX/190/21
To the Rev. Mr Booth's at Woolton near Liverpool (to DDX/190/34)
August 2nd, 1771

[1] John (b. 1756) and William (b. 1758) Langton were at school at Woolton Academy, housed in Woolton Hall, the former seat of the Molyneux family.
[2] The Revd Bartholomew Booth was the headmaster of the Woolton Academy.
[3] William Shepherd, partner in the firm of Langton Shepherd and Birley, and Mrs Jane Langton's uncle.

[4] Thomas Langton always preferred mail delivery by private hand to save expense for the recipient.

[5] Margaret Feilden, wife of Joseph Feilden, textile merchant of Blackburn, was Jane Langton's sister.

[6] Mary Rigby, half sister of Jane Langton and Margaret Feilden.

[7] Cecily Langton, born 1760.

[8] There were three brothers at home but here, presumably, the two older are meant as Tom (b. 1770) was only a baby. Zachary was born in 1762 and Cornelius in 1763.

[9] Bathing at Lytham was thought to be particularly therapeutic. Sea-bathing was increasingly popular as a cure for a variety of ills. See John Walton, *The English Seaside Resort*, Leicester, 1982.

[10] 'Clever' here means better in health, active as opposed to infirm, having ordinary healthy activity (O.E.D.).

[11] Kirkham Free School, the endowed grammar school.

[12] Second master of the free school.

[13, 14] The sons of Hugh Hornby, the rival flax merchant: Hugh was born in 1765 and John in 1763.

[15] The spas were still much sought after for the curative properties of their waters, but the sea-bathing resorts were gradually to supersede them in popularity.

[16] Thomas Langton's sister Tabitha (1730–1801).

[17] John Threlfall, master of the free school for fifty-six years, husband of Thomas Langton's sister Sarah (1720–91). See memorial tablet in Kirkham parish church.

[18] Edward Bolton, son of Thomas Langton's first cousin, Tabitha. See memorial tablet in Askham Parish Church.

[19] Son of Thomas Langton's sister, Ann (1718–1807) who was married to Cuthbert Bradkirk. See memorial tablet in Kirkham parish church.

[20] Thomas Langton often referred to the boys' uncles and aunts as 'Mr' and 'Mrs', though never to Aunt Tabitha as 'Miss Langton'; she was sometimes 'Aunt Langton'. 'Aunt Rigby', also unmarried, was never accorded her Christian name.

(DDX/190/22)

Kirkham   September 2nd, 1771

My dear lads,

I have the pleasure to inform you that I got safe home the day after I left you and found all here pretty well. I was not willing to let this opportunity slip to inform you of it by Mrs Chapman, who is now returning to Prescot, having been upon a visit to your aunt. She is a very agreeable lady and proposes to call of you at Woolton with this letter in a few days after she gets home. She brings a pair of breeches for Will which was left here and which he may perhaps have occasion for. I shall be expecting to have a long letter from him in a post or two after you receive this with a particular account how you go on, and he must also remember to write to his Aunt Rigby and his Mama, and you must one of you answer your sister's letter. Your Aunt Tabby also expects to hear from you, and I would have Will write to Mr Bolton to let him know how his son James goes on, and what improvement he makes in his books etc. as a letter from him will be very acceptable. I hope it will be unnecessary in me to remind you of your duty to your Maker, and a proper attention and regard to the studies you are engaged in. Your good inclinations I trust will always prompt you to it. Your Mama, who I hope is much better, joins me in our best wishes for you, as does your aunts and all your friends here.[1] Your brothers and sister send their love to you, and often remember you. I beg my compliments to Mr Booth and the ladies and am, in haste,

Your most affectionate father,
Thomas Langton

Note to DDX/190/22. September 2nd, 1771

[1] In the eighteenth century 'friends' was more or less a generic term for all the acquaintances of the befriended, of varying degrees of intimacy. Thomas Langton uses the term in practically every letter.

(DDX/190/23)
Kirkham   October 25th, 1771

Dear Will,

I received your agreeable letter of the 10th instant and am glad to hear your brother and you have made such improvements in your writing and accounts,[1] as well as your other studies. It is a great satisfaction to me to hear such pleasing accounts and I hope you will continue to deserve them. Mr Bolton, whose stay was very short at Woolton, was well pleased with his son James, but he wants much to have a letter from him. I desire you will see that he writes to him the next week. Mr Threlfall shewed me your letter to him, with which he was well pleased, and desires to be remembered to you and your brother and the rest of the boys of his acquaintance. We had intended to have come to Liverpool this month, as it is the season the scholars are instructed in writing,[2] and from thence to Woolton to see you, but the unseasonableness of the weather deterred us. However, I hope to see you soon perhaps in a fortnight and your Uncle Hankinson[3] and our new vicar, Mr Shuttleworth,[4] say they will come along with me. As I hope to see you so soon I shall have the less to say now, only I beg my respectful compliments to Mr Booth and the ladies, my love to my nephew Richard Bradkirk and little Bolton[5] and with my affectionate regards for your brother, to whom I will write next, and yourself, I remain,

Dear Will, your affectionate father,
Thomas Langton

Your brothers have both made great proficiency in their writing this month and
propose to give you each a letter soon.
Miss Hankinson[6] of Preston is now with
us and I hope will make a long stay.
Your mother is still not very well but I
hope no worse, and in a little time I
hope will get the better of her disorder.[7]
She is of a very tender constitution, and
cannot stir much abroad without catching cold.

Death conq Death[8]

Notes to DDX/190/23. October 25th, 1771

[1] Throughout the two years of his sons' schooling, Thomas Langton was to reiterate the importance of writing and accounts, the pivotal skills of his business world.

[2] Obviously the master (the Mr Threlfall mentioned above) took no part in the writing instruction, which might have been an extra and perhaps taught by a visiting writing master. A year later Zachary was attending a writing school in October (DDX/190/37).

[3] The husband of Thomas Langton's sister, Susannah, his second wife (1731–1801). A lawyer from Preston, he handled the firm's legal affairs.

[4] The incumbent of Kirkham parish church from 1771 to 1813.

[5] The only son of the Boltons, James, was to die at nineteen and is included in the memorial tablet to his father in Askham Parish Church in the following lugubrious terms: 'who said to corruption Thou art my father, to the worm Thou art my mother and my sister.'

⁶ Mr Hankinson's sister.
⁷ Thomas Langton speaks of illness in terms of a dis-order of the harmony of the human constitution. Recovery was imposing order again. This was in line with the medical thinking of the time.
⁸ This strange addition in another hand may have been taken from a copy book. The rest is obliterated by a smudge caused by deterioration of the paper.

(DDX/190/24)

Kirkham   November 16th, 1771

My dear lads,

This will advise you that I got well home, and found all your friends here pretty well. I hope you would get safe to Woolton and in good time the day we left you as the chaise would be ready to take you at 12 o' the clock, and you would get to Woolton to dinner if you set out at that hour. I paid the chaise hire and the fee to the chaise boy, that you would have nothing to pay him. Mr Bolton was well pleased to hear his son was well. He wishes to hear often from him and desires you will see that he writes once a fortnight at least. I hope Mr Booth would not take it amiss that I kept you so long at Woolton. I beg my kind compliments to him and the ladies. I was sorry I had not the pleasure to see him when I was at Woolton. I want much to see some of your best writing and desire you will both of you when you write give me a specimen of it in a line or two. Mr Threlfall had a letter today from Newark acquainting him that his son¹ was very bad and not expected to recover. Mr Threlfall goes there directly. Your aunt and he are both in great affliction. I hope to have a letter from one of you tomorrow, but if you should not have wrote, do not fail to let me hear from you the next week. Your mother is much as usual and the rest of your friends pretty well. They all join me in best wishes for you both.

I am, my dear lads,
Most affectionately yours,
Thomas Langton

Note to DDX/190/24. November 16th, 1771

¹ William Threlfall, a doctor in Newark, and later Newcastle, where he died in 1773, aged 23. He was the only child.

(DDX/190/25)
Kirkham November 29th, 1771

Dear Jack,

I was duly favoured with yours of the 15th instant by which I find
you got well to Woolton. I was pleased to receive the specimen of
your and your brother's writing as I think you are both improved
but I could wish that you would both of you take a little more care
in your common or ordinary writing which would be of greater
benefit to you. I shall expect soon to hear from your brother Will. I
hope you are both well pleased with your clothes. If you find any
of your clothes at any time out of repair, or as you seem to intimate
that you want a new pair of breeches, you must desire Mr Booth to
get them for you from Mr Carver or any other person he chooses to
make use of, and shall leave it to yourselves of what kind of stuff
you like, only desire that Mr Booth will pay for them, and place them
to my account if he buys them from any other person but Mr Carver.
I have not opportunity at present to send you a list of your books
but will do it soon, but you do not need to send any of them home.
It will be time enough to do that when you come home in summer,
unless you could send a few of those that are useless to you in your
cousin Richard Bradkirk's box, who, I understand, continues his
resolution of leaving the school at Christmas.[1] Your sister and
brothers Zachary and Cornelius are very desirous to have a letter
from you at your first opportunity. They are engaged in going to the
Dancing School every day we have Mr Bradley here, and your
brother Zachary is one of the finest dancers of the young ones in the
school. Your Uncle Threlfall has had several letters from Newark
which give him an account that your cousin William is got much
better and is in a promising way to recover his late indisposition.
Your mother is rather better. She desires to be particularly remembered to you and proposes to write to you soon. The rest of your
friends here are all well. Your mother joins me in our best wishes for
you and your brother and with proper compliments to Mr Booth
and the ladies, I remain,

Dear Jack, Your most affectionate father,
Thomas Langton

My love to your cousin Richard.
They are all well at home except his

sister Peggy who is in the measles but
mending finely.

Note to DDX/190/25. November 29th, 1771

[1] The commemorative plaque to Richard Bradkirk in Kirkham parish church
was erected by his sisters, one of whom was Mrs John Langton, wife of the
John of the letters. Richard Bradkirk never married.

(DDX/190/26)
Kirkham December 20th, 1771

Dear Will,

William Whiteside who came here last Sunday acquainted me that
he had been with you the preceding week at Childwall and that you
and your brother were both well. This I was glad to hear as you
seemed to intimate in your brother Zachary's letter that you had
been a little out of order. This will come by Thomas Brewer, who
brings horses for your cousin Richard Bradkirk, who I suppose will
return hither on Sunday or Monday. I this day received yours of the
16th instant and find you are going to read Livy, and that you had
got some other books from Mr Booth, which was well. I send you
by Thomas Brewer Livy[1] and some paper agreeable to your desire,
with Zachary's French grammar which is the book I fancy you desire
to be sent you. Your brother Zachary is very busy writing to you to
come along with this and as he takes great pleasure in receiving a
letter from you I hope you won't fail to write to him again soon, and
your brother Cornelius is very anxious to hear from his brother John
or you. Poor lad, he is but very indifferent in his old way and his
eyes seem to fail him much, which gives me a great deal of uneasiness
and anxiety on his account. I learnt by a letter you wrote to your
mother that you had lost half a guinea which I gave you at Liverpool.
It seems rather careless and negligent in you not to take more care
of your money, but I hope it will in future be an instructive lesson
to you, not only in keeping your money safe but also in laying it out
with prudence and economy. I do not mean that you should appear
parsimonious, neither would I have you too fluent of your money,
as it is not expected that boys of your age should have a large sum

or spend much. On the contrary when you lay out anything let it be done with prudence and frugality and I hope your own natural dispositions will lead you to nothing unbecoming or vicious.[2] I send you by Thomas Brewer a moidore, 27/–,[3] which will be sent to you and your brother by Mr Yates, and I shall expect to have a particular account from you how you lay it out, as well as what I have already given you. Miss Hankinson is still at Kirkham with us. She desires to be remembered to you and your brother and little J. Bolton, who I hope is well, as does all your friends here. We hope to hear from you how you spend your Christmas. We daily remember you, and are uneasy unless we often hear from you. I propose to write to John the next time I write and I hope to have a letter from him soon, as does his sister. I enclose you a schedule of your books which you took from home and you must add to them what books you buy. Pray take care of them and see that you [*] of them. Your Aunt Tabby desires to have a letter from your brother. You must remind him, and a letter to any of us is the same thing.

I hope your mother is much better and against you come home I have no doubt she will be pretty well. All your friends here join me in our best wishes for you and with proper compliments to Mr Booth and the ladies, I remain,

Dear Will,
Most affectionately yours,
Thomas Langton

[*]   Partially obliterated.

Notes to DDX/190/26. December 20th, 1771

[1] Thomas Langton was educated at Clitheroe Grammar School which followed a severely classical curriculum. The Livy was no doubt one of his school books.

[2] The prudent management of money was of paramount importance to Thomas Langton and he frequently urged his sons to make a full account of their expenditure.

[3] A moidore was a Portuguese coin, of legal tender in England in the eighteenth century. As Thomas Langton says, it was valued at twenty-seven shillings.

(DDX/190/27)
Kirkham January 11th, 1772

Dear Will,

By Mr William Whiteside who returns from hence in the morning
on his way to Liverpool I send this, who promises to forward it by
the first opportunity to you at Woolton. He has also a small box for
you and your brother which comes herewith and contains a bun such
as your mother used to make for you in Lent, a dozen minced pies,
being Christmas time, and a pound roll of chocolate[1] for you and
your particular acquaintance to regale yourselves with. But pray to
take care not to use it in such a manner as may give any umbrage to
Mr Booth or any of the family, by which means you may cause him
to be offended at you, which I beg you will always avoid as much
as possible. How you intend to use the chocolate I cannot say, but
I hope you will not go to any public house to have it made[2] as it will
bring you to other unnecessary expenses, and likewise be disagreeable to Mr Booth. I understand you spent your time very agreeably
at Liverpool this Christmas. It was very obliging of Mrs Roughsedge[3] to send for you, and to show you such respect during your
stay there. You should have acquainted me what day you went there
and how long you stayed. I hope your behaviour was such as to make
you respected by the family, and that you gave as little trouble as
you well could to the house. I hope the four books of Livy was what
you wanted and will prevent your buying them. I was sorry to find
the moidore I sent you was bad. I was surprized to hear it, as I had
not the least thoughts of its being bad. Pray what did you do with
it? If any of your friends took it from you you should let me know
that I may exchange it. I am glad to hear that Master Rigby and you
are on better terms and more agreeable with each other. You would
be sorry to part with your cousin Richard Bradkirk from school. I
do not hear he has fixed upon any business as yet to go to, but
Liverpool seems to be the object of his choice. Mrs Dannett[4] and
Master Harry[5] are now at your Uncle Shepherd's. He enquired
particularly after you and was pleased to hear you was well. Your
Aunt Hankinson has been much out of order lately, but I hope she
is now recovering apace, and will very soon grow quite well again.
Your mother I hope grows better daily, but poor Cornelius I fear is
no better. Youth and a good constitution may perhaps enable him
to get the better of it. Miss Hankinson left us upon your aunt's
indisposition to be with her a while, but I hope she will return to us

again soon. Your Aunt Shepherd is still but poorly, yet I hope no worse than she has been of sometimes. Pray have you got another writing master yet? I should be glad you were kept pretty duly to your writing, and to see you make good proficiency therein, as well as in accounts. Mr and Mrs Bolton are now in Cheshire and have some thoughts of returning by Woolton to see their son James. Very likely they may be with you before you receive this. If not, would not have you mention it to James, for lest something should happen to prevent them. Your Mama and all your brothers and sister as well as the rest of your friends here desire to be properly remembered to you and your brother and the rest of your acquaintance known to them, and with my best wishes for you both (as you are to accept this letter as addressed to you equally) I remain,

Your affectionate father,
Thomas Langton

Notes to DDX/190/27. January 11th, 1772

[1] The roll of chocolate would be a paste or cake composed of the seeds of the cacao fruit roasted and ground, sweetened and flavoured with vanilla and other substances.

[2] It would need to be dissolved in boiling water or milk to make a beverage.

[3,4] Mrs Elizabeth Roughsedge and Mrs Alice Dannett were sisters, née Hankinson, originating in Kirkham, who married Liverpool men.

[5] Master Harry was Henry Dannett, who in the future was to be master of Kirkham School from 1808 to 1814. His brother Thomas became rector of Liverpool.

(DDX/190/28)
Kirkham February 7th, 1772

My dear lads,

I was very agreeably pleased to receive your last letter, which advised me that you had received the box I sent you by William Whiteside, and that the contents therein pleased you. Your mother was not willing to let Christmas pass without sending you something to remind you of our Christmas cheer. If the chocolate does not bring you into any disagreeable company, I shall have no objection to your entertaining and amusing yourselves in the manner you describe, provided it meets with Mr Booth's approbation and concurrence and it does not bring you into expenses improper for you. I am sorry to find Mr Booth should take it amiss that William Whiteside should call to see you at Woolton.[1] He may perhaps think it draws you in a public house, which is disagreeable to him, but I will write to him and give him an intimation that I would not have him go see you any more unless he should be coming over to Kirkham, when I should be glad to hear of you by him. I will do it in such a manner that he cannot take it amiss, or suspect you giving me any intimation of it. I am sorry to say your brother Nely is no better. He continues much as usual, his eyesight very bad and the violent pain in his head occasionally troubles him,[2] but as it is an affliction under the hands of Providence, we must submit to it, and, poor lad, he bears his illness with the greatest patience and resignation. He is very glad to hear from you at any time, and very often talks of you. Your mother is still but very poorly,[3] but I hope before the holidays she will be got quite well, and then I shall be glad to see Mr Fazakerley or any of your acquaintance at Kirkham, about which I will write to you in the interim. I am glad the Livys were right. I will exchange the 27/– with Mr Yates when I see him. Your Aunt Hankinson is got pretty well recovered, and Miss Hankinson is now with us at Kirkham. She is very cheerful enlivening company, and is very agreeable to your mother. As Mrs Roughsedge behaved so very civilly to you at Liverpool I would have you behave well to young Loxham, and assist him in anything that you can, which will be very agreeable to her. Master H. Dannett was returned from hence when I received yours. His mother is still here. Your Aunt Shepherd is still confined and poorly, but I hope no worse. All your friends here enquire frequently after you. Your cousin Richard is still with us, but they talk of fixing him at Liverpool with Mr Richard Robinson, a broker, but how soon he goes I cannot say. He has nothing to do here and the sooner he gets into business the better.[4] I wish he may prove diligent and active when he enters upon a fresh scene of life. Without diligence and application, business of any kind will avail little. I find you have got another writing master which will call your attention to that part of your duty again, and, as good and correct writing is very commendable in business of any kind, I beg you will both of you exert your endeavours to improve on it. Whatever your accounts master recommends to you I would have you adhere to, and you may buy the book you mention to set down any rules in any branch of that science you find requisite. Mr and Mrs Bolton acquainted me that you spent a day with them at Childwall. They speak very favourably of you, and were very proud to find their son James so well and in such good spirits. All your friends beg to be remembered to you and with my most cordial good wishes for you, I remain,

My dear lads,
Your affectionate father,
Thomas Langton

Notes to DDX/190/28. February 7th, 1772

[1] The apparent familiarity between William Whiteside, obviously someone in a fairly menial station, and the Langton family suggests that, at this stage, there were few of those pretensions to gentility which are suggested in the recollections of the Shepherd Birley Notebook.

[2,3] There is no mention of medical consultation for these two chronic sufferers.

[4] Thomas Langton's disappointment at his nephew's idleness is characteristic. It also offers him an opportunity to point the moral to his sons. The prospective employer appears in Gore's *Liverpool Directory* of 1767 as Richard Robinson, Broker, Hackin's Hey.

(DDX/190/29)
Kirkham   March 4th, 1772

Dear Will,

I received yours dated February 27th only this post acquainting me that Mr Booth was going to quit Woolton at May next and to fix a school in Essex.[1] I am very sorry to hear it as I was very well satisfied with your situation. I find you have an inclination to go along with him, but it is a very great distance from home, which is not so eligible. However, I should be glad to know Mr Booth's proposals, as well as the place he fixes on and the mode he proposes to adopt. It would be more agreeable to me to fix you in a private academy for a year or two where the number of boys did not exceed the number you mention, but I am apprehensive if he limits himself to that number he will expect higher terms than will be agreeable to me and perhaps not have the same advantages in different masters as you have now. However, let me have a line from you by the return of the post with Mr Booth's proposals and plan for the conducting his school in as full a manner as you can, and I will immediately write back to you. I would have you also mention the names of his present scholars that propose to go along with him. As your brother's time for being continued at school will be so short, I think I shall not incline to send him anywhere, but perhaps fix him with a master for writing and accounts for a few months at Liverpool, or some other place where he may incline to be fixed, as I would willingly make your situations agreeable to you on this account. I should be glad to hear as early from you as possible. I have required Mr Yates to furnish you with what cash you may need and as it may be uncertain how soon I may see you at Woolton, I would have you have all your books and everything ready for an immediate removal as my stay can be but very short whenever I come. In the meantime I beg my compliments to Mr Booth and the ladies, and with my tenderest wishes for you and your brother, I remain,

Your affectionate father,
Thomas Langton

Note to DDX/190/29. March 4th, 1772

[1] The school was to move to High Beach, Waltham Abbey, Essex. Mr Booth sold Woolton Hall.

(DDX/190/30)

Kirkham   March 11th, 1772

Dear Will,

I wrote to you last week in answer to yours giving me an account that Mr Booth had sold Woolton and was going to live in Essex. I have since then received a letter from Mrs Bardsley giving me the same account and that Mr Booth intends taking only 20 boys at 40 guineas a year, and proposes to give the preference to any of his present pupils who incline to go along with him. I find your inclination is very great to go along with him if it is thought prudent to continue you longer at school, and as you are very young, but just turned of fourteen years old, I think you will think it too early to be put to business, which will subject you to an apprenticeship of seven years,[1] and I should rather choose to put you under a master where you would have the opportunity of making a further proficiency in the French language as well as writing and accounts, though these last are what is chiefly to be regarded. If Mr Booth only takes twenty pupils I can hardly think he will have the different masters for instruction which he has now at Woolton and I can come to no resolution about it at present till I hear from you, which I expect will give me a particular account both of the place where Mr Booth proposes to live at and whether the situation be good and healthy, as some parts of Essex are reputed to be far otherways and whether he proposes to proceed upon the same plan as he does now at Woolton. I fancy he means the 40 guineas a year as a full compensation for everything without any further charge for washing, fire etc. but I should be glad to have his particular terms.[2] Pray does Mrs Bardsley and Miss Valence go along with him? I propose for you to stay with Mr Booth at Woolton as long as he continues his school, which you must acquaint me of, and in the meantime must determine as to the other. I hope to hear from you very soon, as I cannot give Mr Booth a letter till I receive your answer. I send this to Liverpool by your Aunt Bradkirk who is going from hence in the morning to put your cousin Richard apprentice there. He is to be with one Mr Robinson, a broker. He has promised to forward this letter to you soon. I beg my proper respects to Mr Booth and the ladies and with my sincere good wishes for your brother and yourself, I remain,

Dear Will,
Your affectionate father,
Thomas Langton

Your mother and brother Cornelius continue much as usual.
The rest of your friends are pretty well.

Notes to DDX/190/30. March 11th, 1772

[1] The Statute of Artificers, passed in 1653, was still in force. It enacted that every craftsman in town or country had for seven years to learn his craft under a master who was responsible for him. Apprenticeships were originally between the ages of sixteen and twenty-three, and at twenty-four a man could marry and set up in business on his own. However, by the eighteenth century some apprenticeships were completed at twenty-one, so Will, at fourteen, would be able to embark on his at once. Although his father thought him too young there were many instances in the Kirkham apprentice records of pauper children apprenticed much younger, one at eight years old.
[2] The terms at High Beach were considerably higher than those quoted in *The Virginia Gazette* in 1766 for Woolton Academy.

(DDX/190/31)
Kirkham   April 17th, 1772

My dear lads,

You would learn from Mr Booth that I had wrote to him to signify my consent that you should both go along with him into the south to perfect your education under his care, as it seems to coincide so much with both your intentions and earnest solicitations, and although it will be attended with a very heavy expense,[1] yet I hope you will sufficiently repay it by your diligent attention to your studies and utmost endeavours for improvement therein. I desire you will particularly attend to your writing as I much desire to see you improve therein. The time is now drawing on that many of your schoolfellows will be leaving you, especially those that do not go along with you, and I expect in about a fortnight or three weeks Mr Bolton will be with you to fetch his son James and if I find it convenient I may perhaps take a ride over with him to Woolton, but if I am disappointed of seeing you then, I will contrive to come over to see you and Mr Booth before you leave Woolton. Pray let me hear from you next week and I should be glad to know which of the scholars now with Mr Booth go along with you, and the time I must send for you from Woolton. According to your letter I was in expectation of seeing Mr Booth at Kirkham in his way to or from Lytham,[2] but as he has not called I presume he has scarcely been there. I have been twice at Blackburn lately,[3] and heard there that Jack was much afflicted with the toothache, and I since find that he has got quit of so troublesome a companion by the assistance of a surgeon.[4] Your brother Zachary is much troubled with the same complaint but he has not resolution sufficient to have his tooth drawn. William Whiteside is now here. I have but just seen him. He tells me he has not seen you lately but hears you are both well. Your Aunt Feilden has got another son,[5] and does well. They are all very well there, enquire much after you, and hope to see you when you leave school. Master Whalley received a letter from Will at the time I was there, and seemed much pleased with it. We are all pretty well here except your mother and Cornelius, who continue much as they were. My proper compliments await on Mr Booth and the ladies and with my best wishes for you both, I remain,

Your affectionate father,
Thomas Langton

I received Will's letter dated April 9th.

Notes to DDX/190/31
April 17th, 1772

[1] Thomas Langton was ever mindful of the cost of his sons' education. He regarded it as an investment, 'of service' to the business, and he expected a sound return.

[2] Mr Booth was apparently intending to sample the health-giving qualities of the resort.

[3] Mrs Langton's sister, Margaret Leyland, married Joseph Feilden, textile manufacturer of Blackburn. There was much social intercourse between the two families.

[4] The surgeons were considered mere craftsmen, unlike their more elevated colleagues of the medical profession the physicians and apothecaries. They were originally joined with the barbers in the Company of Barbers and the connection was severed only in 1745.

[5] Sir William Feilden of Feniscowles, M.P. for Blackburn from 1832 to 1847, created Baronet 1846, died 1850.

(DDX/190/32)
Kirkham   May 1st, 1772

My dear lads,

This will inform you I got safe home and found all pretty well. This gave me great pleasure as I think your mother is much better. Great enquiries was made after you, and all your friends were pleased to hear that you were well, and will be very glad to see you at the time appointed. James Bolton performed his journey very well and was in good spirits when I left them and much rejoiced with the thoughts of seeing Preston. On my arrival at Liverpool I went to Mr Carver's to see your cousin Savige[1] who is very well, and took the opportunity to look at the patterns of their broad cloths. They have a great variety and I told your cousin Savige, and Richard Bradkirk, that I thought you would perhaps incline to come over to Liverpool to choose for yourselves, and Richard Bradkirk said he would write to you to that purpose. If you [*] would have you to see Mr John Yates who will go with you to Mr Carver's[2] and assist you in your choice, but upon calling of Savige as I left Liverpool he told me Mr Booth's servant had called for Mr Carver's pattern card of broad cloths and that they had sent it by him. This I suppose was for you, and if you have fixed upon any colour and cloth which suits your inclination I shall be pleased. I only meant that by going to Liverpool yourselves you might see greater choice, and if you prefer green to any other colour it will be agreeable to me. There was some pretty cloths of that colour. I leave the whole to yourselves, and Mr Carver will send me a bill of the charge that you will have no occasion to say anything on that head. I had a mind to give you a line on this account lest you might be disconcerted upon receiving a letter from R. Bradkirk if you had fixed upon your cloth previous to the receipt of this letter. I beg my compliments to Mr Booth and the ladies and with my best wishes for you both, I remain,

Your affectionate father,
Thomas Langton

I shall expect a letter from you next week.

[*] Totally obliterated.

Notes to DDX/190/32. May 1st, 1772

[1] Savige Leech, who figures more prominently in later letters, was the son of Thomas Langton's sister, Elizabeth, and Savige Leech, a Liverpool broker. For a time they lived in the same street in Liverpool as Mr Booth and it may be through this that Thomas Langton decided to send his sons to Woolton.
[2] Given in Gore's *Liverpool Directory* of 1767 as John Carver, Mercer and Draper, High Street.

(DDX/190/33)

Kirkham   May 17th, 1772

My dear lads,

I received John's letter in one course of post and was glad to find you were both well. I observe you had not then been at Liverpool but rather chose to defer your journey till your clothes were made that you may have the opportunity of going in a better dress, which is very well but I beg you will take care to keep them clean. The choice you have made is agreeable to me and you'll call of Mr Carver at Liverpool and desire he will send me account of the charge by you, that I may send him the money. You must not omit to call of Mrs Roughsedge. She was very obliging to you. I propose to send horses for you on Monday or Tuesday the 25th or 26th of this month, and in the meantime would have you pack up your books and other things in your desk and box and send them to Liverpool, directed to the care of Mr Yates, before you leave Woolton. This should be done this week, and the man that comes for you will bring a leather portmanteau which will hold your clothes, and some shirts for your present use, before your desk may get here. I hope you'll be able to ride through of a day, as we shall be very anxious to see you at home, and on this account it will be requisite you start very early in the morning. I will write to you again by the Monday. It will be necessary you write a line to Mr Yates along with the desk and desire he will ship it by first sloop for Ribble[1] as you will want it. I beg my proper compliments to Mr Booth and the ladies etc. and with my best wishes to you both, I remain,

Your affectionate father,
Thomas Langton

Your mother, I hope, is much better. She
joins with the rest of your friends here in
their best love for you. I have wrote to
Mr Booth by this post.

Note to DDX/190/33. May 17th, 1772

[1] The most convenient way to send goods was often by coastal shipping. The sloop would discharge at Freckleton or Skippool.

(DDX/190/34)
Kirkham May 23rd, 1772

Dear Will,

I find by your letter to Zachary that Mr Booth has already had a sale of his horses, cattle etc,[1] and that he is intending to sell his household goods next week and expects his boys to leave Woolton today or tomorrow. On this account I send horses off for you this morning and expect they will get to Woolton in good time. The tide at Ribble will serve for crossing the river[2] till 2 o'the clock on Sunday afternoon that it will be requisite you start very early in the morning to be in good time to cross the river and I propose to meet you at Tarleton or Rufford. It would do well if you could get part of the way this evening but that I leave to yourselves and you may consult with Thomas Brewer upon it. I am glad to find you have sent off your desk and boxes to Liverpool and they must be forwarded from thence hither by a sloop which Mr Yates no doubt will take care of. I send you by Thomas Brewer two guineas which I fancy will serve you to pay of all your exigencies, and you must give the servants something on leaving Woolton. You may either give it yourselves or leave half a guinea with Mr Booth for that purpose. I have sent money by Thomas Brewer to pay Mr Booth and you must consult with him whether you leave Woolton this evening and go to Liverpool or some other place to make your [* journey] easier tomorrow. I beg you will take care to be early enough at Ribble tomorrow for crossing the river and with my best wishes for you and your brother, I remain,

Your affectionate father,
Thomas Langton

[*] Paper torn. Word substituted.

Notes to DDX/190/34. May 23rd, 1772

[1] This does not imply that Mr Booth had a small farm. The cattle were probably inferior horses. The term 'cattle' could still refer to animals other than cows and was used in coaching circles to designate horses past their best.
[2] The Ribble crossing was from Tarleton to Freckleton. Within living memory residents of Freckleton referred to a building as the Guide's House, and two are clearly marked on Yates's map of 1786. The alteration of the course of the river later made the crossing impossible. In its day it was obviously preferable to the journey round the estuary by Preston. The present day structures and runways of BAe make it difficult to envisage old Freckleton and Warton.

(DDX/190/35)
Kirkham August 9th, 1772

My dear lads,

I was well pleased to find by both your letters, that you got well to
London, though you were but meanly accommodated upon the
road, and your travelling was so quick[1] you would have no opportunity of seeing the country as you passed along. I observe Mr Booth
met you in London and showed you a little of the town on Thursday
morning, and in the afternoon conducted you safe to High Beach. I
was sorry you were disappointed of meeting your aunts in London.
They returned hither directly from Newark, and met you in the stage
between Buxton and Ashbourne, but as your windows was up, they
could not see who was in the coach and did not suspect you were
there. I fancy you would go down to Mr Threlfall's[2] to enquire after
them and would not be a little chagrined in not meeting them as you
expected. I suppose you would see Robert Parkinson as he is in the
shop, and would call upon Mrs Leigh in Wood Street as you promised Mrs Whitehead at Bolton. I shall expect when you write again,
which I desire may be soon, that you will give me a succinct account
of all your proceedings, and should be glad to see a list of the boys
which Mr Booth has under his care. I hope you have received your
box safe before this, and found everything right. If you want anything further you must let me know. You forgot to take your small
book of Geography with you, but I had an opportunity of sending
it the week following by a gentleman to London, who promised to
forward it you on his arrival agreeable to the directions. I hope it is
now with you.

As you will by this time got settled in the school, I desire you will
let me know what discipline is observed with you and the rules and
regulations prescribed you. I hope I do not need to press you to
diligence and application in your studies. You are arrived at years of
discretion to be truly sensible of the great utility it will be of to your
future, and whatever progress you now make, will redound to your
advantage hereafter, and by behaving with prudence and economy
on your first entrance into life, it will become habitual to you and
you will always afterwards reap the benefit of it. You must be very
sensible I am at great expense in giving you so liberal an education,
but I hope your improvements will be adequate thereto, and then I
shall think my money well laid out. But above all things, have a strict
regard and observance of your Maker. Let nothing ever induce you

to swerve from it and then I hope whatever you undertake will succeed and prosper. I have always particularly recommended to you to endeavour to improve in your writing, which is a great advantage to a person in trade, and may be of future service to you. Let me therefore remind you of it and do not scribble and write ill when you write your exercises.

I have no particular news to send you. Your mother is much as you left her and so are the rest of your family. Miss Hankinson is still with us and begs to be remembered to you, and so does all your friends. They are frequently making enquiries after you. Your Aunt Shepherd is still at Lytham but I believe returns tomorrow. I hope she is something better. Your Aunt Hankinson is now at Lytham bathing with Harry, and your Aunt Rigby, who came here last week, goes there tomorrow. I suppose she will stay a fortnight there. She brought your cousin Henry and Cecily Feilden with her. They are all very well. I fancy Harry Feilden must return this week as he only came for a few nights to see your brother Cornelius. I beg you will present my kind respects to Mr Booth and the ladies, and Mr Newby[3] with the rest of the young gentlemen that I am acquainted with, and with every good wish for yourselves, I remain,

Your most affectionate father,
Thomas Langton

I desire you will write soon, and let me
have a long letter with accounts of what
you have seen in London and elsewhere.

Pray tell Mr Booth I should be glad to
receive my last half year's account from
him that I may remit him the money
owing thereon.

Notes to DDX/190/35
At the Rev. Mr Booth's at High Beach to be left at the New Inn
Waltham Abbey, Essex. August 9th, 1772

[1] By the time of the letters the journey from Manchester and Liverpool to London took two days in summer and three in winter. The fare was in the region of £2 2s. for a night coach and £2 10s. for a day coach. In 1771 a 'superior diligence' from Liverpool to London cost £2 15s.
[2] This Mr Threlfall was probably the brother of Uncle Threlfall, or at least some relation. He lived in London and acted as a connection for the

Langton firm. Later Will was instructed to consult him constantly for business advice.

[3] Peter Newby was a Roman Catholic recusant poet whose presence on the Revd Bartholomew Booth's staff spoke of the tolerance and broadmindedness of his employer. Newby thought highly of his employer and eulogised him in verse on several occasions. (See Maurice Whitehead, *Peter Newby: Eighteenth-Century Lancashire Recusant Poet*, Centre for North West Regional Studies Occasional Paper No. 7, Lancaster, 1980; and T. Malone, *Peter Newby, Friend to All Mankind*, Aylesford, 1964.)

(DDX/190/36)

Kirkham   September 7th, 1772

Dear Will,

You will think me long in answering your last letter, but I have been almost constantly abroad ever since I received it. My last journey was to the Assizes[1] at Lancaster from whence I returned on Friday last. I met with Master Rigby who enquired much after you. I was sorry to find you had been so perplexed about your clothes, but it was well they came safe at last, but the charge of 23/– for the carriage was most exorbitant. I met with a gentleman at Preston who was just setting off for London, by whom I sent your book of Geography but I had not time to write along with it. As your stay in London was so short you would have very little time to look about you. However, you must make that up another time. Mr and Mrs Whitehead of Bolton were here about a fortnight ago. They told us Mrs Leigh was then at Bolton and mentioned your calling on her. I was well pleased to learn that Mr Booth had engaged a writing master, and I must repeat my request to you and your brother that you will both use your utmost endeavours to write well. Mr Hornby tells me that his son Thomas[2] is very much improved in his writing and accounts. I would not have him surpass you therein. The plan of business which Mr Booth has laid out for you seems pretty extensive[3] and if you attend to the whole will keep you pretty fully employed. However, if you incline to learn a little music, I am well pleased and give my consent to it provided it does not interfere too much with your other studies, but you must be the best judge of that, and on that account I leave it to your own option, but I should like to know what kind of music you propose to learn, and what will be the expense, as you have no kind of instrument to learn upon, and if you must be obliged to buy any perhaps the charge may be too great. In your next let me know what kind of instrument you begin with, and what you propose to learn. I suppose you will make a beginning on receipt of this letter.

You would be very much surprized, but I presume very agreeably, to see your Uncle Feilden and Mr Thornton at High Beach. They were very well pleased with your situation and much approved of Mr Booth's behaviour. Mr Feilden wrote me from London to acquaint me of their having seen you and mentioned Mr Booth's pressing invitation for your mother and myself to come and stay awhile with him. It was very obliging but I think your mother will not think of taking so long a journey, though the hopes of seeing you both would compensate a good deal for the fatigue such a journey should occasion. Your cousin Cecily Feilden is now at Kirkham and is a very fine girl. Your Aunt Rigby is still with us here and was very well pleased with your letter to her. I expect she will make a long stay with us. I have great hopes your mother is much better than she has been of some time past, and if her disorder does not return upon her again (which may kind Providence forbid) I hope she will in a few months be quite clever again. She has all our most earnest prayers for the restoration of her health and must rely upon Providence for the event. Your brother Cornelius is much the same as you left him and Thomas is got pretty well recovered from the chincough.[4] He improves very much and is a charming boy. He has been talking of his brother Jack and Will all day and says they are gone to London. I received Jack's letter and will write to him soon. If he inclines to learn to dance as he mentions in his letter, I have no objections to it. I had a letter from Mr Feilden on Saturday. He was got well to Blackburn and says that Mr William Whalley has got a letter from John that day and that you were both well. I am now sorry to acquaint you that your Aunt Hankinson has had the misfortune to bury her little boy about a fortnight ago. Poor Harry, he was a very fine endearing lad, and will make his loss more sensibly felt by both Mr Hankinson and my sister. They are both in very great affliction and I fear it will be some time before your aunt will be able to get the better of it. On this occasion we have lost Miss Hankinson's company. She is gone back to be with my sister on this melancholy event happening. Your Uncle Langton[5] is still at Oxford and I suppose proposes to stay the winter there. I had a long letter from him the other day. He enquired much after you and your brother, and was pleased to hear you was agreeably fixed. All your friends here join me in my warmest wishes for your health and welfare and in hopes of hearing from you very soon again, I remain,

Your affectionate father,
Thomas Langton

I will write to John very soon. Your mother desires her best love to you both.

Notes to DDX/190/36. September 7th, 1772

[1] Thomas Langton's name appears in the list of freeholders liable to serve at the assize and sessions of 1778, along with those of his partners, William Shepherd and John Birley. The names of Hugh Hornby and Joseph Hornby, the rival flax merchants, also appear, along with those of the lord of the manor, Thomas Clifton, the master of the school, William Threlfall, and the two medical men, Mr Clayton and Mr Parkinson.

[2] Thomas Hornby, born 1759, a son of the rival flax merchant, Hugh Hornby, was to marry Cecily Langton, Thomas Langton's only surviving daughter. Their eldest son, Hugh, was to be mayor of Liverpool in 1838.

[3] Mr Booth obviously applied teaching methods which treated the pupils as individuals, methods much advocated today.

[4] Chincough is whooping cough. A Langton child had died of this illness.

[5] Uncle Langton was the brother of Thomas Langton's father. He bore the family name Zachary and his father left money in his will to make him a scholar. He won the endowed scholarship from the Kirkham free school in 1714 and after graduating B.A. and M.A. from Magdalen College, Oxford, he entered the Church. During an incumbency near Dublin, Thomas Langton visited him in 1748, leaving a manuscript journal of the visit. Zachary Langton wrote *An Essay Concerning the Human Rational Soul*, his contribution to the theological discourse which presented man as a rational soul in search of virtue as distinct from the immortal soul in search of salvation. He published anonymously in 1753. Anne Langton, Thomas Langton's granddaughter, daughter of his youngest son Tom, spoke of this book in *The Story of Our Family*, published privately in 1881. She wrote: 'His work is in our library but I do not think any of us ever got through it.'

(DDX/190/37)
Kirkham October 15th, 1772

Dear Jack,
It is some time since I wrote to you or your brother, having been
lately much abroad and otherwise engaged in the discharge of our
Baltic ships,[1] which has kept me fully employed. After the death of
your Aunt Hankinson's little boy, she was very much cast down and
almost inconsolable, that I was greatly afraid she would prejudice
her health thereby. This induced us to try to get her abroad a little
and at same time I thought it might be of great service to your
mother, so we agreed to go to Blackpool[2] (Mr and Mrs Hankinson
and Miss Hankinson, your mother, sister and myself, and Mr and
Mrs Bolton was so obliging to be of the party) where we stayed ten
days and I hope it has been of service to them all, though your aunt
is still very low and cannot get up her spirits. We left your Aunt
Tabitha and Aunt Rigby at home to be housekeepers. I have the
pleasure to assure you your mother is abundantly better, and I hope
she will in due time be restored to her former good state of health,
for the reestablishment of which we must rely upon the bounteous
hand of Providence and earnestly implore his aid and assistance with
whom are the issues of life and death. Miss Hankinson is now in
Preston. She has received your brother's letter and will write to him
very soon. Your Aunt Rigby will stay with us all winter and your
Aunt Tabitha will stay with us most of that time, as she does not
intend to go to her house till spring. Mrs Shepherd is not yet returned
from Lytham. I hope she is something better than when you was
here. Your Uncle Langton is still at Oxford and I believe proposes
to stay there the winter. I had a letter from him last post wherein he
enquires particularly after you and your brother. Mr and Mrs Bolton
only left Wesham yesterday being gone to Preston for the winter.[3]
They propose to return early again in the spring. They had a letter
from James on Sunday. He was very well and wanted them to send
him a Chester faring.[4] I understand by your brother's letter that Mr
Booth has taken the care of the writing into his own hands. Your
brother sent me a specimen of his writing and I think he is much
improved and by care and diligence he will make a good writer. I
should be glad to see how you improve in your writing, and to know
the plan of business you pursue, what books you read and how your
time is chiefly employed and what masters you have to instruct you.
You mentioned your desire to learn to dance, to which I wrote your

brother that I consented if it was your desire and should be glad to know whether you pursue it and what time is allotted to that purpose and whether your brother learns or no. If it is his desire I shall have no objections. I fancy he has made a beginning in learning to play upon the flute. I hope he will take care not to injure his health by playing too much upon it, as wind music has a dangerous tendency that ways especially to young boys while they are growing. As the winter season is coming on I am afraid you will find High Beach not quite so comfortable as Woolton. However, I hope you will make your situation as agreeable as you can and guard as much as possible against catching colds. If you have any occasion for clothes of any kind let me know, as I would not have you to want any necessary proper for you, and take care that your shoes be good and that you do not go wet of your feet. I hope you will always be frugal in laying out your money and when you have occasion for a supply, I shall expect from you, according to your promise, an account how you have expended your last stock and will then furnish [* you] with anything which may be needful. Mr William Whalley was here this week and went out one day a-hunting with Mr Clifton.⁵ He has purchased a horse and I have given him an invitation to spend a few days at Christmas. He desired his compliments to you and your brother. I expect your Uncle Feilden here the next week to take the diversion of coursing for a few days. They are all very well at Blackburn. Mr Anyon is dead and Mr Shuttleworth has given the chapel of Wrea Green to your Uncle Threlfall where he does duty every Sunday in the afternoon, and at Singleton as usual in the morning. All your friends here are well. Zachary has been at Writing School⁶ for a month and improved much. Cornelius much the same as you left him. Mr Parkinson from Cambridge⁷ is now over here and enquires much after you. Your mother and the rest of the family join me in our best wishes for you and your brother, and hoping to have a letter from you as soon as you receive this, I remain, dear Jack,

Your affectionate father,
Thomas Langton

[*] Word omitted, but required by sense.

Notes to DDX/190/37. October 15th, 1772

¹ These Baltic ships would dock in the Wyre estuary at Wardleys which was a busy wharf at this time. Warehouses were available on the banks of the river and Thomas Langton's father had goods insured for over a thousand pounds

in a warehouse at Staynall as early as 1750. Riga flax was considered the best in Russia, Königsberg hemp the best in the world.
[2] Blackpool was no doubt chosen in preference to Lytham as it provided a wider range of diversions.
[3] Preston, the social centre of the county, held a winter season, with assemblies, card parties and plays. Cecily was twelve, and this visit seems to be something akin to a finishing. Between the Boltons and the Hankinsons she was away until the spring. She had already learnt to dance, as her father remarked to her brothers in November 1771.
[4] This should mean that James Bolton asked his parents for a faring, or souvenir, of the fair at Chester. However, it appears from the letter dated 26 December 1772 that he was already at Chester and could have obtained his own faring.
[5] Mr Clifton, the lord of the manor, was of the gentry and lived in Lytham Hall, recently rebuilt by John Carr as his first important commission. As the Langton house guest was consorting with him, the social standing of the merchant family would be enhanced.
[6] We know from the 1771 October letter that October was the month in which the boys were instructed in writing. The instruction is obviously not given by the usual teachers at the grammar school.
[7] As this Mr Parkinson was 'from Cambridge' he was no doubt Thomas Parkinson who was the 1764 Barker Exhibitioner from the grammar school. In 1771 he was elected a Fellow of Christ's College and was admitted to the M.A. in 1772. He subsequently became chancellor of the diocese of Chester, prebendary of St Paul's and a Fellow of the Royal Society.

(DDX/190/38)

Kirkham   November 10th, 1772

Dear Will,

I begin to think it long since I received a letter from you. I wrote to your brother a long letter and have expected his answer, but I hope to hear from him in a post or two, or I shall be greatly disappointed. I told him that it was agreeable to me that you should learn to play upon the German flute[1] though I preferred other instruments if you had opportunity, as wind music is too apt to prey upon the constitution when closely applied to but I beg you will be careful in that respect and not injure your health by it. Pray let me know how you go on and whether you think you can make any proficiency in it. I presume you have no harpsichord at High Beach nor opportunity of learning to play upon it. I also mentioned that I would have you learn to dance, if you inclined to it. I think it gives young people a pretty easy manner and an agreeable behaviour. As the present expense of your education will be great, I hope no part of your time will be idly thrown away but that you will in every respect aim at improvement and shew your friends on your return that your time has not been spent in vain. This will make your own characters amiable and will also bring credit and reputation to Mr Booth.

Your Uncle and Aunt Feilden came here about 3 weeks ago to spend a few days with us, and as she was a nurse she brought her little son William and his nurse along with her. The child within a few days after they came was seized with a violent fever occasioned, I apprehend, from his getting teeth, and he has lain ever since in great pain that we have not expected his life from one day to another. He has for these few days past been rather easier that we have now hopes he may get the better of it, and as soon as he is in a condition to be moved, I fancy we shall lose your Aunt Feilden. Your Aunt Rigby, I expect, will stay the winter with us and my sister Tabitha will also be with us as she will not go to her house before spring. Your mother I hope still continues to grow better though the late hurry we have had with your Aunt Feilden's little boy's indisposition has rather fluttered and depressed her spirits a little, but she keeps up surprisingly and if we could but get her to go out a little more into cheerful enlivening company, which we endeavour to do as much as possible, I have great hopes she would soon be as well as ever. Your brother Cornelius continues much as he was, but seems very happy and contented, very fond of being out of doors among his play fellows. I have James Parkinson,[2] (our servant Ann's brother) to attend him constantly. I desire you will write to your mother in a post or two (I would not have you mention anything particular of her disorder). It would be very pleasing to her. She often mentions you both with a deal of pleasure and is much pleased when she finds that [* you] have wrote to any of your friends. Your Aunt Shepherd is still but poorly, though much better than she was, and I hope she will be able to get the better of her disorder. The rest of your friends are all pretty well. They all unite with me in our best wishes for you and your brother. I fancy your sister will write to you the next week. She will then send you all the news for which I refer you to her. I have not[hing] to add only that I am,

Dear Will,
Your affectionate father,
Thomas Langton

N.B.
This post has just brought me your
brother's letter. I am glad to hear you
are both well. Tell him I think he is improved in his writing and hope he will
continue his endeavours still to improve.
I will write to him soon, and hope to
have a letter from you very soon.

[*] Word omitted but required by sense.

Notes to DDX/190/38. November 10th, 1772

[1] The side-blown flute as distinct from the English flute, or recorder.
[2] This Parkinson is obviously not connected with the previous Mr Parkinson
and Thomas Langton is at pains to identify him. Once again Cornelius's
playing happily in the streets of Kirkham among his play fellows does not
suggest social exclusiveness at this stage.

(DDX/190/39)
Kirkham December 6th, 1772

Dear Will,

I have received your letter but it was without date, and since that I
have the favour of Mr Booth's letter with your last Woolton account
and the small balance of £3 3s. 7d. shall be paid him at my first
convenience. I will send him a small bill[1] and order him to give you
the money out above discharging this account, as I would not choose
to have the accounts inter-mixed. Pray make my compliments to him
and let him know I have received his letter and will write to him very
soon. I have now the pleasure to acquaint you that your Aunt
Feilden's little boy is got quite well again. They left us about 10 days
ago, got well to Blackburn and he got no cold with his journey and
continues well. Your brother Zachary goes to Blackburn this Christmas to spend a fortnight with your cousin Henry Feilden. Your
mother received your letter the last post. It gave her great pleasure
to hear from you and I would have you and your brother to write
to her occasionally. I am in great hopes she is going better daily. I
was at Preston yesterday and told Miss Hankinson the purport of

your letter. She said she would write to you in a post or two. Your sister is now at Preston on a visit to Mrs Bolton. She went there the last week and left the annexed letter to be forwarded to you when I wrote you. I find you will be almost left to yourselves these Christmas holidays. If the weather is favourable you will have good time to see the country in the neighbourhood of you, and to write to all your friends.[2] I should be glad to find you make a little proficiency in your music though I do not wish you to take up your time too much with it to neglect your other more necessary studies.

I find Mr Booth has got a young gentleman from Lynn who has been at an academy in Holland sometime. This may be mutually advantageous to you as he must have some knowledge of the languages and be pretty conversant in the French and Dutch. You say you have begun to learn High Dutch,[3] which I am glad to hear, and would have you to prosecute this study if Mr Booth thinks it eligible. Whatever books you have a desire of I would have you to buy them and if Mr Booth thinks a Dutch dictionary or any other French books necessary, I would have you to get them and if you want any money let me know and I will send it you. Although the Dutch language may be spoke at Konigsburg[4] and at other places in the Baltic, yet the persons we correspond with there are all Englishmen that seldom have any occasion to write any other language. However, it may be of use to you some time, and as you have the opportunity, would have you to prosecute it. Your brother Thomas is got a fine chattering lad. He talks very fluently and frequently mentions his brothers that are gone to London. Cornelius is pretty well in health, and much as you left him. Your Aunt Rigby and Aunt Tabby, who are still with us, desire to be remembered to you. So does all your friends. I hope to hear from you very soon. I have great pleasure in hearing from you both and desire you write me in a post or two. I expect to hear daily from your brother. My best wishes attend you both. I remain,

Your affectionate father,
Thomas Langton

Dear Brother,

I now sit down to write to excuse for my long silence. My Aunt and Uncle Feilden has been here and my cousin Will who has had a very bad illness here. My Aunt Tabby is at Preston and I believe I am to

go when she comes back and stay part of the winter there.[5] My
Mama has got a bad cold and sends her love to you both along with
my Papa and all friends and desires to know if you want anything.
I must have done, for my Papa has something to write here.[6]

I am, dear brother,
Your ever affectionate sister,
C. Langton

P.S.
Pray give my compliments to my
brother and tell him I will write to him
very soon, but if he is in anxiety to
know what is become of Mr Gaunt,
why, he is at Warton.

Notes to DDX/190/39. December 6th, 1772

[1] The complexity of the bill system is sometimes confusing. Here Thomas
Langton means that Mr Booth is to give the boys any surplus after the
discharge of the school expenses. Thomas Langton has difficulty in obtaining
a suitable bill and payment is in fact deferred until March.
[2] Throughout their schooldays the boys shouldered a considerable burden of
obligatory correspondence. There is an ironic *non sequitur* here. Favourable
weather would imply outdoor pursuits rather than indoor letter-writing, but
Thomas Langton had no doubt where his sons' duty lay and expected them
to discharge it, come what might.
[3] High Dutch is German.
[4] Königsberg was celebrated for its hemp.
[5] Cecily has been told of the family's plans for her winter.
[6] Presumably at the writing table.

(DDX/190/40)
Kirkham   December 26th, 1772

Dear Jack,

I was duly favoured with yours of the 13th of this month and was
pleased to find you were both well. It always gives us pleasure to
hear from you and would have you or your brother to write often.
If we are not so regular in our correspondence you must excuse us.

Your sister is now at Preston on a visit to Mrs Bolton[1] and I fancy will stay there during the holidays. They have got their son home from Chester and after Christmas they are to bring him back, when your sister is to go to your Aunt Hankinson's to stay a while. I fancy we shall not see her at home again before March at soonest. Your brother Zachary is gone to Blackburn to spend his Christmas with your cousin Harry Feilden[2] and does not return before the close of the holidays. I have not had an opportunity to get a proper bill to send Mr Booth yet, and as the half year is now come I will defer it till I send him one for your schooling which I will do soon. If you or your brother should want any money in the meantime I desire you will get it from Mr Booth who I dare say will readily supply you with what you want. As you have a few days now to spend, I expect you will be going into the country, which may cause you to want a little cash. Your cousin Savige Leech is now here at your Uncle Threlfall's. He has been here a week, and is to return on Thursday next. Your cousin Richard Bradkirk and Master Yates came over here last night to spend a few days. I am to have some company to dine with me today at my Christmas entertainment, which makes me rather in a hurry, that you must excuse me adding any more only my proper respects to Mr Booth and the ladies, and my best wishes for your brother and yourself concludes me, Dear Jack,

Your affectionate father,
Thomas Langton

Your mother is I hope rather better and
her best wishes attend you both.

Notes to DDX/190/40. December 26th, 1772

[1] It is worth noting that, although Mrs Langton was an invalid, Cecily was not expected to stay at home all the time. No doubt the maiden aunts were earning their keep.
[2] The close social connections between the Langtons and the Feildens were kept up to the end of their lives. This kinship tie was particularly strong but there was no marriage between the cousins.

(DDX/190/41)
Kirkham   January 28th, 1773

Dear Will,

Mr Richard Parkinson,[1] who has been here above a month, is now returning back and expects to arrive there on Tuesday next. I take this opportunity by him of writing to you, and have sent you 5 guineas which may serve to supply you both as your exigencies require it. I expect you will have many letters from your friends by him. He promises me to go over to High Beach very shortly to see you when you will have an opportunity of hearing all the news of this country. Your sister is still at Preston, with your Aunt Hankinson. She proposed to write to you by this conveyance, so did Miss Hankinson and your aunt. You will also have a letter from your mother. I hope she is much better. It always gives her fresh spirits when she hears from you. She has a very tender regard for you both and I hope your future behaviour will merit her affection and kindness for you. I find you have been much confined at High Beach these holidays, the unseasonableness of the weather not permitting you to stir much but as a finer season comes on you may perhaps have liberty to see a little of the country, and it will be very agreeable to me that you accept Mrs Leigh's kind invitation to stay a little while with her in London when a convenient opportunity offers. I hope you will take particular care not to skate upon any water where there may be the least danger. We sometimes hear of fatal accidents attending this diversion. If you should at any time want a little money as you may want shoes, stockings or other necessaries, I shall willingly allow it you and would have you ask Mr Booth to let you have it. I intend to send him a bill after Candlemas for fifty or sixty pounds. I have confidence in you both that you will not misapply your money, so would not limit you. Pray in your next let me know the condition your clothes are in, and whether you will want anything of that sort soon. I could wish you to appear clean and decently dressed when you go to London. When you return home will be time enough to render an account of your expenses and disbursements, in which I expect you will be very exact. You complain of having got a little cold. Pray be careful of yourselves. A bad cold is a troublesome companion and sometimes very difficult to get quit of it. Your cousin Savige Leech was here a fortnight at Christmas. He is a fine boy, I think much improved, but very low in stature. He would be glad to hear from you. You may direct to him with Mr Carver in

Liverpool. Your cousin Richard Bradkirk stayed 3 weeks here this Christmas.

I have only to recommend to you both a due attention to your studies, and a proper application to your improvement in your writing. Good writing is a fine and very useful accomplishment in business and should require your utmost attention to acquire it.

With my proper respects to Mr Booth and best wishes for you and your brother whom I hope to hear from soon, I remain,

Your affectionate father,
Thomas Langton

P.S.
You have enclosed, a letter from your
mother. You will be satisfied of the good
wishes and attention she has for your future welfare, and I would have you to
burn it[2] after you have properly digested
her good advice.

Notes to DDX/190/41. January 28th, 1773

[1] This Parkinson, in delicate health and lodging with Mr and Mrs Threlfall in London, has no connection with the two previous Parkinsons.
[2] The curious injunction to burn their mother's letter is inexplicable. There is no suggestion that she is suffering from a contagious disease and no other reason could readily explain the course of action prescribed.

(DDX/190/42)
Kirkham   February 5th, 1773

Dear Jack,

I wrote to your brother Will by Mr Richard Parkinson who had been here and was to be in London on his return last Tuesday. He promised me to come and see you at High Beach as next Sunday or that day sen-night following, but perhaps he may be stopped for a week longer. I gave him 5 guineas for you and your brother to supply you in case of your wanting a little cash for present necessity, as I find your brother had exhausted his fund and was forced to apply to you to assist him, having bought a new hat, German flute, I hope it is a good one, and some other necessaries. You may probably receive this before you see Mr Parkinson or receive your letters by him, as you will have a number of them from many of your friends. You'll please to give my compliments to Mr Booth and desire he will give you permission to wait of him and attend him during the time he can stay with you. He is a well disposed young man and I hope he will find his health greatly amended by his journey into Lancashire. Pray remember me to him.

If you have received any money from Mr Booth I will answer it to him again. I propose towards the close of this month to send him a bill for £50 which you may acquaint [* him] with. As I wrote so lately by Mr Parkinson I shall have nothing more now to add only to request that I may frequently hear from you, which gives us all pleasure. Your sister is still at Preston. They are all well there. Your mother is pretty clever and well and the rest of your friends are very hearty. They all join me in our best wishes for you and your brother, which concludes me, Dear Jack,

Your affectionate father,
Thomas Langton

[*] Word omitted but demanded by sense.

(DDX/190/43)

Kirkham   February 19th, 1773

Dear Will,

I received your brother's letter of the 7th instant as also yours of the 12th, and your mother had one from your brother same day, which she was well pleased with, and your brother Zachary has received your last letter to-day, which gives him great pleasure and he intends to write to you again soon. I find you have been in London previous to this last on a visit to some of your schoolfellows, but you do not mention to whom. Pray in your next let me know to whom you was obliged. I presume you would call of Mr Parkinson as I find you have got the 5 guineas I sent you and would then see Mr and Mrs

Threlfall with whom Mr Parkinson lives. I was a little surprized at
the account your brother gave me of the disaster you met with in
London.[1] It was a little unthinking of you to trust your money into
a stranger's hands to get change. You might be sure you would never
see him again, but I hope it will teach you better caution in future.
I fancy you have traversed the streets of London pretty well as you
are become so well acquainted as to go anywhere in the town by the
direction of your map. However, I would have you to be cautious
not to ramble too far, and as Mrs Leigh has been so obliging as to
give you an invitation to stay a few days with her that you will give
them as little trouble as you well can during your stay as her late
indisposition may not bear it. If your brother wants stockings and
is bent upon having a pair or two of silk stockings, I shall not object
to it but I think worsted is full as suitable for the season. I am willing
to allow you anything you want in reason,[2] and hope your own
discretion will lead you to no extravagances. You need not repay Mr
Booth the 2 guineas you borrowed of him. I have a bill by me which
will recompense him to the half year, but as you will not be at High
Beach I will defer sending it to him for a week or ten days. Your old
acquaintances, Miss Roughsedges, of Liverpool, are now in London,
or at Mr Bromley's in Essex. They will be very glad to see you and
I dare say you will meet with them at Mrs Loxham's, where Mrs
Leigh will be so kind to direct you. If they should not be there I
would have you to call upon Mrs Loxham with our compliments
and to enquire after Mrs Whitehead of this town[3] who is now with
her brother in Essex, not far from Waltham Abbey. You will there
also hear of Mr Thomas Wilson, who was with your Uncle Hankinson and is now in London, who I dare say would be glad to see
you.[4]

I have a relation in London who I dare say would be glad to see
you also and you may perhaps remember his name. It is Mr Zachary
Taylor.[5] I am not sure, but I think he lodges at Mr George Lindsay's,
watch maker, in the Strand, a little below the Exeter Exchange. I
desire you will enquire after him and you can learn from this account
the place of his abode that you will wait of him with my proper
compliments. He will be enquiring after your Uncle Langton, who
is now at Oxford. I had a letter from him last post, is very well and
always enquires very kindly after you. I hope to have a letter from
you during your stay in London. Your mother and your Aunt
Rigby, who is now here, joins me in our most cordial good wishes
for you and your brother and Mr and Mrs Leigh, where I expect this

will find you. We are greatly obliged to them for the kindly notice
they take of you and hope if they come into Lancashire this summer
that we shall have the pleasure to see them at Kirkham. We were
greatly disappointed in not seeing them last year when Mr and Mrs
Whitehead was so good as to call of us. The post is just come in that
I have not time to add any further only that I am, Dear Will,

Most affectionately yours,
Thomas Langton

All your friends send their love to you
and your brother.

Notes to DDX/190/43
To Mr William Langton at Mrs Leigh, London. February 19th, 1773

[1] Thomas Langton issued only a mild rebuke upon the imprudent conduct
with the stranger. The boys had confessed their folly and their father was
content for them to learn from their experience. For one so well aware of the
value of money his attitude told much about his affection for his sons.
[2] This statement may be taken at its face value. Thomas Langton was an
indulgent father within reasonable limits. He genuinely considered the wishes
of the boys, as his permission to buy silk stockings instead of worsted shows.
[3] Mrs Whitehead was Mrs Langton's cousin, married to the vicar of Bolton.
She was a native of Kirkham.
[4] In addition to their epistolary commitments, the boys were to pursue a
formidable round of visits on behalf of their family.
[5] Zachary Taylor inherited his Christian name from the same source as
Zachary Langton and Uncle Langton. Cornelius Langton, who came to
Kirkham about 1687, married the daughter of the master of the free school,
Zachary Taylor. The Zachary Taylor of this letter was probably the master's
grandson.

(DDX/190/44)

Kirkham   March 14th, 1773

Dear Will,

I duly received your last of the 28th ultimo from which I find you
were returned from your visit to Mrs Leigh. I make no doubt but
you were very agreeably entertained during your stay in London and
you would have an opportunity of seeing everything which was

worth notice. You were much obliged to Mr Meynell and at some convenient opportunity you may perhaps return the obligation. I find Miss Roughsedges are not yet gone to London but they propose it some time this spring. If you should go there again I would have you just call of Mr Loxham,[1] and present our compliments. You may then enquire after Mrs Whitehead of this town, who is with her brother in Essex, and after Master Loxham your old schoolfellow. Mr Parkinson was very obliging in letting you have so much of his company while you were in London as well as Mr Thomas Wilson. I find he is expected at Preston this summer. I am glad you had the opportunity to see Mr Taylor. You would let him know that your Uncle Langton was at Oxford. I wrote to Mr Booth on this day sen-night, and therein sent him two bills value £61.14.8. I shall expect in a few posts to have a line from him to acknowledge the receipt of them. Your sister came home from Preston only last Tuesday where she left all your friends very well. I understand she had a letter from you this post and proposes to write you very soon. She complains that her brother John does not answer her last letter and I think it long since I had a line from him. I have not anything material further to say. Your friends here are all pretty well and desire to be remembered to you. Your Aunt Langton[2] only is troubled with a bad cold and confined to the house which makes her very weak and feeble, as she is now advanced in years. Your Aunt Tabby and Aunt Rigby are with us, the former expects a letter from you every post. My best wishes wait you and your brother and proper compliments to Mr Booth etc. concludes me,

Dear Will,
Your affectionate father,
Thomas Langton

Note to DDX/190/44. March 14th, 1773

[1] Edward Loxham, hatter and sword cutler, married to Jane Hankinson of Kirkham, sister of Alice Dannett and Elizabeth Roughsedge.
[2] Not Uncle Langton's wife, but his sister Abigail who died at Kirkham in 1776.

(DDX/190/45)

Kirkham   March 26th, 1773

Dear Will,

Your letter to your mother came duly to hand which gave her much pleasure and to-day your aunt has received a letter from you. I was pleased to find you had been so agreeably entertained during your stay in London. If you could without much inconveniency call of Mrs Whitehead who is with Mrs Loxham, it would be agreeable to me. I understand it is not far distant from High Beach. It will be agreeable to me that you purchase any books which either Mr Booth or Mr Newby may recommend to you. I understand Mr Newby is purposing to leave Mr Booth and that he would be glad to fix in some part of Lancashire and prefers the neighbourhood of Preston if there was a prospect of its answering his expectation.[1] I should be glad to do him any service if it lays in my power, but at present I can say nothing to the purpose. Perhaps we may have the pleasure to see him at Kirkham soon and may then hear some more about his intention. I should be very glad on your account if he was to fix somewhere in this neighbourhood. I have a letter from Mr Booth to-day acknowledging receipt of the two bills I had remitted him, value £61. 14. 8. on your account, and he therein acquaints me that on Mr Newby's being obliged to come into this country at Easter your summer vacation takes place then, and that he proposed you and your brother to come down with him by the Manchester stage which sets out from the Swan with Two Necks in Lad Lane[2] on Easter Sunday in the evening. I have wrote him to-night by the post and this serves also to acquaint you that your Uncle Shepherd[3] and his three daughters, Miss Shepherds, are intending to set out from hence for London on Monday next, but as they make Oxford in their road it may be a week or more before they get into London and Mr Shepherd has promised to go over to High Beach to see you as soon as he gets to London. He will then settle with Mr Booth and discharge your account and I would have you to pack up all your clothes in your box but what you will want on your journey and get them to London that you may see them forwarded by the carrier to Preston. You will direct them to me at Kirkham. You will also hold yourself in readiness to depart from High Beach on Mr Shepherd's coming there as I could wish you to stay a few days in London before you leave the country and you must call of all your friends to take leave of them. Among the rest you must not forget Mr Taylor.

Perhaps Mrs Leigh may ask you to lodge with them while you are in Town and if you have opportunity call of Mrs Loxham. Mr Wilson may perhaps have time on his hands to show you the way. If you have time and incline to it, your brother and you may buy yourselves each a suit of superfine cloth and get them made in London, and Mrs Leigh will recommend you to proper persons to purchase them.[4] You may get what money you want from Mr Shepherd who I have desired to give it you, and as to the mode of your return, whether it be with Mr Newby or otherways, I shall leave it to you and Mr Shepherd, but will write you again by him on that head or by Mr Joseph Hornby who, I hear, is intending for London next week. Your friends here are all pretty well. Miss Hankinson does not set out for London this three weeks,[5] that I expect you will scarce see her there. As you will so soon hear from me again, I have only to add my best wishes attend you and your brother and that I am, in haste,

Your affectionate father,
Thomas Langton

Notes to DDX/190/45
To High Beach Essex (and 46). March 26th, 1773

[1] Mr Booth was selling up the school at High Beach and emigrating to America. Peter Newby was returning to Lancashire and his expectation was to start a school of his own in the neighbourhood of Preston. Although Thomas Langton is not optimistic about this venture, Newby succeeded in starting a school at Burton in Kendal and in 1775 moved it to Great Eccleston, which was a centre for Roman Catholic recusants, visited from time to time by the Roman Catholic mission for baptism and confirmation sub rosa. Subsequently he moved to Haighton, near to Fernyhalgh, the location of the celebrated Roman Catholic school run until 1760 by Dame Alice. He was eventually forced out of business when Stonyhurst was established as a school for moneyed Roman Catholics following the closure of the Jesuit school on the continent at the French Revolution.

[2] The Swan with Two Necks in Lad Lane was for many years the starting post for the Manchester and Liverpool coaches.

[3] William Shepherd, the uncle of Thomas Langton's wife and the first partner of the Langton firm.

[4] The boys are to be given suits made by a London tailor, of even greater status value than the Liverpool-made ones of the previous year. London clothes and materials were much sought after by socially-aspiring provincials.

[5] Visits to London were made by an assortment of people, by no means all of them on business. They are in no way daunted by the rigours of travel and there are no references to discomfort. This suggests that travelling in the English roads was perhaps not always as unsatisfactory as some writers such as Arthur Young made out. Perhaps the northern stock was hardier.

(DDX/190/46)
Kirkham   April 2nd, 1773

Dear Jack,

I wrote to your brother William in answer to his letter as well as to a letter I received from Mr Booth signifying to me his intention that as Mr Newby was going into Lancashire at Easter he intended his summer vacation to take place at that time. This I find he had not communicated to you when you wrote, but as my letter must be now with you no doubt you will be preparing to have everything in readiness to take your departure from High Beach as I expect Mr Shepherd will be with you in a day or two when he will pay Mr Booth the balance of your account and also furnish you with what money you may want. You will take care to see your box forwarded from High Beach and also from London and as you will want another box to pack your new suits in which you will now get made in London before you leave it you will take care also to see it packed up and forwarded. Mr Shepherd has something to buy for your Aunt Rigby and your mother[1] which is intended to come in the same box. Mr Richard Birley[2] and Mr Hornby are setting out for London on Monday next. What [* stay] they may make there I cannot say but I was in hopes they would have gone a week sooner and would then have very probably fallen in very opportunely for you to have returned back with them. I leave the mode of your return to Mr Shepherd and yourselves. If you could get everything you want done, to have come with Mr Newby by Manchester might be agreeable. Otherways you must regulate your return as Mr Shepherd may advise you. If you come by Manchester, your Uncle Feilden has been so obliging to offer to send horses for you from thence to Blackburn, where you may stay a day or two, and I will send horses from hence for you thither. Please to give me a line as soon as you determine upon your journey and what day you intend to leave London and to what place and time I am to send horses to meet you. If you come by Manchester you must give Mr Feilden a line to Blackburn to let him know what day you will be there, or you may get Mr Birley to mention it in his letter when he writes home. I cannot say anything to you about Mr Newby at this time. It is very uncertain whether a scheme of that kind may answer at Preston or no,[3] but he may probably take a ride over on his coming into Lancashire. I fear he would meet with few persons here that would encourage it, though there is no doubt that he might get an agreeable farm in this country. All your friends here are pretty well. They join me in due respects to you and your brother. You have always our best wishes. I remain,

Dear Jack,
Your affectionate father,
Thomas Langton

If you want each a new hat you must
buy such as you like. And should you
not leave something with the servants at
High Beach? This as you think proper.

[*] Paper torn but probable word substituted.

Notes to DDX/190/46. April 2nd, 1773

[1] It was common to give commissions of this sort to relatives travelling to London so that the provinces could reflect the capital in fashion.
[2] Richard Birley was the brother of John, partner in the firm. He settled in Blackburn.
[3] Thomas Langton obviously thought a farm more likely to succeed than a school.

(DDX/190/47)

Hotwells, Bristol   June 19th, 1775

Dear Will,

I begin to be very impatient to hear from some of my friends, though I cannot yet receive a letter in reply to my last. However, I hope a post or two may relieve me from my anxiety and satisfy me that you are all well. As Doctor Rigge[1] was prevented from going to Bath on Wednesday and was uncertain what day he should go, I put off my journey until Sunday when Mr Cockin and I took a ride there and dined and spent the remainder of the day with Mr and Mrs Hornby.[2] She is very well and Mr Hornby much better than expected. I think he stands a fair chance of getting the better of his disorder if he will but stay a sufficient time that the waters may have a proper effect. I expect them here on Wednesday to dine with me. Bath is a sweet place.[3] I often wished to have some of you with me. I will not attempt a description of it, but improvements are making there every year.[4] The country about the Hotwells[5] is much pleasanter, and more agreeable rides. The downs are very pleasant, you have fine extensive prospects over the whole country well inhabited and interspersed with a number of fine houses chiefly belonging to the Bristol merchants.[6] I wrote to my Uncle Langton and to Cecily on my coming here and have received an answer from them both. Cecily is very well but wonders much that she has not had a letter from her aunt since her return from Chester.[7] My uncle is very pressing with me to come to Oxford to see the Grand Encoemia or commemoration, which is to be held there the 5th, 6th, and 7th of July next, where Lord North[8] is expected to attend the celebrity, and is therefore likely to be very grand and most brilliant as great preparations are making to render the whole as splendid as possible. In this case he would return with me back to the Hotwells and to Bath. But I think I shall hardly acquiesce with the proposals, as I shall not think of returning here again after I once leave it, unless it was upon a further tour into the west, but as Dr Rigge advises me to continue here 6 weeks I shall be inclined to return home as speedily as possible afterwards as my absence will be longer from home than I intended when I left Kirkham. The waters have hitherto agreed pretty well with me and I hope will be of service to me. I ride out every day as do most of the people which come to this place. Here is a good deal of company, but mostly invalid, and many of them appear to be in the last stages of life, but from the accounts which are given surprising are the cures which these waters have effected.

We have various accounts here of our North American affairs[9] and as various are the sentiments of the people, but the generality look upon it in a very serious light and are very fearful of the consequences. I hope you have received some letters from thence since I left home with remittances or I fear it will be long, VERY LONG, before we get anything from that quarter.[10] I do not hear that any particular accounts are received here from any part of North America since the late unfortunate affair at Boston[11] which are to be depended on, but I shall be in Bristol again tomorrow and if any accounts which may be interesting arrive here, you shall be advised in my next.

Mr Hornby tells me the Riga vessels are all arrived there and those that are wholly to be laden with flax will be immediately dispatched but those that are to lade timber or part timber will be detained as no balks[12] are yet come down. They have one vessel there which lades all flax which may be soon expected if this is the case. I fear they will have new flax at market a long time before us.[13] Pray what accounts have you from London and Hull of its quality? I have seen none here nor do I think much is imported to this place. I find by the Liverpool Imports[14] two vessels are arrived there from Riga. One is wholly laden for Messrs Heywoods and the other for the Warrington sail canvas makers[15] and Mr Dawson of Liverpool. I fancy you will learn their prices.

Tuesday morning, June 20th

Mr Cockin is just come here and has brought me John's letter. I think myself obliged to him for taking the earliest opportunity in writing to me and giving me so agreeable an account of my friends. I shall expect to hear from some of you every post with a particular of what passes. Mr Calvert's order will lessen your stock of No. 1 and 2.[16] I am glad to see Captain Potts in such forwardness and that he may be expected so soon with you but I am sorry to see he brings so much wheat. I fear it will meet with a dull sale, and it may be a doubt whether the present low prices of wheat may not subject it to the payment of the high duty.[17] I shall be glad to find C. B.'s note is paid, but I have no dependence on it. If it should come back, security should be immediately insisted on.[18] I wonder Mr Taylor should not have wrote you of the condition of the 2 remaining bales of Ancona Hemp[19] which I left to be landed. He would no doubt answer Mr Birley's letter and say whether the hemp was forwarded to J. Ratcliffe. As soon as the freight is fixed with Captain Bell it would be best to order the damaged hemp or to endeavour to sell it to Jonathan Deane and let it be sent to Lancaster directly from Liverpool. As it was taken so early after it was wet, and dried, I think the loss will not be so great and if you could dispose of it at about 10/– per cent loss might do well. I am glad to find the insurance on the Betsey and Tindale are both done so low. A bill should be sent to Mr Sowerby for last year's account.

I find James Haighton has sold all the cattle except one, and has bought a mare. Let me know upon what account they are, and what share of them are for my account and what for the company.

This comes under cover to Mr Cockin to save you the postage. I beg my respects to him. His brother has received his letter and Mrs Cockin is very glad to hear of her sons. Remember me also to all my friends. I often think of you and shall be glad to get home again but as I am come so far and have hopes to receive benefit from my journey I must persevere and follow the doctor's prescriptions.

My best wishes await on you all and concludes me

Dear Will,
Most affectionately yours,
Thomas Langton

When you want any money you must apply for it to Mr Birley who will charge it to my account.

Notes to DDX/190/47. June 19th, 1775

[1] Dr Rigge was the physician at the Hotwells Spa and appears by name in Tobias Smollett's novel *Humphry Clinker* in which the novelist, a physician by profession, is adversely critical of the efficacy of the spa cures.

[2] The Kirkham flax merchants were now able to join the clientele of the fashionable spas, a mark of their upward social mobility dependent upon their increasing affluence.

[3] Bath was considered a winter spa and had a wide range of diversions to cater for the fitter patients and the various entourages accompanying them. Bristol Hotwells, more a summer spa, vied with Bath in providing equivalent entertainment.

[4] Bath was virtually rebuilt in the eighteenth century, largely to the plans of the Woods, father and son. The Royal Crescent was started in 1767.

[5] The Hotwells was on the bank of the Avon, through the mud of which at low tide oozed a white warm liquid which was piped as spa water. The water was sold in bottles, and even reached the continent. There is virtually nothing left today of the spa buildings and the spring is blocked by constructions introduced when the suspension bridge was built and the course of the river changed. A dejected colonnade façade is the only remnant of former splendour.

[6] The Bristol merchants were wealthy, trading in slaves and American produce, but not with the Baltic. The chief port after London in the early eighteenth century, Bristol was to be superseded by Liverpool by the end.

[7] The Langtons relied heavily on family correspondence.

[8] Lord North became Prime Minister in 1770.

[9] The struggle for American independence had finally come to open warfare in April 1775.

[10] In fact they were to wait until 1782 for the first payment from their American contacts. (See letter dated 13 August 1782, DDX/190/65.)

[11] As the Boston Tea Party—when the colonists had thrown a cargo into the sea rather than pay the duty on tea—took place in 1773, this reference is likely to be to the skirmishes in 1775 at Lexington Green leading to open hostilities which sent the British forces back to Boston, which was defended by the New Englanders and became under siege.

[12] Balk is the name given to the roughly-squared trunks which were later to be cut into planks.

[13] The Hornbys, though socially friends, were commercially rivals, and Thomas Langton never forgot it.

[14] The list of Liverpool imports would be available in Bristol.

[15] Warrington was the most important centre of sailmaking in the north of England, to a much larger extent than Kirkham.

[16] Sailcoth was made in seven qualities of which numbers 1 and 2 were the best.

[17] Although less severe than under the Corn Laws of the nineteenth century, low prices for home grown grain were balanced by high duties on imported grain. Here, it would be Baltic produce.

[18] If the promissory note proved invalid, Will was to negotiate some security with the debtor.

[19] Ancona was a European exporter of hemp. The port was important in eighteenth-century trade.

(DDX/190/48)
Hotwells, Bristol   July 12th, 1775

Dear Will,

I have just received your letter of the 9th instant and same post has brought me a letter from your sister whom I have the pleasure to tell you is very well and hearty and also that I am got quite recovered from my colic and I hope it has greatly relieved some of the complaint at my breast[1] as I find myself better since than I have been of some time past and it gives me great hopes that I shall receive benefit from my journey and during my stay at this place. I was now thinking of returning and mentioned my intention to Dr Rigge but he strongly recommends my staying a fortnight or three weeks longer which he thinks necessary. I go down to the Pump Room every morning and drink two half pint glasses of the water before breakfast at about half an hour's distance between them and afterwards if the weather will permit I ride out upon the downs for an hour or two, and at noon I go to the pump room again and drink two glasses same as in the morning. I dine about three and then walk out pretty frequently to Bristol which is but about a mile. In the evening I go to the Long Rooms for about an hour, sup about eight, of water gruel and generally retire to bed before ten. Thus you see how I spend my time. I do not know whether the temperate and fine air upon these downs or the gentle and healthful exercise of riding with regularity and sobriety may not tend as much to restore me to a good state of health as drinking the Hotwell waters[2] but upon the whole I think myself much better than when I first came here. I may probably in my next say when I hope to return, and although everything tends to make this place agreeable yet I shall be very glad to see my family and friends at Kirkham.

I was glad to see you had attended the discharge of Captain Potts who has delivered you a dry cargo which is very agreeable. I hope the quality of the flax will please the chaps[3] and that you may meet with ready sale but they are generally tardy in laying their stocks so early being desirous of seeing the whole importation arrive first. I wait with much impatience to hear some account of the Tindale. I am afraid she will make a late voyage.[4] I observe Captain Potts has brought something for me. You'll take care of it till I return and settle with him for the value. I hope H. Feilden was well pleased with his journey to Wyre and I make no doubt you would endeavour to make Kirkham agreeable to him. I wish Mr Birley may be able to dispose of the wheat to his mind at Liverpool and that he may close with some of the flaxmen there for some Riga flax.

I hope they will have good diversion at the races.[5] I shall rejoice to hear you have got the hay well in and you'll pay all charges attending it.[6] I am sorry to hear your aunt has been poorly. I hope this will find her much better.

Pray remember me to all my friends. I find John did not go to Liverpool races. I shall be glad to have a line from him when he can spare time from business. I am going to-morrow to Bath to see Mr and Mrs Hornby who I hear are pretty well and that Mr Hornby continues clever.[7] My love and best wishes attend you all. I am,

Dear Will,
Most affectionately yours,
Thomas Langton

Notes to DDX/190/48. July 12th, 1775

[1] This is the only specific reference to Thomas Langton's illness. As the Hotwells water was considered efficacious for chest complaints he might have been suffering from bronchitis or pleurisy.

[2] Other observers thought the air and exercise as valuable restoratives as the water. Richard Joseph Sulivan, writing in 1785, reported that one of the physicians had said to him that it was of no consequence whether the benefit to the invalids proceeded from the water or the Downs and that it was more probable that the Downs might be entitled to the merit of a moiety of the cure at least.(Surely not Dr Rigge!)

[3] The chapmen were the middlemen who bought the raw material and sold to the manufacturers. The Langton firm dealt in flax as well as sailcloth importing more than they required for themselves. Chapmen is sometimes abbreviated to 'chaps' in the letters and is indeed the origin of the colloquialism.

[4] The *Tindale* was bound for the Baltic and a late voyage would mean that she would be stranded all winter as the Baltic ports were closed from October/November to March/April.

[5] Thomas Langton's children participated in pastimes appropriate to their station. Horse racing was popular with the gentry and the monied burgesses. It was by now regulated by the Jockey Club, and had grown more respectable than formerly. There had been races at Preston since 1669, and at Liverpool since the early seventeenth century.

[6] Kirkham was still predominantly a country town. Agricultural land was comparatively extensive within its official confines.

[7] See note 10, DDX/190/21.

(DDX/190/49)

Hotwells, Bristol   July 24th, 1775

Dear Will,

I was agreeably favoured with yours of the 18th instant and should have wrote to you by the return of that post, but I was prevented by some friends calling upon me. I hope I continue still to gain ground and am in great expectation that I shall receive benefit from my long excursion. I do assure you I am heartily tired and often wish myself with you. I this morning to my doctor. I proposed to leave this place on Thursday or Friday next but he said it was necessary I should be bled again and that I should scarce be able to think of it before this day sen-night.[1] However, to put myself in the greatest forwardness I sent for my apothecary to perform the operation who came about two hours ago and took a large basin of blood from me that you must not now expect a long letter. He came with his large gold headed cane and umbrella and told me he had just been taking leave of Lord Strathmore who was leaving the Wells in the morning.[2] I fancy I shall have a large bill to pay him and I fancy I have paid a good many.[3]

As I continue my resolution to return by Oxford I could wish to receive a line from some of you to meet me there and hope I may get there about the 1st of August at furthest. I shall only stay there 2 or 3 days and then return home but you will hear from me again. Do not write to me any more here as I hope your letters would not reach me while I stay but let me have one to meet me at Oxford. If you write by Friday's post it will be sure to find me there and you may order it to be left at the Post Office till called for. I am obliged to Mr Bolton for his letter which came very duly. Remember me to him and Mrs Bolton and if he would add one line at the foot of yours, would oblige me to know what is doing in the north.

It gave me much satisfaction to find the Tindale was got to Narva. I doubt not he will meet with good dispatch there and I shall be glad to hear of his arrival with you. I find the wheat is sold at Liverpool, the price is low, and that you have made some progress in the sale of the Riga flax. I hope you have got all the hay safe housed as we have had a tolerable fine week here. I have a letter from Mr Feilden to-day. He tells me he sent for his son Henry that morning and hourly expects him. I hope you made Kirkham agreeable to him. He tells me Mr and Mrs Hornby was got home, where I dare say they will enjoy themselves after so long an absence. Pray remember me to them, also to all my friends. Pray what stay does Miss Shepherds make at Harrogate? I fancy they will return before me. I am glad to hear you all continue pretty well. My best wishes attend you, being always,

Most affectionately yours,
Thomas Langton

I have bought you a pair of very hand-some knee buckles but I have yet met with no stock buckle that pleased me.

I hear from Cecily that they are all well at Chester. This comes under cover to Mr Cockin. Pray remember me to him.

Notes to DDX/190/49. July 24th, 1775

[1] Dr Rigge seems determined to have his pound of flesh by keeping Thomas Langton as long as possible.

[2] An apothecary was officially of lower professional status than a physician, intended for making up prescriptions and keeping a shop. However, there were apothecaries and apothecaries. Old Apothecary Parkinson, resident in Kirkham in the time of the letters though not attendant on the Langton

household, acted in all respects as a general practitioner as well as keeping a shop for his drugs. This dandified, name-dropping apothecary at the Hotwells was on to a good thing, performing the menial duties of medicine for generous remuneration.
[3] That Thomas Langton was prepared to contemplate the expenditure of so much money speaks well for the reputation of the spas. He would never have embarked upon the cure if he did not think it had a good chance of being 'of service'.

(DDX/190/50)

Woodstock   August 8th, 1775

Dear Will,

I have only just time to inform you that I left Oxford last night, having met with great civility from many gentlemen there and it was with great difficulty I could get away as the races began that day and great diversion was expected. I left my uncle[1] very well. He enquired much after all his friends in Lancashire and I presume will not be long before he comes to see them. I am just going to see Blenheim,[2] and may probably call at Ditchley[3] or Heythrop.[4] I propose to get to Birmingham tomorrow night, but as I have some thoughts of making Chester in my way, it may be Saturday or probably Sunday before I get home where I hope to meet all my friends well and in good spirits which would give me great satisfaction after so long an absence from them. My best wishes attend you all, being most sincerely,

Yours,
Thomas Langton

I did not draw for any money at Oxford
as I proposed.

Notes to DDX/190/50. August 8th, 1775

[1] Uncle Zachary Langton, the scholar.
[2] It is typical of Thomas Langton that he makes use of his journey home to see stately homes and to visit relations. In this way he would be getting his money's worth. Blenheim, completed in 1722–3, was a popular port of call already. Sir William Chambers was at work from 1766 to 1775 on the temples of Flora and Diana, the last additions to the grounds.

³ Ditchley Park, built by James Gibbs between 1720 and 1731 for the second
Earl of Lichfield, grandson of Charles II and Barbara Villiers.
⁴ Heythrop House, a baroque palace built for the first Duke of Shrewsbury,
designed by Thomas Archer, started about 1706 and roofed in 1709.

                                                    (DDX/190/51)
                                    London   June 15th, 1776

Dear John,

I take the earliest opportunity to advise you of our safe arrival here
this day about noon. We got to Warrington the first night but it was
with some difficulty we could leave our friends at Prescot. Poor Mrs
Crook continues in much the same as she was when Mrs Leaf wrote
to Mrs Bradkirk and although she is very much emaciated yet she
may continue some time, perhaps years, though in her present distressed situation without any the least glimpse of hope of her getting
the better of her disorder, a release might be happy for her. On
Thursday we left Warrington about six o'th'clock and got to Lichfield
that night, next day to Brickhill and to-day to this place. Mr Threlfall
went to Barnet in hopes to meet us, but we missed each other. I spent
the afternoon with Mr Turner and he has [* told] Zachary that he
shall often have the pleasure of seeing him at Hampstead as he has a
house within a few doors of the Academy.¹ William Threlfall only
came back this evening about 9 o'th'clock. We have taken our lodgings with him, and have the pleasing prospect of spending our time
here very agreeably. Zachary is very much surprized² with London,
and as the school time does not begin till Monday sen-night he will
have all the week to see the amusements and variety of this place. I
have not had the opportunity of seeing any more of my friends. I shall
be more particular in that respect in my next. I hope to have a line
from some of you to advise what is going on with you.

    I must conclude, having Mr Threlfall at my elbow, who begs to
be particularly remembered to all friends at Kirkham and with my
most sanguine good wishes for you all,
I remain,

                        Most affectionately yours,
                            Thomas Langton

Zachary begs to be remembered to all his
brothers, sister, and the rest of his
friends.

[*] Word omitted.

Notes to DDX/190/51. June 15th, 1776

[1] The purpose of this excursion was to place Zachary in the Hampstead
Academy. Thomas Langton had considered Essex too far from home when
his sons had asked his permission to move with the Woolton Academy to
High Beach in 1772. Four years later London seems to present no such
problem.

[2] Surprized or no, Zachary was to spend most of the rest of his life in London.
When he left school, his father set him up as a wholesale linen draper and he acted
as a contact for the Kirkham firm. He was to become master of the Skinners'
Company, a burgess of the City of London and a member of the Common
Council. Later still, he abandoned the textile trade and was one of the driving
forces behind the resuscitation of Pickfords, the carriers. (See Gerald L.
Turnbull, *Traffic and Transport. An Economic History of Pickfords*, 1979.)

(DDX/190/52)
[This letter is headed Kirkham,
but clearly London is intended.]
June 24th, 1776

Dear Will,

I have yours of the 20th instant for which I thank you. It gave me
both concern and much pleasure. I am sorry to find your brother
John's complaint hangs on him. I beg he will take care of himself,
and if the bleeding[1] and other precautions he has taken has not the
good effect I wish I would have him consult Dr Clayton, and follow
his advice, but I hope by proper care he will be freed from his cough.
But my surprize was very great on finding that poor Tom has had
the small pox.[2] I should have been very unhappy if I had heard of it
before he had got well again. Is it not early for him to go abroad so
soon?, and have you taken proper care to give him some physic which
is certainly necessary after such a disorder,[3] which often leaves bad
humours[4] lurking in the blood after it, if proper precautions are not
taken to prevent it. You were certainly right in calling in Dr Clayton

on this occasion.[5] I am glad you have Miss Bolton still with you. I hope I shall find her on my return. I am afraid Cecily was too precipitate in her journey to Blackburn, as she was not only hurrying my lad away too soon but leaving Miss Bolton. I am certain her inducement was to meet Miss Starkie,[6] being fixed between them, and Miss Bolton is very obliging in excusing it. Her habit and hat were forwarded by the London carriers to Preston and will be there on Tuesday next at furthest. I did not see them but they say they are very neat and handsome. Messrs Pontin and Coats do nothing in the men's wear, that I was obliged to apply elsewhere for your clothes. I bought the cloth of Mr Threlfall's friend, and employed your old tailor to make them, who has promised to do them in the neatest and genteelest manner,[7] but it will be the beginning of next week before they are finished as part of the trimmings are to make which will take up some time. I have no objection to your Ormskirk expedition on my return but I fear your clothes will not arrive in your time, however, they shall be sent from hence without delay as soon as finished.

If Captain Potts arrives with you before my return you must write to Blackburn to acquaint them of it, and that you expect Henry and John Feilden whom I promised should go to see the ship.[8] Zachary I believe could wish to be with them, but I bring him to-morrow to Hampstead, when he begins his schooling. I am pleased with the situation, approve much of Mr Alexander, and hope he will be agreeably fixed. I have made him a parlour boarder,[9] which will make it more eligible to him, and I think of greater service to him. We have been much taken up with seeing the amusements of this place, which are various, elegant and some of them expensive, but it would take up too much time to be too particular. As Mr Threlfall returns with me it will be the latter end of next week before I leave London, and I shall have a day or two to spend in Oxford with my uncle. Mr and Mrs Leigh enquire very kindly after you. We have dined with them and they propose to make an excursion to Kirkham during their stay in Lancashire in the course of the summer.

I have a letter from Mr Shepherd. They are agreeably fixed in lodgings at the Hotwells[10] but I fear I shall not be able to return with him into Lancashire, as Mr Threlfall cannot leave home before the middle of next week. You say nothing of Dn Dobson. I wish to hear how he goes on. I heartily wish for his recovery but I fear there is but little hopes. I have given my sister's cottons to Mr Threlfall who has promised to get them done for her. I hope she continues pretty

well. Pray my love to her and Miss Bolton and the rest of my friends
with you. I will write to Cecily at Blackburn. I am,

Dear Will, with my most sanguine
good wishes for you all,
Most affectionately yours,
Thomas Langton

Notes to DDX/190/52. June 24th, 1776

[1] The letting of blood (phlebotomy) was commonly used in treating a vast
variety of illnesses. It was not necessarily performed by a physician. Here
John was being bled before a consultation with the doctor.

[2] Although the Langtons had lost one child because of smallpox, it would
appear that Tom had not been inoculated against the disease. Inoculation was
common, increasing in popularity as the century progressed from its introduction into England by Lady Mary Wortley Montague in about 1717.

[3] A mild laxative was one of the standard procedures in treating smallpox.

[4] The humoral theory of disease, the guiding principle of medieval medicine,
was still, in a modified form, the basis of medical thinking. Although the
original humours of blood, phlegm, black bile and yellow bile had now come
to be seen as all aspects of the one humour, blood, the balance between them
still constituted the idea of health. Thomas Langton is obviously acquainted
with the term, even if he does not use it accurately.

[5] The implication here is that on some previous occasion he had not thought
them justified.

[6] Jinnet Starkie, elder daughter of Dr Starkie of Redvales, near Bury. She was
later to die when upon a visit to Kirkham (see DDX/190/64). Will Langton
married her sister, Mary, in 1791.

[7] Like others aspiring to social distinction, the Langtons had their clothes
made in London when possible. Commissions were given to members of the
family visiting the capital.

[8] The ship would be in the Wyre estuary, at Skippool or Wardleys.

[9] A full boarder.

[10] Another flax merchant consorts with the Quality at a health spa.

(DDX/190/53)
Liverpool   March 1st, 1777.
2 o'th'clock

Dear Will,

I got here last night but rather too late to do anything that evening. I this morning breakfasted with Mr Brock and afterwards we went in quest of Savige,[1] who we found after some time, and I am sorry to say it affected me very much to see him in such a distressed condition[2] and I am afraid he is so habituated to his present dissolute state that he will not easily be reclaimed. What must be done is at present difficult to determine but we are to meet together again this evening to come to some conclusion, but I fear he will scarce meet us. After dinner at Ormskirk we went to drink a glass of wine with Mr Hill and he returns with me on Tuesday to Kirkham, and I understand purposes to be your guest, so you must consult with your aunt and sister and make some provision for it. I do not mean anything very extraordinary but such as your aunt may think sufficient. If you would get a few flookings,[3] might be agreeable.

I have been able to attend little to business today, being chiefly taken up with Savige. I received from G. Brewer £20 and expect to get something more from him on my return. I have signed the letter of licence[4] to Benjamin Davis[5] and it goes up to London again in the morning by the diligence. I received Mr Birley's letter this morning, but have nothing particular to reply to it. I am in haste with proper respects to everybody.

Dear Will,
Your affectionate father,
Thomas Langton

Notes to DDX/190/53. March 1st, 1777

[1] Savige Leech, son of Thomas Langton's late sister, Elizabeth, appeared last in the letters as a boy of some promise working for a mercer and draper in Liverpool.
[2] There is no indication of the 'distressed condition' into which Savige Leech had sunk. Whatever it was, he appeared to be physically weakened by it and, indeed, lived only until 1779, dying at the age of twenty.
[3] Hambleton flookings were a species of freshwater mussel found on the banks of the River Wyre. They were considered a delicacy.
[4] Letters of licence were writings granted to a debtor by his creditors giving him respite and time for payment of his debts.

⁵ This is not the Captain Davis who appears as a co-partner with the Langtons in several ventures. His Christian name was Joseph.

(DDX/190/54)
Kirkham   September 16th, 1777

Dear Will,

I am this morning going to Preston to accompany Mr and Mrs Threlfall to Preston on their return journey to London, and Mrs Leigh whom I have entrusted with the delivery of this letter, is now with us. Captain Storey is expected up at the warehouses¹ today that we shall begin to discharge in the morning, and I hope we shall finish on Saturday. The weather is fine and suitable for the purpose which will greatly forward us. Mr Hornby will finish today.

Mr John Birley is gone to Blackburn and returns on Wednesday. We have got invoices of Captain Thursby's cargo. He has been a month at sea and we may expect him against the following [*]ring, but no account of his passing the Sound.² Messrs Muilmans³ have drawn on us for £1600, and I this day remit Messrs Turner and Co.⁴ £1000 in account thereof. Nothing further occurs worth notice and as the vessel will be discharged the time of your return is left to yourself and you'll let me know when you would have the horses sent you. I have fixed for our Bolton journey but will advise you when we determine on it.

I enclose you a London Bill value £13. 2. 0. as you will have my hat and other things to pay and you may perhaps be short of cash. You may pay it to Mr Philips and account for it on your return. John is gone to Fazakerley again. My proper compliments await all our friends, particularly the family you are with. I am

Dear Will,
Your affectionate father,
Thomas Langton

We have got E. Bradshaw's house end down and are very busy rebuilding it.

[*] Paper torn.

Notes to DDX/190/54. To London, September 16th, 1777

[1] These would be the warehouses at Wardleys.

[2] The Lloyds List published a list of vessels passing the Sound on the Baltic voyage.

[3] Muilmans and Sons were a financial house based on Amsterdam with agents in London. They served many Baltic merchants.

[4] Turner and Threlfall, linen drapers, 170 Fleet Street, London. The Threlfall partner is almost certainly the Mr Threlfall of the letters, domiciled in London.

(DDX/190/55)

Kirkham   July 19th, 1778

Dear Will,

Mr Threlfall[1] has just sent to acquaint me he is setting out for Liverpool, and I refer you to him for what I have to say on Savige Leech's account. He will go with you to him, but it will not suit me at this distance to take his affairs into my hands, were he disposed to adopt that plan. Mr and Mrs Hankinson will be in Liverpool the latter end of the week, and I shall send his balance[2] by him with a release for him to execute.

I find you have wrote to Messrs Collins and given them permission to draw on you for £1200, through the hands of Messrs Muilman and Sons. As this is the case you must be sure to lodge the proper credit with Messrs Turner and Threlfall, but if you could speedily collect a pretty large sum, would have been better to have remitted to Messrs Muilmans immediately. If you can obtain a pretty large bill from Mr Blair in the course of this week would have you enclose it to these gentlemen, as the value will be wanted there, and Messrs Collins and Co. may be advised in [* due] course but if I remember right Messrs Muilmans order was that you were to account with them for the balance of the cargo, and it would be much less trouble to yourselves in the negotiation.[3] Mr Threlfall is waiting, so must conclude. If I can spare time, will write you by the post tonight. Our best wishes attend you. I am,

Dear William,

Most affectionately yours,
Thomas Langton

Mr Threlfall will acquaint you that your
brother Thomas has been very ill, but he
is, I hope, recovering again.

[*] Word omitted.

Notes to DDX/190/55. To Liverpool, July 19th, 1778

[1] Uncle Threlfall, master of the school, also uncle to Savige Leech.
[2] The balance of the legacy due to Savige Leech by his grandfather John
Langton's will of 1762.
[3] This paragraph illustrates the complexity of the bill system under which
firms operated. Defoe had said in 1745 that credit was the basis of trade and
it was still so in 1778.

(DDX/190/56)
Kirkham July 23rd, 1778

Dear Will,

Mr Threlfall[1] returned home last night and brings us account that
you are well but busily employed in your tobacco preparing for the
sale.[2] He gives me a very unpromising account of poor Savige. He
seems bent upon his own destruction, and if he will not hearken to
the advice of his friends, he will soon be reduced to poverty. He has
a very gloomy prospect before him, but as he has brought the whole
upon himself by his own misconduct he must abide by the consequences. I enclose you a release which Mr Hankinson drew up for
him to execute on my paying him the balance due for his moiety of
my father's legacy which amounts to £39. 8. 6. and as Mr Hankinson
is now in Liverpool I wish you would get it executed and settled
during his stay there and it would do well if you would get the
money properly applied in discharge of his debts. William Anderton
is amongst the list of his creditors and you may perhaps assist him
in getting his money.

  The sale of the tobacco at Lancaster was very dull and only two
chaps appeared. Seven hogsheads were only sold at 13s to 15s per

pound[3] and those called in by the sellers, and no better prospect offering they stopped the sale. It was of much inferior quality to ours. Mr Birley sold 2 hogsheads at 18s per pound abating 10/6 at one of the hogsheads. He received the value for them which will go in part of the duties, freight, etc. We paid the prime entry[4] and as soon as we receive the other charges we will render you account of the sales and charges attending it. The samples of the remaining hogsheads would be sent you on Wednesday by the coach for Liverpool which would be there the same evening that you will have got them, otherwise you will apply at the inn the stage comes to for them. We wish you may obtain the price you mention, but we fear you will be disappointed in your expectations. However, the most must be made of it for payment to enable you to pay your acceptances[5] and it is thought for the benefit of the sale to accept payment in bills at three months.[6] You must discount[7] the bills but perhaps bills within a month of one may be accepted in payment of Mr Swarbrick's[8] drafts especially if you take them up some time before they become due. We shall be impatient to know the event of the sale and shall be looking for a letter at Preston on Saturday, unless Captain Briars who is the bearer of this return home tomorrow evening.

We shall be glad to see a state of the wheat account and how the measure turns out. We observe by Mr Yate's letter to Mr Birley by Mr Threlfall that you have remitted £1000 to Messrs Muilman and Sons on that account and were preparing to send Messrs Collins and Co.[9] the account sales by Saturday night's post with a remittance to Messrs Muilmans for the balance at same time. This will be very early and punctual remittance and may make small amends for the loss of the cargo. It may also be a means to establish your credit with Messrs Muilmans, but if you gave them no information of your further intention of such an early remittance, it might do very well to send the balance after you have received advice of their receiving this bill and perhaps some of the bills arising from the sales of the tobacco might answer the purpose. You must be careful before you close the account to get all the expenses and disbursements attending this business (and it would do well to discharge them) that you may have no after charge[10] to make and you will have settled, closed and paid Captain Meyer his freight in full previous thereto. We find you have sold all the sago powder to Messrs Drummond and Son[11] at 15s per pound, to be paid on delivery in good bills at 3 months, and that you were induced to close the sale on Mr Teasdale's recommendation of it. You'll render us the account of it at your first opportunity and remit us the bills for the amount. We are glad to find Mr G. H. Eggers gives you hopes that Captain Williams will be at liberty to depart upon his voyage by Monday next. Pray forward him as much as possible and as the season is so far advanced we hope his own prudence will dictate to him to lose no time in the prosecution of his voyage to prevent a winter's passage. We shall wait with great impatience to hear of his sailing. We should have been very happy to have engaged Messrs Mason and Bourne's[12] vessel if we could have been freed from our engagement for the Bersham. Another time we should be glad to give them a freight for a good ship and of suitable burthen.[13]

The Young Peter, Captain Daniel Hanburgh, sailed from Pillau the 29th of last month, pray advise us when she appears in the Sound List. We send you enclosed bill of lading of the flax and the captain's receipt for 16 decker of matts.[14] We wish soon to hear of her arrival with you. I send you enclosed 2 bills value £60 out of which you will pay

Savige Leech's balance of	£39. 8. 6.
and you must receive from him the charge of the release which Mr Hankinson will acquaint you of and I must desire you will pay Mr Zachary Leafe of Prescot on Mr Crook's account which is in	£24.14. 6
full to the 8th July last and take his receipt	
on the back of the enclosed letter	£64. 2. 6. [sic][15]

and you may charge me with the balance which shall be sent you.

You'll send me the release by Mr Hankinson if you get it executed, but do not pay any part of the money before you get the release signed by him.[16] All your friends join me in our best wishes for you. Your Uncle Feilden is now at Blackpool or Lytham along with Mr R. Birley. They came to go down Wyre on Tuesday on a fishing along with a party from hence but their success was bad and the weather most unseasonable. They went this morning to Blackpool and Lytham and propose to return here this evening. Your brother was of the party. The ladies are gone from hence today to pay [*] to Captain Bones. Your brother and some others are gone with them. The day proves favourable for them. Your sister and he set out from hence on Sunday for Fazackerley. They stay all night at Ormskirk. Perhaps you may contrive to meet them there, which would be very agreeable. Your sister will be with Miss Heskeths,

who accompany her to Fazackerley. From this you will surmise with
good reason that your brother Thomas is much better. I wish I could
say he was perfectly well, but I think him mending apace or I should
not have given Cecily leave to have left him.[17] I am,

Dear William,
Yours most affectionately,
Thomas Langton

Charles Caldwell and Co.[18] on B. Burton Forbes and Gregory[19] 10.0.0.
John Watson and Sons[20] on William Rawlinson   50.0.0.
                                                                      60.0.0.

I will give you the particulars of the flax by the Young Peter in my
next.

[*] Paper torn.

Notes to DDX/190/56. To Liverpool, July 23rd, 1778

[1] Again Uncle Threlfall from Kirkham.
[2] At John Owen Parr's warehouse in Liverpool.
[3] A hogshead was a liquid measure, usually about fifty gallons, and also the cask containing it.
[4] Prime entry was an entry of two thirds of a ship's cargo liable to duty made before discharge on which an estimate of duty was paid.
[5] Will must be careful to see he has enough ready money to pay the bills drawn on him in the credit chain. An acceptance was the agreement of the drawee of a bill of exchange to carry out the order of the drawer. After acceptance the drawee was known as the acceptor.
[6] The bill must be honoured at the end of three months.
[7] Discount here means that Will must deduct an amount from the face value of the bills for cashing-in previous to the date of maturity.
[8] Mr Swarbrick was the Langton agent in Jamaica.
[9] As this seems to be a general cargo that Will is discharging, Messrs Collins may be the Collins and Co. of 2 Lower Thames Street, London, dealers in rum. Will was to send by post to the firm so it was not likely to be in Liverpool.
[10] This is not a technical insurance term. It merely means that there will be no further charge later.
[11] As sago comes neither from America nor Russia, the powder must either have been bought from a trader or shipped by the Langtons from the Indies. There is no evidence of such venturing, so the sago must be assumed bought from another merchant. John Drummond of 39 Stanley Street is given in the 1790 Liverpool directory as tobacconist and household broker.
[12] Mason Bourne, timber merchants of 27 Mason Street, Liverpool.
[13] A ship of suitable tonnage.
[14] A matt was a bag made of matting to hold flax, sugar, coffee etc. Decker is probably an alternative to 'dicker', which was used to describe bundles of ten

hides, and here probably means bundles of ten matts. It was an acceptable alternative to dicker but was not usually applied to flax. There were many regional variations of commercial terms.

[15] Thomas Langton wrongly adds this up to £64 2s. 6d., in spite of his insistence upon Accounts.

[16] The release was a form of receipt signifying the transaction was completed.

[17] Cecily, the only girl, had to act in *loco parentis* to her youngest brother. On the other hand she was allowed to go on long visits and was not expected to stay at home all the time.

[18] This was the firm of C. Caldwell and Co., bankers, of 37 Paradise Street, Liverpool.

[19] B. Burton Forbes and Gregory were merchants of 17 Aldermanbury, London.

[20] Linen draper of 135 Oxford Street, London.

(DDX/190/64)
(February 7th, 1780)

Dear Will,

I am most sorry to say that Miss Starkie[1] is now no more. Judge of my situation. I am distressed beyond measure and am afraid of the consequences for my dear Cecily. There is now no occasion for Dr Hay's attendance. If I and my whole family are so far distressed what must poor Mrs Starkie feel when she receives the fatal account. I am in the greatest distress and wish you would immediately proceed to Blackburn. Take a Post Chaise and desire your Aunt Feilden will come immediately back with you. Do not lose any time and leave a proper person to await Mrs Starkie's coming but I hope you may get back to Preston as soon as she can almost get there. If you can go with the greater expedition take 4 horses. Your own discretion must direct you. I am almost distracted for fear of my dear Cecily.[2]

I am yours
T. Langton

Notes to DDX/190/64 (following 56).
This letter is unheaded and undated and obviously written in great distress.

[1] Jinnet Starkie was the daughter of Dr Joseph Starkie of Redvales, near Bury. Will Langton was to marry her sister Mary in 1791. The name is spelt variously: Starky (as in Will's genealogical notes); Starkie (as here); Starkey

as in the following notice in the *Manchester Mercury* of 22 February 1780:
'On Monday sen'night died at Kirkham of putrid sore throat and Fever
[?diphtheria] Miss Starkey, daughter of the late Jos. Starkey of Redvales, near
Bury, Esq.' This would date the letter 7 February. I am indebted to Mrs R.
B. Hirst of Bury Reference Library for tracing this information.
² Thomas Langton's concern for his daughter is very clear. He is also mindful
of the greater grief which the dead girl's mother will experience.

(DDX/190/57)
Lancaster, September 18th, 1780

Dear Will,

We got well here last night but found a very crowded town, chiefly
Sir Thomas Egerton's¹ friends. I dined with them at the Ordinary
but left them very soon after dinner and retired to the ladies. We got
lodgings next door to the King's Arms. We had many visitors, scarce
one of the gentlemen but called of the ladies. The election was carried
on very smoothly, and without the least thought of any opposition
that the call of the freeholders on the part of Mr Stanley² was quite
unnecessary. If there had been any contest you would have had a
messenger this morning. You will learn every particular from your
neighbours. I have scarce time to write, as we are preparing to
prosecute our journey to Kendal this evening. The ladies are very
well and in high spirits. Miss Bassnet begs her best respects to you,
and orders me to acquaint you that she is highly delighted and quite
in spirits and as merry as you can conceive. We met Mr Hill here.
He will come to see you on our return. I hear nothing worth
troubling you with. Nothing talked about but the business of the
day, and all quite happy. Sir Thomas first offered his services and
was followed by Mr Stanley and after the return was made they
returned their thanks to the freeholders. Sir Thomas was short but
very concise. Mr Stanley went upon a larger ground, and acquitted
himself pretty well.

Mr Feilden is now with us. He desires you will prevail upon Mr
Venables to go to Blackburn next Saturday evening, as he is going
into Cheshire on Sunday and would accompany him if their route
agreed, but he wishes to see him, and begs he will contrive to be there
on Saturday night. My horse will be ready for him.

The whole party join in best wishes to you and all friends. I am,

Dear Will,
Yours etc.,
Thomas Langton

I will write you from Keswick.

Notes to DDX/190/57. September 18th, 1780

[1] Sir Thomas Egerton was a Tory and represented Lancashire from 1772 to 1784 when he was raised to the peerage as Earl of Wilton and Viscount Grey of Wilton. During the American War he raised a regiment of Fencible Infantry called the Royal Lancashire Volunteers.

[2] The 1780 election was called on the death of the Hon. T. Stanley, who had been Whig member of Parliament for Lancashire from 1776 to 1779. He was the second son of Lord Strange, himself Lancashire M.P. from 1741 to 1771. The Mr Stanley of the letter was Thomas Stanley, a representative of the younger branch of the House of Derby. He was the son of the Rector of Winwick. He was to represent the county until 1812.

(DDX/190/58)
Ambleside   September 21st, 1780

Dear Will,

You would receive my letter by William Parke from Lancaster. I had scarce time to drop you a line from thence, we were in such a hurry and confusion. We set forward on our journey about 2 o'th'clock on Monday even. Pretty fine afternoon but after the agreeable entertainment at Lancaster we could not pursue our journey with the spirit we ought to have done. We drank tea at Burton[1] which took up too much of our time and it was after 6 before we left that place. Nothing to be seen here except a pretty site of a house of a Mr Pearson's. From hence we went by Milnthorpe with the hopes of seeing a pleasant country, but we passed by Levens Park[2] and Sizergh Hall[3] too late to partake of any pleasure in the views as we passed along. We however, though late, got to Kendal. We took up our quarters at the Lion and the ladies immediately went to Alderman Gurnal's. We supped with him there and breakfasted with them also in the morning and afterwards took a view of Kendal. I assure you we made a handsome parade,[4] many enquiries made after us and not a little gazing, but we gave them fine liberty to feast their eyes, and about 11 o'th'clock we mounted our palfreys again, agreeably accompanied with two Miss Gurnals and their brother, intending to pursue our route to Windermere Lake. Bowness was the place of rendezvous where we arrived safe, ordered dinner and a boat to carry us to Mr English's island.[5] Here we regaled ourselves with the beauties of the place as well as delicious fruits etc., but I do not mean to enter upon the descriptive part of our tour. I leave that to Mr Parr whom we have made treasurer and secretary and keeps a regular diary which will be published by subscription upon our return and may bring in some cash towards defraying the expense of our tour.[6] After dinner we took a boat and sailed upwards of 4 miles to the head of the lake and within 2 miles of Ambleside the place we intended to sleep at. Met with tolerable accommodations and a communicative landlord.

In the morning, Wednesday the 20th, instead of pursuing our direct route to Keswick we were induced to turn out of our road to view the lakes of Coniston and Esthwaite and I must say we were amply repaid by the agreeable prospects which were varied from every hill we ascended.[7] Nothing transpired from the ladies but heavenly and glorious epithets and astonishment at the tremendous and romantic scenes we viewed. We dined at Hawkshead,[8] were elegantly entertained there and reasonably. We met a pretty red haired girl and it was with difficulty we could get J. Parr from the place, and at last was forced to leave him. This was high entertainment for the ladies and afforded us a good hearty laugh. In the evening we went to view the waterfall at Sir Michael le Fleming's[9] as we had done the waterfalls at Ambleside in the morning. We slept again at Ambleside and I now lay down my pen as the post is going from hence to resume it again on our arrival at Keswick.

We are now arrived at Keswick. We got here to dinner after a very agreeable ride though not without a little rain, but the beauty of the country we passed along fully compensated for every other inconveniency. We found Mr Standen here and his party. Their stay was but short for they passed us at Ambleside this morning, though unknowing, and after dinner went forward to Whitehaven. A party of gentlemen and ladies were dining with Mr Pocklington at his house upon the island[10] that prevented our going there but we took a boat with 4 oars and sailed round Derwentwater Lake and are just returned. Drank tea at our inn and everyone sat down in the same room, the ladies at one table, and your brother, Mr Parr and myself at another writing letters. After this business is over, we are to concert a plan for tomorrow's excursion but it will in some measure depend upon the weather. If a fine day (with which we have been hitherto favoured) we propose to see the top of Skiddaw, the highest hill in the country, afterwards to take a cold repast with us in the boat to the head of the lake, dine there, and go into Borrowdale, another favourite excursion for all parties of pleasure who visit these rural and romantic mountains.[11] I suppose the following day, Saturday, may probably bring us to Askham,[12] but what route we shall take from thence, and how long our stay may be there I can not say. The ladies are so highly entertained with their excursion, it will be with difficulty I shall get them home again. The horses have all behaved remarkably well, but none more so than Little Orpheus, who will, I make no doubt, go through the journey very well. This I am sure will please Cornelius. We very often think of you and wish you with us. We are happy in our party and I only want to hear from you what is doing at home. I shall expect to have a letter from you this evening and shall wait the post's arrival about 11 o'th'clock before I retire.

I wish you may be able to advise me of some or all the ships' safe arrival, or whether you have any further account from Mr Threlfall relative to his Lancashire journey. I shall also expect to hear from you while I stay at Askham. I suppose we may probably leave there on Tuesday that a letter put into the office in Sunday evening will find me there, and may in some measure govern us as to the lengthening our tour, or returning directly back again. I fear you have no more promising accounts from the Navy Office.[13] As Mr Hornby will be now returned he may probably give you some more interesting intelligence if he will be open and free. If any letters come for me you may open them as Zachary may perhaps write on this subject.

Miss Bassnet and Cecily both present their best love to you and wish you could transport yourself to us for a few days. They say it would enliven the scene. We are so happy and pleased with our excursion that we shall certainly proceed from Carlisle to Gretna Green.

I will write you again from Askham. In the meantime, you must pay our respectful compliments to all our friends and the whole party join me in our sanguine good wishes for yourself, Cornelius and little Tom. I am, Dear Will,

Most affectionately yours,
Thomas Langton

I cannot let this letter go without assuring my dear Will that I have not had a wish ungratified since I left K–M except for the addition of his company—we are all well, astonished and delighted beyond description. You may be assured I will write to you from Askham. (Postscript in Cecily's hand but unsigned.)[14]

Notes to DDX/190/58. September 21st, 1780

[1] Burton in Kendal.

[2] Levens Hall had passed into the Grahame family as the result of a wager in 1692. Sir James Grahame engaged the king's gardener, who had recently redesigned the gardens in Hampton Court, to lay out the Levens Hall gardens and park, and his design obtains today. The house developed from a fortified manor into a mansion house with additions in the Elizabethan and Jacobean periods.

[3] Sizergh Castle, like its neighbour Levens Hall, started as a fortified pele tower and the pele still stands, now flanked by a great hall and later additions. The Stricklands have been in unbroken possession and their adherence to the Stuart cause led them to share the exile of James II in France. The gardens were laid out in their present form in the latter half of the eighteenth century. Both Levens and Sizergh had obviously been noted by the Langton party as worth seeing.

[4] The parade, when the fashionable promenaded with a certain self-consciousness, was very much a feature of eighteenth-century gracious living. It is significant that Thomas Langton comments on the 'gazing' of the natives and the many enquiries which were made after the well-dressed strangers. He obviously felt his party socially superior to the general populace.

[5] Now called Belle Isle, this is the largest island in Windermere Lake. West in his *Guide* put two stations, or viewpoints, on it and a visit was compulsory for any tourists in quest of the picturesque. Wordsworth was to speak disparagingly of Mr English and the house he built on the island. He went on to speak of Mr English's house as 'the first house that was built in the Lake District for the sake of the beauty of the country'. The house was built in 1774, and as it is circular, must have been of considerable interest to tourists.

[6] This diary does not appear to have been published. No reference is made to it in the Langton papers. The Parrs were father and son of the Liverpool merchant firm of John Owen Parr & Co. DDX/190/65 is addressed to Will at the Parr warehouse.

[7] West's *Guide*, published in 1778 and the first book written with the express purpose of helping tourists make the most of their visit to this area of mountains and lakes, began the tour in the Coniston district, having approached over the sands of Morecambe Bay, a common route at the time. We do not know what induced the Langton party to make the detour from the direct route to Keswick.

[8] It is interesting to remember that Wordsworth would be a pupil at Hawkshead grammar school at the time of the Langton visit.

[9] Rydal Hall. The two waterfalls in the grounds were much visited. Wordsworth was to dismiss them with the tart utterance, 'The waterfalls of Rydal are pointed out to everyone'.

¹⁰ Vicar's Island in Derwentwater, another favourite vantage point. The house was owned by a Mr Pocklington who, in emulation of Mr English, in Wordsworth's words, 'played strange pranks by his buildings and plantations upon Vicar's Island, which his admiration, such as it was, of the country, and probably a wish to be a leader in a new fashion, had led him to purchase'.

¹¹ Thomas Langton had made no mention of the scenery of Ireland when he visited there in 1768. Now he was in the fashion, and had learnt what to see and how to see it.

¹² Askham Hall was the home of the Boltons who had previously lived for a time near Kirkham. They were relations of Thomas Langton through his cousin Tabitha. See letters dated 2 August 1771 and 6 December 1772, et al.

¹³ The Navy Office delayed payment of the 1780 order until 1781, although the Hornby account was cleared earlier.

¹⁴ Cecily gives the reaction of the typical Laker of her day to the splendours of the Lake District.

(DDX/190/61)

Askham   September 25th, 1780

Dear Will,

I hope you would receive my letter from Keswick. The beauties of that place kept us longer there than we expected. We did not leave it before yesterday. We set out early and got here to dinner. We found Mr and Mrs Bolton and Miss Gorst[1] very well and had been expecting us some days. We are all very well. Our horses behave extraordinarily and will tempt us to lengthen our tour. At present we come to no resolution further than seeing Carlisle on Wednesday from which place I will write you when we may probably have fixed our route. As I mentioned to you before I will not enter into the descriptive part of our tour; that you will see when you read our journal at our return. We reached the highest summits of Skiddaw Saturday, went through the Vale of Borrowdale to view the stupendous rocks where the eagle builds his nests[2] and round the lakes of both Derwentwater and Bassenthwaite water. The poor girls were on horseback upwards of seven hours without any refreshment and came back sufficiently tired.

I must now acknowledge the receipt of your letter. I sent to the office at Penrith for it last night. It brought me the pleasing account of the arrival of the Baltic convoy at Hull and that the Maria, John and Mary and Catharine were got safe there. This was very acceptable as it frees us from any apprehensions of loss by the fire at Cronstadt[3] of which I was in some fear on account of the Catharine. This flax will no doubt be immediately forwarded by the canal,[4] and I hope you will have both Davis and Holland in Wyre very soon and I hope to find that you have made some progress in the sale of their cargoes on my return.

I find you received the haunch of venison, but it gives me pain it should not prove so good as could be wished. Mr Bolton is rather unhappy about it and I wish I had not given him the particular account you sent me. Appearances to be sure was against it, but from the time of its being killed, there was no doubt of its being good. We had a haunch of the same venison today, and I must say it was the best I ever eat. Indeed the trip we made in it was a convincing proof. I think the haunch weighed 22½ lbs and was 3 inches thick of fat.

We were very kindly received here though so numerous a party, and as we stay a few days it will relieve Cecily and Miss Bassnet a good deal. They are very anxious to lengthen our tour which must convince you we are very well and in good spirits.

I have just now recollected that Friday next is Michaelmas Day and our Vestry meeting,[5] which Mr France[6] proposed to attend and Mr Rigg and he promised to dine with me. If they come you must make an apology for me and entertain them in the best manner you can, but as I am abroad Mr Shepherd may probably engage them. You will however make my best respects to them and all my friends. We never forget you when we come to evening potation but drink the friends at home. I find Mr J. Hornby has joined the other party and that they will be at home before us. I wish I could hear good news from the Navy Office.

Miss Bassnet and Cecily beg to be particularly remembered to you and so does Jack and Mr Parr. We are happy in our party which is pleasing. My best wishes attend you, Cornelius, Tom and all my friends. This family all join me in the same good wishes.

I am, dear Will,
Most affectionately yours,
Thomas Langton

Notes to DDX/190/61 following 58. September 25th, 1780

[1] See note 18, DDX/190/21. The Bolton ancestral home was Askham Hall, near Penrith, today the residence of Lord Lonsdale. Miss Gorst was Mrs Bolton's sister.

[2] The stupendous rocks of Borrowdale were a feature of many writings about the Lake District. West in his guide draws attention to the haunts of eagles and Thomas Gray, some years earlier, was so alarmed by the menacing splendours of the scenery that he would proceed no further than Grange in Borrowdale for fear of avalanches.

[3] Cronstadt was the port of St Petersburg.

[4] Thomas Langton was now taking canal transport as a matter of course. The goods would go via the Aire Navigation and the Yorkshire end of the Leeds and Liverpool canal to Kildwick and would eventually reach Kirkham via the Rufford branch of the Lancashire end of the Leeds and Liverpool and the remains of the Douglas Navigation to the Ribble crossing from Tarleton to Freckleton. There would have to be a considerable road haulage *en route*, but it would be a quicker way than by sea round Scotland. (See Mike Clarke, *The Leeds and Liverpool Canal*, Carnegie Press, 1990.) The canal was not completed until 1816.

[5] The select vestry at Kirkham parish church was known as the Thirtymen, two thirtymen representing each of the fifteen townships of the parish.

[6] Mr France represented Little Eccleston and lived at Little Eccleston Hall and later at Rawcliffe Hall. He is not recorded as attending the meeting.

(DDX/190/62)

Kirkham   October 10th, 1780

Dear Will,

This, I make no doubt, will find you safe arrived in London. I hope you and your colleagues had an agreeable journey and found all your friends in London well. I got well home on Saturday evening. Mr J. Birley and Mr W. Yate[1] who came here on Sunday set off yesterday to attend the Fair at Lancaster, and W. Birley and J. Parr are gone this morning to Wyre in hopes of seeing Captain Davis come up the river, but I fear they will be disappointed as there will scarce be water sufficient. Captain Holland is arrived at Whitehaven the 6th instant. I think he may stand a chance of getting in today and coming up the river, if he meets with a good pilot. If they return from Wyre before the post goes out I will let you know whether they get up or not. You must enquire of Messrs Dickinson and Lloyd[2] about the canvas shipped them by the London, Captain Evans, and whether they have got it into their possession. Messrs Birkbeck Blakes and Co.[3] advised us of its lying there and you'll see that it is properly delivered. You'll acquaint Mr Gale[4] of the Providence's arrival at Whitehaven, on her arrival in our river and after the delivery of her cargo we will send him the needful to recover our over insurance. We shall forward him a few bales of canvas as soon as we can for sale. Probably the next coasters will take it to Liverpool. We have got by last post Bill of Lading of 235 bobbins 12 heads flax shipped by the Esther, Captain Harley, from Petersburg[5] for Hull which was left out by the Providence. The remainder of the flax lying at Petersburg is all bought [*] in for London account on speculation at 24 Rubles, a high price indeed.[6]

We have an order from Messrs Hartley of Whitehaven for 136 Bolts canvas for exportation. No sloop offering from hence, it must go by Liverpool and we shall be forced to send it by the canal.[7] Messrs Alexander Anderson and Davidson[8] advise the sale of the Navy Bill[9] at 11% discount, net amount £990 19 0 sold. They advise to have delivered to Messrs Birkbeck Blake and Co. a quantity of canvas, say 20 Bolts No. 6 the 2nd instant and on the 6th instant further 15 Bolts No. 2, 10 ditto 3, 8 ditto 4, 7 ditto 5, 15 ditto 6, and 10 ditto 7,[10] so that I hope you will have opportunity of running of our canvas in this period without reducing the price which you should avoid doing if possible unless you can sell on short credit which you should endeavour to do and also bring our different agents to sell at six months credit, as the value will be then wanted against our next importation. J. Hornby tells me this morning that he thinks there will be a demand for canvas in London this winter for private sale. The demand only comes on in November and generally holds till March or April. It would be very eligible if you would agree with any person for the delivery of a quantity of canvas without going through our agents' hands and subjecting us to the payment of their high charges and commissions. Mr Threlfall may probably recommend you to some merchant etc. I wish you may get the canvas on hand of at present prices which being Government canvas[11] should be done if possible. I wonder A. A. & D[12] makes no progress in sales. I apprehend their Scotch canvas prejudices the sale of ours. Press Messrs Dickinson and Lloyd to make speedy sales. I do not remember their rendering sales of the last parcel they sold. The Industry, Captain Wark, from Dantzig is arrived at Hull on board whom was 4 casks of ashes[13] shipped by Roberts Balfour and Smithson but was taken by a French privateer[14] (and ransomed) of 14 guns about 60 leagues from the land and arrived at Hull the 5th instant. The Captain, not having proper instructions, has ransomed the ship etc. for near £1500 more than they are worth, having given

£4500 for the ransom and the ship and cargo is not worth more than £3000 that probably nothing will be done until advice is received of the safe arrival of the hostage and then probably both ship and cargo may be sold on account of the captors. This is an unparalleled case with us, and we must [†] it and conform to what the proprietors of the cargo do but you will acquaint Mr Anderson Junior with it as he made our insurances and if the cargo is sold we shall be obliged to purchase the ashes again as we are near out.

We have a letter this post from Mr Thomas Stefanelli of Leghorn with an order for 60 Bolts canvas to be shipped by a vessel from Liverpool but that you may better understand the mode on which he grounds his order and likewise his proposal for future transactions, I enclose you his letter and would have you call upon Mr Thomas Lansdown (No. 139 Cheapside) to know whether he will accept our draft for the amount of this canvas after the Bounty of discount use[15] taken off, agreeable to the proposal in his letter and whether he will in future stand guaranty on any goods we may send Mr Stefanelli. It may be proper to enquire very particularly into his character and stability[16] which Mr Lansdown will readily inform you if he is a person worth our future notice and we waive to give him any reply till we have your answer by return of post when you will return us his letter.

You will find J. Parr is still with us, but nothing further said or done about your future connections.[17] I presume he returns tomorrow. I have been busy about your house today but will give you a more particular account next post, as I have neither room on my paper nor leisure to do it, and you must excuse all inaccuracies as I have not time to revise what I write.

Miss Patten is very well and in good spirits. I am taking the whole party to the warehouse in the morning after breakfast to weigh them to see what improvements a wholesome country air is capable of providing. She begs her duty and proper respects to every one of her friends and will write soon. Miss Bassnet joins in the same request with Cecily but particularly in her best love to yourself, and Miss Patten says and mine too Sir. This evening we celebrate your brother Tom's birthday being 10 years old. He is got clever again and goes to school. I suppose you would surprize Zachary much at first sight. My best wishes await you both. We received his letter this post. I expect to write you again next post and shall hope to hear from you. I am with proper compliments to all my friends,

Dear Will,
Most affectionately yours,
(not signed)

The William is got on this side Stanah
Lane End and Herbert about Burn
Naze,[18] that we are preparing for discharging tomorrow. Holland does not
yet appear.

[*] Paper torn.
[†] Indecipherable.

Notes to DDX/190/62. To London, October 10th, 1780

[1] John Birley, the Langton partner, married Margaret Yate of Liverpool in
1776. William Yate was his brother-in-law.
[2] Messrs Dickinson and Lloyd were linen drapers on the Royal Exchange.
[3] Birkbeck Blake and Co. were merchants of 9 Great St Helens, London.
[4] Richard Gale, 6 Ironmonger Lane, London, warehouseman.
[5] Petersburg flax was made up in bundles of twelve, nine or six heads, which
were called bobbins, and they were tied up with strips, each sort having a
stated number. Twelve head was the best, and six head the worst, quality. (See
A. J. Warden, *The Linen Trade*, 1864, reprinted 1967.)
[6] Thomas Langton used both the Roman Ru and the Cyrillic Py to represent
the two first letters of Ruble. From 1733 to 1803 the Ruble averaged 30–40
pence.
[7] Thomas Langton here prefers a coastal vessel for the journey to Liverpool
if one were possible, perhaps because of the canal tolls, or because he was
more accustomed to using the coastal service.
[8] Merchants, of 56 Lothbury, London.
[9] Navy Bills were sold on the stock exchange and in other financial transactions.
[10] These references are to the seven qualities of sailcloth. A bolt was a measure
of cloth, but was not uniform in application.
[11] As government canvas the sailcloth would have to conform to certain
standards.
[12] Alexander Anderson and Davidson, merchants, 56 Lothbury, London.
[13] Danzig had long been a leading exporter of ashes for the bleaching process
in cloth production. Wood ash was put in pots and leached with water to give
a ley which was rubbed on the cloth. The potassium carbonate thus formed
was known as potash. Pearl ash was a partly purified form of potash.
[14] The French and American privateers preyed upon British ships wherever
they could. This necessitated the British ships' sailing in convoy for protection, but they were nevertheless vulnerable.
[15] From the 1740s bounties, or subsidies, had been paid upon British linen

exported. The Act establishing these bounties had been renewed in 1778. The subsidies continued until 1832.

[16] It was good practice to establish whether a prospective client was 'sufficient', i.e. a sound proposition. The reputation of men of business was crucial in the enquiries made prior to accepting a new client.

[17] There is no indication as to what these future connections might be. It is possible that Will was contemplating marriage, as he was building a house and his father mentions it immediately after the reference to the future connections. As J. Parr seems to be involved we may assume the intended bride was a connection of the Liverpool merchant family with whom the Langtons dealt. Will did not marry until 1791, and his wife was Mary Starkie or Starky, daughter of Dr Joseph Starkie of Redvales, near Bury, sister of Cecily Langton's friend Jinnet.

[18] Stanah Lane End and Burn Naze are points on the Wyre estuary on the way to the quays at Wardleys and Skippool.

(DDX/190/63)

Kirkham   October 22nd, 1780

Dear Will,

I wrote you last post a few lines under cover of a frank covering several enclosures, but had scarce time to do it as the post was waiting at the door in the dark. I now send you Captain Holland's Protest[1] attested by himself, his mate and boatswain, which will certify the Underwriters of his coming North About,[2] and save us the trouble and expense of getting a fresh affidavit, which is no trifle as we have no magistrate near us.[3] You will deliver it to Mr Gale and after he has done with it, he may deliver it back to you as it will be wanted at Hull, but you must acquaint Mr Gale that we expect there will be a General Average[4] for the loss of the anchor and cable, and that we shall be called upon for our proportion which our Underwriters must make good to us and we shall make out our account for the Over Insurance.[5]

We have Messrs Anderson's account of the insurance on the Nancy, Captain Davis, for Jamaica. This Vessel is still at Lancaster[6] but expected to sail soon and take the convoy.[7] Mr Swarbrick[8] only left Preston this morning with his wife for Manchester and on Tuesday morning they proceed from thence for London in the diligence that he cannot be expected to arrive in London before

Thursday. He will go to the Swan, Lad Lane, and wishes to see you there as soon as you can with conveniency. If you enquire there you will learn what time the Manchester diligence gets in, and if he can meet with good lodgings near you he may probably engage them.

Mr Wilson wrote to know the date of his will. Please to acquaint Mr Swarbrick it is the 17th October instant and not the 18th. I wish he may be in time for the convoy. I am afraid the vessel will be too late.

We have Dickinson and Lloyds accounts sales, which shall be examined and we hope they will retain the freight to make good on the damages. You'll press them to finish sales of the last eight bales, and we shall furnish them with a fresh supply. Cloth comes in very fluently, and we must find a vent for it. Our fabric will improve as greater attention will be paid to the weavers.[9] We hope Mr Gale will be able to dispose of the quantity he proposed. It will be all government canvas and he may depend of its being good. His exerting himself at this time will oblige us and bring some advantage to himself. You would see by our letter to him that we had great complaints against the quality of the whole cargo by the Providence. We think little attention was paid to our interest by the House at St Petersburg.[10] The damage on the flax by Captain Holland was great but it will not amount to an average,[11] neither will the William's though it was rather more, but we have got this latter estimated by William Brown and Thomas Adamson, and shall draw up a State of the Loss from their valuation,[12] from which we hope Mr Anderson will recover the loss from the £300 insured on the profits.[13]

We observe you have got the warrant from Mr Bromley for 50 Bolts canvas same as last proportion and that the same will be sent down to Deptford.[14] We wish you may get it immediately surveyed and a Bill taken out for the whole so as to close all warrants finally. The value of the Bill will be much wanted.[15] The writings for our purchase[16] were sent by Mr Nabb from Preston yesterday to Mr Santor (Mr Hankinson's agent) ready engrossed, and I have a letter from Mr Smith this post to desire they may be sent to Mr Allen his attorney as Mr Goring who is one of the parties and lives in the country will be in town about the middle of the week when all the parties was to be ready to execute them. I would have you to call of Mr Santor and desire he will wait upon Mr Allen with the deeds and fix a time when they are to be executed. You may perhaps go with him at the time and if everything is done requisite to the perfecting of the title, you may pay the purchase money and receive the deeds, and Mr Santor will take care that you have all the old deeds delivered to you according to the abstract of schedule which Mr Wilson would send him. For this purpose I enclose you a Preston

Bank Bill[17] on Denison, value £600
and our draft on Anderson and Davidson for £260

which will make the full amount of the purchase money. I have not advised Messrs A & D that you must mention it to them and get both Bills accepted before you pay them, unless you can get bank bills for the value,[18] but I would not allow Mr Denison any discounts so do not ask him for them, as the bill will speedily be in cash.[19] They expect to have an allowance of interest on the purchase money or the rents till Whitsuntide, but as Mr Hankinson and my sister are now here and will stay a few days I will talk to him about it and will write you again on Tuesday which will be in time. I will then send you Mr Smith's letter.

I delivered your letter to Mr Hankinson. He is fully apprized of the case you represent and bids me tell you that Justice and not Humanity must be the rule of his conduct. He says Mr Gornall has no plea for his demand and that the other persons have fully authenticated their claims. I am sorry for Mr Gornall but I find he has no prospect of getting anything.

I enclose you sundry receipts for Duchy rents[20] for Mr John Birley and Mr Thomas Birley and Mr Hankinson. They desire you will apply for them at the Duchy Office[21] which the enclosed handbill will direct you in and purchase for them their several quit rents.[22] You must pay the money and take their leases which you will bring down with you. Mr Thomas Birley's may be included in one lease. Dr Clayton has also applied to me to send his receipt for same purpose. You shall have it in my next.

Pray when do you think of returning? I do not by mentioning this press your return sooner than you wish it. I will write to Mr Feilden tomorrow about his son. I have not room to say more only my best wishes await you.

I am, Dear Will,

Yours affectionately,
Thomas Langton

We wish you may succeed in Mr Gale's
sale of 200 Bolts Navy canvas. Don't

scruple to allow 10% discount for
money rather than reduce the price for
Navy canvas. If you find any persons
selling at reduced prices learn their
names and advise us.

Notes to DDX/190/63. To London, October 22nd, 1780

[1] When insurance was claimed for loss at sea the ship's captain had to submit a Protest or statement that he had followed the accepted route and had sailed in convoy.

[2] Captain Holland is stating that he took the route around the north of Scotland on his way to join the convoy at Hull.

[3] It is interesting to note that none of the Kirkham burgesses was of sufficient standing in the county to be appointed to the Bench.

[4] In marine insurance the term 'general average' refers to the division of liability between the interested parties, i.e. all who have an interest in the voyage, of any sacrifices made or expenditure incurred for the common good. Here it would seem that the share of the cost of the anchor and cable which had been lost on the voyage was to be met by the insurance though originally general average was independent of insurance and probably preceded it.

[5] Over insurance is defined in the *Digest of Law of Shipping and Marine Insurance*, Newson, London, 1883, as: 'If in the case of an open policy on goods or freight the goods be over insured, i.e. in excess of the interest of the insured, a portion of the premium corresponding to the excess must be returned. This is generally termed a return for *over insurance*'.

[6] This vessel appears in the 1780 archive of Gillows, cabinet-makers, of Lancaster. They were using the ship to export furniture to the colonies.

[7] The American convoy assembled at Portsmouth.

[8] Mr Swarbrick was the agent for the Gillows as well as the Langtons.

[9] This is the only reference in the letters to the workers.

[10] Importers were at the mercy of the agents in the countries where they traded. Tom Langton was to be sent to Riga as a prospective partner in an export firm there (Thorley Morison) to oversee the Kirkham firm's interests as well as to further his own career.

[11] An average is not related to the general average discussed above. It refers to the amount insured, and here the implication is that the firm undertook to stand a certain amount before any claim. The loss did not exceed that amount.

[12] It was necessary to have two independent assessors when a claim was made.

[13] This refers to the over insurance mentioned above.

[14] The firm provided canvas to the dockyards at both Deptford and Woolwich, but more frequently to the former.

[15] The Langton firm was experiencing a cash flow crisis. 1780 was a difficult year for them, though it did not prevent them from embarking upon several new ventures such as the tour of the Lakes and the acquisition of property in London.

[16] This purchase was probably the London premises in which Zachary was to

operate as a warehouseman dealing in Manchester goods and as a merchant. His premises were in Bread Street.

[17] The Langtons used banks as well as the bills drawn on other merchants. Banking in the north was in its infancy. Denison was the London house guaranteeing the Preston bill.

[18] Will was to establish that the bills would be honoured when he presented them.

[19] As the bill would be soon encashed and therefore at the end of its journey, there was no necessity for Will to ask for a discount.

[20] The Duchy of Lancaster is still an extensive property owner in Lancashire.

[21] The Duchy office was situated in the Savoy.

[22] A quit rent was a rent usually of small amount paid by a freeholder or a copyholder in lieu of services which might be required of him.

(DDX/190/59)
Kirkham   October 24th, 1780

Dear Will,

I wrote you on Sunday the 22nd instant enclosing you two Bills for £860 at 14 days date which was intended to go to Messrs Goring and Smith for the purchase of our lands from them when the writings are settled and every requisite duly performed which Mr Santor is to take care of as he has Messrs Hankinson and Wilson's directions about it and you must see him to fix what is to be done and when you are to go with him to see the writings executed and to pay the money. He has an abstract of what writings or deeds are to be delivered you or convenants entered into to produce any when required which cannot with propriety be parted with, which Mr Santor will be a proper judge of, and which Messrs H. & W. will point out to him. In regard to the interest money claimed by Messrs Goring and Smith, I proposed to allow them interest (after 4% per annum) on the purchase money from Candlemas last till it was paid, but as the affair had been protracted through them or their agent Mr Barcroft beyond the time which was expected, it appears very hard to pay it, and by the enclosed letter they propose to accept the Whitsuntide rent in lieu of it, by which I suppose they mean half a year's rent though it will be only about 3 months from Candlemas to Whitsuntide. What the rents are called I do not know, but you have a fair plea to renounce the interest as they were untenanted at

Candlemas and will not this year make above the half rent. However you must settle it with them on the best terms you can and at the worst comply with their proposal in the enclosed letter. They have acted in a very free and candid manner in this business and I would not have you to behave otherways but leave it in some measure to themselves. Mr Irving's money was paid in May and your brother's about same time that the whole was advanced in one time if the business had been finished.

I wish you may soon get another warrant as we shall be obliged to raise more money than our own resources will furnish us with and I partly understand the Blackburn Bills C. & B. £1300 odd must be soon replaced. We must then probably be obliged to have recourse to our London friends. Little yet done in the sales of flax and no present prospect of doing much while Messrs H. and Co. sell so low. They are determined to put off their flax at any rate. They have sold their Petersburg 12 heads[1] so low as 40 shillings per hundredweight, 6 at 9 months which will mean at least 12 months credit. We find you have drawn of B. and B. for £150 at 10 days. We presume it was done with their concurrence and that they had so much collected on our account. Pray press them to extend their sales as much as possible and to get quit of the canvas on hand. Don't scruple to allow 10% for prompt payment. It is more eligible than reducing the price. If the navy cloth with A. and D. should be all sold we can very speedily replace it. I wish Mr Gale may put off the 300 Bolts with the allowance of 10% discount. Pray press him to exert himself in the sale of it. As your journey will be attended with a considerable expense, I wish you may be able to complete the sales which will be some compensation, and any agreeable connections you may form for future advantage may alleviate it. It would be pleasing to find that you could make any agreements or contracts for canvas sales without the charge of commissions. Mr Threlfall might perhaps assist you in it. You might in that case have a greater plea for a small reduction in price. Although the price of iron is so high in London we don't find it sells readily at £17–£17 10 0, the prices we ask, but ours is very strong, and not so saleable. Mr Hornby's was much slenderer and finer drawn. Indeed it was old sable[2] but they sold it at £17.5.0 to £18 per ton, a good deal of it at the former price. We don't think it will advance here before Christmas.

We have wrote to Hull to get the proper affidavits of the ship's sailing with convoy to enable Mr Anderson to procure us the returns, and we have wrote for Captain Davis's Protest which will answer the same end. We wish to find he gets our Riga insurance done by good men. Before you receive this you will, I expect, see Mr Swarbrick. I wish you to show him and his wife every civility you can.[3] He will acquaint you what bills he draws on us. He must do it as sparingly at present as he can; he knows our necessitous situation.[4]

Mr Earle[5] is very well satisfied of Mr Lansdown's sufficiency but does not say much of Stefanelli. I fancy we shall have no further correspondence with him as it may disgust our Leghorn friends.

If Mr Threlfall finds it necessary that we prove our debt against the estate of Mr Garford, we will do it on receiving his or your answer. You say what remains unpaid is £16. 16. 6. I am writing to Mr Feilden and expect to hear from him but probably he may write to you about his son's return. I fear he will not consent to it. Your sister and Miss Patten I believe go to spend their Christmas at Blackburn. They were out a-hunting yesterday and brought a hare back with them. Your Uncle Hankinson was their conductor. Miss Patten rode Little Orpheus, the first she ever rode single and Cecily rode her new nag which I bought of Mr Swarbrick. They were out with the Kirkham Dogs. You must remember me particularly to Zachary. I will renew my correspondence with him on your return. We have heard nothing from Mr Leigh, though I heard at Blackburn he was in the country. I have a letter from Mr Whitehead to-day but he does not mention him. I suppose he must be returned to London.

You will make my proper respects to Mr and Mrs Threlfall and all the family and to Mr Turner, Mr and Mrs Leigh and all my friends. Cecily and Miss Patten both join me herein. We have no letter from you to-day.

I am, Dear Will,
Yours affectionately,
Thomas Langton

Mr Kearsley has just gone from here. He has broke up Nathan Kearsley and comes back next week to attend the sale. He has behaved in a most humane manner to him.

There is an arrear of rent due to Mr Clifton of £10. 5. as per enclosed account which you must deduct from the account of Messrs Goring and Smith and gain a receipt upon it. Back of the Bill. You'll bring Mr Smith's credit back.

Mr Threlfall will go with you to the Duchy Office about the purchase of the Quit rents.

Cecily desires you will get Mrs Threlfall to buy her 3 or 4 pretty fine book muslin handkerchiefs and you'll pay for them and bring them with you. May bring me ½ dozen bottles of the Universal Balsam[6] with you and Mrs Threlfall will not forget the table linen.

Your house I expect will be finished all but the plastering and the windows putting in this week. I have palisadoed it very handsomely from the corner of Irving's field to the east end of the house from the lane. It looks spacious and noble and gives a good space before the house.

Notes to DDX/190/59 (following 63). To London, October 24th, 1780

[1] See note 2, DDX/190/62, 10 October 1780.
[2] Old sable—a superior quality of Russian iron, so called from being originally stamped with a sable.
[3] As so much depended upon the good offices of the overseas agent it was politic to be as accommodating as possible to Mr Swarbrick on his visit to England.
[4] Thomas Langton stresses again the financial problems of the firm.
[5] Mr Earle was one of the Earles of Liverpool, prosperous merchants, into whose family Will's son Joseph was to marry and in whose business Tom's son William was put to learn the ropes. Joseph became the first secretary of the Bank of Liverpool and William a banker and savant in Manchester, managing director of the Manchester and Salford Bank and treasurer and secretary of the Chetham Society.
[6] Although Thomas Langton was sceptical about the efficacy of doctors he was credulous enough to ask for a patent medicine, one of the many with which the age abounded, which purported to be a panacea, for what else could something claiming to be a 'universal balsam' offer?

(DDX/190/60)

Kirkham   October 27th, 1780

Dear Will,

We have yours of the 23rd instant. Have no account today from Mr Anderson of our insurance being done, but from his engagements must excuse it and shall expect to hear from him by Sunday's post. We will endeavour to get the certificates sent you from Hull of the ships sailing from Elsinore with Convoy etc., but they are often tedious in pushing these matters forward.[1] It may be some time before we can get the account of the general average[2] by the Providence adjusted but as we are charged with it we will furnish Mr Gale with the account. We do not see any probability of the damages by either Davis or Holland amounting to an average on the whole cargo, but we will send Mr Anderson the estimated account of the loss that he may get us an average on the £300 insured on the profits by Davis.[3] We have not made affidavit to Garford's debt and from what you say it will not be worth while, so shall waive it till your return and if then necessary may be done, but if there is not effects to pay the charges of the statute there can be no dividend expected. As to Rowley's affairs I never expect anything coming from thence. We have received a dividend of 10/- in the pound on our debt, except that part which we claimed upon Thackery and failed in our cause. This we should be paid if there is any effects before any other dividend is made and if we could obtain this we should come better off than I expected.

I wish you may get the 150 Bolts surveyed that you may take out a Bill for them. I hope you will succeed in it. We are much surprized to find so many of the Warrington people[4] are up and running down the prices of canvas so much. We must do the same as others and we wonder Messrs Anderson and Davidson should make any engagements for Messrs Gaskells[5] at a reduced price without acquainting you of it. Although you still adhere to the old price, they should have made you the offer of taking a share of the contract sale they made for Messrs Gaskells and of supplying a part of it. You must therefore immediately fix with all our agents to sell at 15s per yard for No. 1, at 12 months or at 14s per yard prompt payment. These are the prices which you say the Warrington people offer at, but if you can make an engagement for a quantity I would allow them 10% discount for money, which is more advantageous to the buyer than 1s per yard but you should see some of the chaps yourself and endeavour to make an acquaintance with them which may be of future advantage and at present may save the commission on the sales. Messrs Birkbeck, Blake and Co. and Mr Gale only charge 2½% commission; to the rest we pay 4% for standard Del Credere.[6] You should press B. B. & Co. to exert themselves in the sales for us and they should always advise us when they have orders from their other employers to reduce the prices. We are at present determined to sell, and would wish to do it on the shortest credit. As we are at present circumstanced it is most eligible to us and at all times we run the less risk of making bad debts by selling for speedy payment. We wish to have our canvas with A. & D. run off and you can order any quantity to any other person who can dispose it. We hope Messrs Dickinson and Lloyd will have put off the 8 Bales; if not you must give them liberty to reduce the price and allow 10% discount. By this means they may quit the whole together.

Pray have you ever seen Mr Hatton Turner? He was very friendly with me. Zachary knows him. I would have you form an acquaintance with him. He may befriend you in the sales or some other respect and you may give him encouragement by doing it. We shall be glad to give him some consignments in future. I dare say he would give you a list of some good chaps, *sailmakers etc.* or go with you to them upon a promise of this kind, but still you must be upon your guard with him as he is agent for most of the Warrington makers.

Messrs Hornbys have notice from Mr Loxham and their other agents of the price being got to 15s per yard No. 1 and I have no doubt they will give orders to sell on same terms if not lower. You must therefore exert yourself to quit our stock on hand.

No demand yet for flax. Surely it must come on after Christmas. If you see Messrs Atkinsons enquire the prices and particularly of Italian or Ancona hemp,[7] and you will have a good opportunity by being with Mr Rigby of seeing what is done, and getting some acquaintance with the dealers in iron. It may be of service another time.

I observe you intend returning with Mr Rigby through Oxford, but you do not intimate the time. I am going with John Leech[8] on Monday to Liverpool. He proceeds from thence by Manchester to Oxford unless some better opportunity should offer from Liverpool. I hear nothing from Mr Feilden about his son. Our Navy Bill is dated the 1st May 1779. Pray enquire when it is probable those Bills will be paid.[9] We shall have occasion for the cash soon. I wait to hear you have received the Bills £860 and how you succeed in the settling that business. Remember me to Zachary and all my friends.

I am,
Dear Will,
Most affectionately yours,
Thomas Langton

Notes to DDX/190/60. To London, October 27th, 1780

[1] Insurance matters were delayed as long then as today.
[2] See note 4, DDX/190/63.

³ As Captain Davis was a partner in several Langton ventures it is to be supposed that he was one in this as Thomas Langton obviously expects to share in the insurance payments.
⁴ The market for sailcloth was experiencing cut-throat competition.
⁵ Messrs Gaskell were Liverpool flax merchants holding a Navy contract in excess of those of the Kirkham firms.
⁶ A *Del Credere* agent was one who received goods on consignment, selling only to buyers able to pay, thus guaranteeing payment. (Italian *del*—of the; *credere*—to believe or trust.)
⁷ The Langtons did not rely exclusively upon Baltic raw material.
⁸ The younger brother of the unfortunate Savige, John Langton Leech M.A., who was to become the vicar of St John's Church, Blackburn and vicar of Askham in Westmorland. As this latter was in the gift of the Boltons some strings had been pulled, as he could not carry out both cures simultaneously although he held them concurrently.
⁹ Thomas Langton wanted cash for this bill. He had been waiting for it all summer.

(DDX/190/65)
Kirkham   August 13th, 1782

Dear Will,

We have yours of yesterday. Are sorry you did not get our letter in time, as you would have made a better bargain with Mr Lawrence. We shall incline to look on a while as to the hemp in hopes our Riga pass¹ may arrive at Hull. The conveyance from thence by Kildwick² will be very speedy. If you find the remains of the Petersburg 12 heads³ please you as to colour and quality, would have you ship it by the first canal boat to Freckleton⁴ as we fear we may be short for the long shades,⁵ and as it will clear the parcel it should be charged as low as any has been sold at. This will only leave the Petersburg 9 heads and the Riga 3 bands⁶ for sale. Pray do you hear any more of Roger Gaskell about the Livonia?⁷ You have annexed the weight of the hemp, which you'll fix in the books and allow the discounts.

You will also see we have shipped pretty largely by the Delight who would sail last night and will be with you in a few days. You'll order the 11 bales of Navy canvas for Anderson and Co., the bale for Messrs Gales and that for Birkbeck to be sent on board the Duke's flats⁸ to take the first conveyance by the canal boats.⁹ The bales for Newry[10] must be shipped by first vessel going there as it is wanted and the twine may remain for further orders when you can sell it. By the annexed particulars you may make out the entry on the canvas for Newry. We are glad to find the Leeward fleet[11] are [*] and as they were but four day's sail from hence when the vessel passed them we hope they are out of all danger of combined [*], especially those bound for St George's Channel.[12]

We have by this post a letter from Messrs Thompson and Rowlandson of Barbados advising that they would ship us £150 currency in this fleet by the Devonshire, Jos. Jackson, for Lancaster and in full confidence of its safe arrival we have determined to risk it.[13] You'll ship the flax on the Delight's return. We wish you would enquire of Terry Scott and Co. whether they have any account of the Barbados sailing with convoy that they can furnish us with the documents to enable us to get our return for convoy. You are to bring Mr Parr's whiskey forward with you but I shall scarce expect to see you before Saturday. If you cross Ribble, come in the cart and let the Guide take the whiskey. I would meet you if I knew the time and place. We have partly run matters over with Peter Kenyon. Have not time to add.

I am, Yours,
Thomas Langton

[*] Words obliterated.

Notes to DDX/190/65 (following 60)
To Mr William Langton at Messrs John Owen Parr & Co., Liverpool
August 13th, 1782

[1] Pass is the third quality of Russian hemp and was mainly used for ropes.
[2] Thomas Langton was now contemplating a canal dispatch with some enthusiasm. Kildwick is near Skipton.
[3] See note 2, DDX/190/62.
[4] See note 4, DDX/190/62, but the Rufford branch was now completed.
[5] Long shades appears to be a term of local application as it is not generally known in textile nomenclature. It seems from the context to apply to certain lengths of sailcloth. 'Shades' was sometimes used in Lancashire for 'sheds' but that use seems inappropriate in the letters.
[6] The Riga marks for flax included Risten Threeband, which was the flax rejected from the superior Drujana and Marienburg cuts. It had been judged by the brackers (inspectors) to be below the higher standard but was suitable for coarser linen.
[7] Livonian flax was denominated at Riga HD Hoffs Threeband. This flax was suitable for sailcloth as the fibre was strong and the yield on the heckle considerable. (See Warden, *The Linen Trade*.)

[8] The Duke's flats were the barges plying the Bridgwater canal. Once again Thomas Langton welcomed the canal as a means of transport.
[9] The bales would be conveyed by the Weaver Navigation to the Trent and Mersey canal for the first part of their journey to London, which by now could be reached by canal from the north.
[10] It is interesting to note that the firm was shipping finished cloth to Ireland, not importing flax. In the early days of Thomas Langton's father, Ireland was probably the sole source of supply for the firm's raw material.
[11] The fleet coming from the Leeward Islands.
[12] The approach to England between Ireland and the Bristol Channel.
[13] This was probably the first payment from America during the American War.

(DDX/190/66)
Oxford   March 2nd, 1786
3 o'th'clock

Dear Will,

We are just this moment arrived here and my first business was to send to Mr Richard Curtis who, I found, was the apothecary that my uncle made use of and who wrote the letter to me and I was much concerned to be told by him that he died on Tuesday morning about 5 o'clock, worn out with old age[1] and without any bodily pains or particular complaints. He told me he sealed up his bureau immediately and he proposes to call of me about 6 o'th'clock this evening to go down to the house to examine his papers. He does not know whether he made a will or not nor shall I be able to give you any further information in this letter nor what I shall do about his interment. If he has left no written or particular directions I shall most certainly bury here in the most private and decent manner. I should have been very happy to have seen him alive, but we must submit to the dispensations of Providence.[2] I will write you again by next mail, but the mail at present [is] up very irregularly,[3] and I fear you will not get this before Monday unless you send to the Office on Sunday. If so you may probably get two letters together, but I will write to Mr Hankinson and desire him to take the letter from the Office and send it you.

I must now give you some particulars of our journey which has been very tedious and uncomfortable having been twice dug out of the snow, and frequently obliged to take four horses. We got to Wigan on Monday evening, on Tuesday breakfasted at Warrington and proceeded directly forward, after calling of Mrs Bent, whom I referred to your letter, and Mr Lee, who declines taking any more yarn;⁴ at Knutsford we had no great signs of heavy snow nor till we reached Congleton where we found the Mail Coach had with difficulty passed to Newcastle with the addition of two horses and we were obliged to take four horses or be left on the road. Indeed in some places it was deep and troublesome but better than I expected from the account we had. We were however obliged to pursue our journey that day in the same manner to Wollerley Bridge, where we took up our lodgings and next morning with 4 horses to Sutton Coldfield. Here we ventured with 2 horses to Birmingham as we found the road began to be more tracked where we arrived safe to breakfast after travelling in the snow upwards of 25 miles. We got that night to Shipton, and this morning we set out with 2 horses, but it was in this stage we were twice assisted by a number of men with spades to make our way through the snow to Chapel House. However, we had resolution to pursue our journey to Woodstock where we made breakfast and dinner together and got here about 3 o'th'clock not a little fatigued. I hope not to be detained here long so that you need not write to me here but the letters you send may probably find me in London where I shall hope to have a letter from you. I am at present very unhappy in my situation, though I might expect this event, yet the first account shocked me as I wished to have found him alive. We have bore our journey much better than I could have expected, and your sister is very well only much tired. We have yet seen none of our friends but probably may before we sleep. Our best wishes attend you all. As this event will cause an alteration in all your drapes,⁵ it will be necessary you set about it and you will acquaint all our friends and if your aunt should not be returned you will give her a line to Bank. I will write J. Leech and desire him to acquaint my sister Bradkirk.

[Unsigned]

Notes to DDX/190/66. March 2nd, 1786

¹ Uncle Zachary Langton was eighty-eight when he died.
² Thomas Langton puts the duration of human life in the hands of Providence, the name he uses for God.
³ This is the only reference to the uncertainties of the post, and this complaint is obviously owing to the difficulty presented by the snow 'at present'.

Thomas Langton preferred personal delivery by friends where it could be arranged, but this was as much because of the saving in postage as anything.
[4] Even on the way to his uncle's funeral, Thomas Langton made the most of any opportunity to engage in business.
[5] The family was to observe the customary procedures of mourning.

(DDX/190/68)

Hull   June 10th, 1787

Dear Sirs,[1]

We arrived here last night and found Mr Thorley[2] was still at Harrogate and as it was after 8 o'th'clock and past the time of doing business we did not meet his bookkeeper in the counting house nor have I yet seen him. I went to enquire after Captain Davis of Mr Tong and found he was sailed that very day about noon, or perhaps not 2 hours before. Captain Maychel not yet arrived. My first enquiry was for Captain Appleton the Master of the Cave, whom we found, and who went with us to Mr Tong's, but previous to this we went to look at the Cave who was lying alongside the dock when Tom took a view of his cabin and his lodgings. I find these vessels are not calculated for the accommodation of passengers. The cabins are very small and confined. Tom is to have the Captain's bed of one side the cabin and the Captain his bed on the other side. He appears to be a very good tempered intelligent man and says he will do everything to make the voyage comfortable. Tuesday is the day he hopes to sail, but I think it will be Wednesday. He expects to arrive in 4 or 5 days at Elsinore after he sails. He delivers part of his cargo at Liebau, but hopes a single day will clear him there and that he may arrive at Riga in less than a week from his leaving Elsinore. Tom at present seems in pretty good spirits. As I have not seen anything of the Thorleys or their connections I can say nothing as to our flax etc. but I will write you again before I leave this place, when I may probably give you some account what route we mean to take in our return.

Mr Feilden is very well. We have hitherto had a very pleasant journey.[3] He joins me with Tom in our kindest regards to all our friends.

I am,

Dear Sirs,
Most affectionately yours,
Thomas Langton

Notes to DDX/190/68 (following 66)
Messrs Langton Birley & Co., Kirkham, Lancashire June 10th, 1787

[1] This letter, unusually addressed to 'Dear Sirs', was no doubt considered a business letter to the firm as Tom was embarking on a career abroad which was an extension of the firm's interests.

[2] Tom Langton was sent to the firm of Thorley Morison and Co. in Riga with the understanding that he would have a partnership at twenty-one. His daughter recorded that his partnership was deferred because he felt injustice was being done to another employee, but he eventually became a partner. He returned to England only when the international situation of the French Revolutionary Wars became a threat. He came home about 1800, marrying in 1802. Thorley Morison was one of the foremost merchant houses in Russia. (See Anne Langton, *The Story of Our Family, op. cit.*) Tom's brother, Will, in his genealogical notes in 1798 designated Tom 'one of the principal merchants' of Riga (DDX/190/103).

[3] Although the journey would have been cross-country and not on the principal turnpiked roads, Thomas Langton makes no reference to the condition of the roads or the inconvenience of travel. His 'very pleasant journey' is in sharp contrast to the dramatic discomforts made so much of by such writers as Arthur Young (see, for example, Young's *A Six Months Tour Through the North of England*, 1771, reprinted N.Y., 1967). This kind of evidence suggests that the state of the roads was not as deplorable as scholars long supposed and supports John Chartres' reinterpretation to this effect (J. A. Chartres, 'Road Carrying in England in the seventeenth century', *Econ. Hist. Rev.*, 1977).

(DDX/190/67)
Kirkham   April 23rd, 1788

Dear Will,

I received your letter in due course but you may judge of my surprize when I found you were going to make a longer tour and even to cross the channel for the continent without making anyone here in the least acquainted with your intention.[1] You may undoubtedly make it a very pleasant tour, but at same time I apprehend it will prove a very expensive one, and where you can have little prospect of its turning to any advantage in trade in our line of commerce. Yet I cannot help thinking if you pay a little attention to business but you will be able to form some connections which may be of use in the mercantile line, for at any seaport you come to, may easily find out how they are supplied with canvas and on what terms, so as to judge how the prices would stand with our long shades. If you could open a new market for them your journey might not prove useless.[2] I suppose they are chiefly supplied with Russia canvas, which is broader than ours, say about 27 inches, and will probably come lower in price in proportion, but I apprehend ours would be preferred as to its fabric. A good recommendation to a good mercantile house in any place would give you a suitable introduction and at the same time that your inquiries tended to our line of business I should endeavour to get a general knowledge of their imports and exports particularly in the West India products, say cotton particularly for to be acquainted with their prices occasionally might some time be of service,[3] as we are near enough to Liverpool to attend to the sale of any article.[4]

Don't forget to make particular enquiries how they are supplied with tallow, if their dependence is on the Russian or Irish market. There may be a prospect of a fall for the French market, and I think I have heard it has been frequently purchased in London for the French market. But I am afraid your companions, not being conversant in trade, will not give you opportunity of attending much to anything which looks like business.[5]

The Nancy does not yet appear at Liverpool. I fear the flax by her will be delivered in very rough condition, which will be a great prejudice to the sale of it, as well as to ourselves in what we work up. We shall probably go over there on its arrival and acquaint all our chaps of it in hopes of meeting them and making some sales, but there is little prospect of any advantage from it. We do not find yet whether Joseph Hornby purchased any more while he was in London, though we learn he made many enquiries after the article. We are well satisfied you did nothing further with G. & Bagnall. Their account is large, fully enough to trust them at one time. We wish Fenning may succeed in the sales he has in view as the credit of two to three months is no object where there is a prospect of vending a quantity and we think it will be as well to be forwarding a fresh parcel by the Rose on her return,[6] who is arrived at Lancaster, and will be loading again in about three weeks, by whom we shall send all the Navy canvas we can muster, but we are afraid we shall still have some objections made to the carding, which you should have enquired after, and given us full directions about it.[7] We hope to have one half the contract to ship by her, though it will not be the half of each number, only the half of the whole, and chiefly all the light No. 1 which we suppose is most wanted. We hope the Rose will be so soon after the Concord from Ribble who is not yet sailed that we shall scarcely think of taking out a Navy Bill before the Rose arrives and her canvas is delivered.

We observe what you say about Mr Fraser of Quebec. We will write to him and consider of the offer you have made him and we could make him up a fresh assortment more suited to his inclinations if he did not want it immediately.[8] We shall draw upon Dyer Allen & Co.[9] for the last small order. Joseph Hornby and his party came here yesterday but I have not seen any of them, nor have we had opportunity to examine into the papers you sent by him, or to learn anything particular from him.

Messrs Thorley of Riga has resold all our Drujana Cut[10] at 22 and a twelfth Rubles per [*] but no orders yet to enable them to transfer the Risten 3 band[11] though I hope they will do it. As to the Theasonhausen[12] we ordered it to be shipped for us to Liverpool and also the Lithuania Rakitzer[13] unless they could put it off at 26 Rubles per [*] which the present prices will not enable them to do. Hemp still continues very high there, much above our limits that we shall have no purchases of any kind further made for us there, and the money they have in hand will be more suitable to us, and more to our advantage to have it remitted to Petersburg than to be transferred back to Amsterdam,[14] which they were proposing to do. No late letters from Tom.

I am sorry to acquaint you that the Norfolk, Captain Gallilee, by whom we had engaged to ship 60 tuns of flax from Petersburg to Liverpool is stranded near Hull on her outward passage, that we shall have this lastage[15] to replace. She was to have been an early ship, and to have brought us an early supply. Captain Bigland and Captain Maychell are ready to proceed on their voyages from Hull to Portsmouth and we shall write very pressingly for their dispatch. Messrs Birchs' drafts for 8000 Rubles have already appeared, and no orders were given to Zachary for their acceptance.[16] We, however, wrote him immediately back to accept their drafts to the amount of £3000.

No further remittance yet from Jonathan Jones Sen. and Thomas Jones Jun. has remitted £50 [†] £100 further. Thomas Jones has

ordered £1 2 6 to pay you for his insurance [†] remitted Messrs
Heywoods[17] for the flax, and to Zachary for to cover all [†] under
acceptance for to the middle of June. We have got £1500 [?] from Mr
Feilden[18] and he offers a further sum if we want it. Have not called
yet upon the Liverpool bank[19] for [*] our balance that we have that
sum still in reserve.

Tom Parr was here at the time I received your letter and much
surprized as well as ourselves to hear of your excursion. Cornelius
and he went to spend a few days with H. Feilden at Blackburn. T.
Parr returned yesterday. We have nothing new here worth noticing.
All your friends pretty well much in the same state you left them. I
hope to hear from you before you leave Paris with what route you
propose to take on your return. If you could purchase a good
hogshead Burgundy *cheap* to ship directly to Liverpool would be
acceptable, but unless it is of the best quality would have nothing to
do with it.

All your friends here unite with me in our sanguine good wishes
for your health and safe return and with the same kind remembrance
to your fellow companions, Wolston Rd. (?) and Joseph.

I remain,
Dear William,
Most affectionately,
Yours,
Thomas Langton

As to your return, I leave it entirely to yourself. I hope you will not
make your stay too long though it is a season when business will be
going slack and it is too long a tour not to make it worth the trouble
that I should certainly not restrain myself to a few days time but
make a little excursion to see the country etc. But if you have any
opportunity of doing anything in business I hope you [*] it.

[*] Indecipherable.
[†] Paper torn.
[?] My query.

Notes to DDX/190/67 (following 68)
Monsieur Langton à l'Hotel de Muscovie, Rue de petits Augustins,
Fauberg St Germain, Paris April 23rd, 1788

[1] Thomas Langton's irritation is plainly evident. Will prudently kept his plans
of the French visit from his father until he was in Paris.

[2] Thomas Langton hoped that some advantage to the firm might yet be salvaged from so expensive a trip.

[3] It is likely that Thomas Langton himself would have felt such enquiries quite compatible with a pleasure excursion abroad. He had made visits of use to the business when he visited Ireland in his own youth.

[4] The commercial instincts of Thomas Langton were always strong.

[5] Even Thomas Langton suspected that defeat was likely.

[6] Although his father acknowledged that Will might have little opportunity to pursue the interests of the firm he nevertheless did not spare him an up-to-date report of the commercial situation. The Rose was a coastal vessel plying between London and Liverpool.

[7] This is a rebuke that Will had been neglectful and also evidence that the canvas did not always pass muster.

[8] Thomas Langton was willing to accommodate customers if a good sale was likely, except when there was a cash flow problem (cf above).

[9] Dyer Allen and Co., merchants, 28 Mincing Lane.

[10] Drujana Cut was the rejections of the Rakitzer.

[11] Risten Threeband was the refuse of the Drujana Cut and of the Marienburg Cut, themselves the rejects of Rakitzer and Crown Marienburg. The flax here had been judged by the brackers (inspectors) to be below the standard required for fine yarn. Crown Marienburg was the most superior of the Riga marks and much liked in Britain. (See note 6, DDX/190/65.)

[12] Theasenhausen Rakitzer was flax grown on the estate of Count Theasenhausen and was of a long harle, strong, even, clean and soft (see Warden, p. 328).

[13] Lithuania Rakitzer was inferior to the other Rakitzers.

[14] Amsterdam was the commercial capital of Europe.

[15] Lastage was the ballast which the stranded ship was carrying on her outward journey. There was virtually no trade in British goods in return for imports from Russia.

[16] Thomas Langton had his sons well trained not to act without his authorisation. By now Zachary was established as a merchant at 61 Bread Street. In the 1790 directory he appeared as a Manchester warehouseman.

[17] Arthur Heywood was a Liverpool merchant banker whose bank, known as Arthur Heywood and Company, was the sole Liverpool bank authorised to exchange newly coined money for old. He traded as a merchant under his own name. (See G. Chandler, *Four Centuries of Banking*, 1964.)

[18] The Feilden brother-in-law had helped in this second period of financial difficulty for the Langton firm. Reliance upon kin was considered preferable to reliance upon more remote business connections.

[19] There was no bank called the Bank of Liverpool until 1831. The Langtons earlier had used the Caldwell bank.

Select Bibliography

PRIMARY SOURCES

Lancashire Record Office

The Langton Papers, DDX/190/1–119
The Birley Papers, DDD/unclassified
Kirkham Apprentice Indentures, PR 827
Clitheroe Grammar School Accounts, DDX/22/5
The Account Book of a Physician in the Poulton-le-Fylde Area, DDS
Accounts for the medicines for Lancaster Prison and the Preston and
    Manchester House of Correction, QSP 2043/13: 2186/55: 2196/6

Public Record Office

Abstract of Navy Contracts 1775–93, Adm/106/3603–3624
British Register of Shipping, CUST 80 72/80 81

Liverpool Record Office (Picton)

The Letter Book of Sparling and Bolden, MD/219/1

Liverpool Record Office (Islington)

Plantation Registers, C/EX2

Guildhall Library

Sun Fire Office Policy 123211

Lancaster City Library

The Lancaster Port Book
Notes from *Gore's Liverpool Advertiser* 1776 onwards, PT8365
Notes from *Williamson's Advertiser* 1756 onwards, PT8366

Lancaster University Library
The Gillow Archive on microfilm. Copy of original in Westminster City
    Library.

Preston Harris Library
The British Courant or Preston Journal

The Hornby Papers
by kind permission of Mrs Jennifer Hornby

PUBLISHED PRIMARY SOURCES

Langton, Anne, *The Story of our Family*, privately printed, 1881 (only known
    copy in Manchester Local History Library).
Langton, Thomas junior, *Letters of Thomas Langton and Mrs Thomas
    Hornby 1815–1818*, privately printed by his grandchildren, Manchester,
    1900 (only known copy in British Library).
Langton, William, ed., *Early Days in Upper Canada*, Toronto, 1926 (British
    Library).
Philips, E. J., ed., *Journals and Letters from Upper Canada*, privately printed,
    Manchester, 1904 (British Library).

UNPUBLISHED THESIS

Borsay, P., 'The English Urban Renaissance', Lancaster, 1981.

ARTICLES

Chartres, J. A., 'Road carrying in England in the seventeenth century', *Econ.
    Hist. Rev.*, 1977, pp. 73–92.
Egnal, Marc and Ernst, Joseph A., 'An economic interpretation of the Ameri-
    can Revolution', *William and Mary Quarterly*, 1972, pp. 3–32.
France, R. Sharpe, 'The highway from Preston into the Fylde', *HSLC*, 1978,
    pp. 92–108.
Hamilton, Bernice, 'The medical profession in the eighteenth century', *Econ.
    Hist. Rev.*, 1951, pp. 141–69.

Jarvis, Rupert C., 'Liverpool statutory registers of British merchant ships', *HSLC*, 1953, pp. 107–21;

——, 'North Lancashire Shipping Registers', *HSLC*, 1958, pp. 124–5.

McIntyre, Sylvia, 'The mineral water trade in the eighteenth century', *Journal of Transport History*, 1973, pp. 1–19.

Money, John, 'The schoolmasters of Birmingham and the West Midlands 1750–1790', *Histoire Sociale—Social History*, 1976, pp. 132–53.

Plumb, J. H., 'The new world of children in eighteenth century England', *Past and Present*, 1975, pp. 64–93.

Schofield, M. M., 'Statutory registers of British merchant ships for North Lancashire in 1786', *HSLC*, 1968, pp. 107–23;

——, 'The letter book of Benjamin Satterthwaite of Lancaster 1737–1744', *HSLC*, 1961, pp. 125–67;

——, 'The Virginia trade of Sparling and Bolden of Liverpool 1788–89', *HSLC*, 1965, pp. 117–65.

Singleton, F. J., 'The flax merchants of Kirkham', *HSLC*, 1977, pp. 73–108.

BOOKS

Place of publication London unless otherwise stated

Aikin, J., *A Description of the Countryside Thirty to Forty Miles Around Manchester*, 1793.

Albion, Robert Greenhalgh, *Forests and Sea Power*, Cambridge U.S., 1936.

Anderson, B. L. and Stoney, P. J. M., eds., *Commerce Industry and Transport. Studies in Economic Change on Merseyside*, Liverpool, 1983.

Baines, Edward, *History of the County Palatine of Lancashire*, Vol. iv, 1835.

Baines, Patricia, *Flax and Linen*, Shire Publications, 1985.

Berg, Maxine, *The Age of Manufactures (1700–1820)*, Fontana History, 1985.

Bicknell, Peter, ed., *The Illustrated Wordworth's Guide to the Lakes*, Exeter, 1984.

Black, Jeremy, *The British and the Grand Tour*, 1985.

Brough, Anthony, *A View of the Importance of the Trade between Great Britain and Russia*, 1787.

Brown, H. G. and Harris, P. J., *Bristol Observed*, Bristol, 1964.

Brookbank, W. and Kennedy, F., eds., *The Diary of Richard Kay of Baldingstone near Bury, Chetham Society*, No. 16, 1908.

Carlisle, Nicholas, *Endowed Grammar Schools*, Vol. i, 1818.

Clark, Peter, ed., *The Early Modern Town*, 1970.

——, *The Transformation of English Provincial Towns 1600–1800*, 1984.

Clarke, M. L., *Greek Studies in England 1700–1830*, Cambridge, 1985.

Coleman, D. C., *The Economy of England 1400–1750*, Oxford, 1977 (1988 edn).

Cooke, G. A., *A Topographical and Statistical Description of the County of Lancashire*, n.d., c.1800.

Corfield, P. J., *The Impact of English Towns 1700–1800*, Oxford, 1982.

Crouzet, François, *The First Industrialists. The Problem of Origins*, Cambridge, 1985.

Crowhurst, Patrick, *The Defence of British Trade 1689–1815*, Folkestone, 1977.

Davidoff, Leonore and Hall, Catherine, *Family Fortunes. Men and Women of the English Middle Class 1780–1850*, 1987.

Davis, Ralph, *The Rise of the English Shipping Industry in the Seventeenth and Eighteenth Centuries*, Newton Abbot, 1962, reprinted 1972.

Dickson, R. W., *General View of Agriculture in Lancashire*, revised for publication by Stevenson, 1815.

Durie, Alastair J., *The Scottish Linen Industry in the Eighteenth Century*, Edinburgh, 1979.

Ehrmann, John, *The British Government and Commercial Negotiations with Europe 1783–1793*, Cambridge, 1962.

Evans, Eric J., *The Forging of the Modern State 1783–1870*, 1983.

Fishwick, Henry, *A History of the Parish of Kirkham in the County of Lancashire*, Chetham Society, 1874.

Floyer, Sir John, *A History of Cold Bathing Both Ancient and Modern*, 1722.

Hamer, Philip M., *The Papers of Henry Laurens*, Columbia S.C., 1970.

Hamilton, E., *The Mordants: An Eighteenth-Century Family*, 1965.

Hans, Nicholas, *New Trends in Education in the Eighteenth Century*, 1951.

Hanway, Jonas, *An Historical Account of the British Trade over the Caspian etc.*, 1753.

Harte, N. B. and Ponting, K., eds., *Essays in Honour of Julia de Lacy Mann*, 1973.

Holmes, Geoffrey, *Augustan Society. Professions State and Society*, 1982.

Holt, John, *General View of Agriculture in the County of Lancaster*, 1784.

Hutton, William, *A Description of Blackpool in Lancashire Frequented for Sea-bathing*, 1788 (R. Sharpe France, ed., 1944).

Jackman, W. T., *The Development of Transportation in Modern England*, 1962 edn.

Jackson, Gordon, *Hull in the Eighteenth Century*, Oxford, 1972.

Jones, M. G., *The Charity School Movement in the Eighteenth Century*, Cambridge, 1938.

King, Lester S., *The Medical World of the Eighteenth Century*, Huntington N.Y., 1971 reprint.

Kirchner, Walter, *Commercial Relations between Russia and Europe 1400–1800*, Bloomington, 1966.

Lenta, A., *Russia in the Eighteenth Century*, 1973.

Malone, Josephine, *Peter Newby*, Aylesford, 1964.

Margetson, Stella, *Leisure and Pleasure in the Eighteenth Century*, 1970.

Marshall, William, *Review and Abstract of the County Reports to the Board of Agriculture*, Vol. I, 1808, reprinted York, 1818.

Mathias, Peter, *The First Industrial Nation*, 1969 (1983 edn);

——, *The Transformation of England*, 1979.

Morris, Christopher, ed., *The Journeys of Celia Fiennes*, 1945.

Notan, Alex, ed., *Silver Renaissance. Essays in Eighteenth-Century English History*, 1961.

Nicholson, Norman, *The Lakers*, 1955.

Oddy, J. Jepson, *European Commerce*, 1805.

Orchard, B. G., *Liverpool's Legion of Honour*, Liverpool, 1893.

Parker, Irene, *Dissenting Academies in England*, Cambridge, 1984.

Parry, Keith, *The Resorts of the Lancashire Coast*, Newton Abbot, 1983.

Pimlott, J. A. R., *The Englishman's Holiday*, 1947.

Plumb, J. A., *The Commercialisation of Leisure in Eighteenth-Century England*, Shenton Lecture, 1974.

Pococke, Richard, *Dr Pococke's Journey into England from Dublin*, Camden Society, 1888–9.

Porter, Roy, *Patients and Practitioners. Lay perceptions of medicine in pre-industrial society*, Cambridge, 1985;

——, *Medical Fringe and Medical Orthodoxy 1700–1850*, 1987.

Pratt, K. A., *Inland Transport and Communication in England*, 1912, Putnam, Peter, ed., Princeton Studies in History, Vol. vii, 1952.

Randolph, George, M.D., *An Enquiry into the Medicinal Virtues of Bristol Water and the Indication of a Cure which it Answers*, Oxford, 1745.

Rather, L. J., *Mind and Body in Eighteenth-Century Medicine*, 1965.

Razzell, Peter, *The Conquest of Smallpox*, 1977.

Robinson, Howard, *Britain's Post Office*, Oxford, 1953.

Robson, Derek, *Some Aspects of Education in Cheshire in the Eighteenth Century*, Chetham Society, 1966.

Rolt, L. T. C., *The Inland Waterways of England*, 1950 (1962 reprint).

Shaw, R. Cunliffe, *Kirkham in Amounderness*, Preston, 1947;

——, with Helen Shaw, *The Records of the Thirtymen of the Parish of Kirkham in Lancashire*, Kendal, 1930.

Stone, Lawrence, *The Family Sex and Marriage in England 1500–1800*, 1977.

Sulivan, Richard Joseph, *A Tour Through Parts of England Scotland and Wales in 1778*, 1785.

Southey, Robert, *Life of John Wesley*, Vol. I, 1830.

Turnbull, Gerald L., *Traffic and Transport. An Economic History of Pickfords*, 1979.

Waddington, Ivan, *The Medical Profession in the Industrial Revolution*, Dublin, 1984.

Wadsworth, A. P. and Mann, J. de Lacy, *The Cotton Trade and Industrial Lancashire*, Manchester, 1931.

Walton, John K., *The English Seaside Resort*, Leicester, 1983;

——, *Lancashire. A Social History*, Manchester, 1987.

Warden, A. J., *The Linen Trade*, 1864 (1967 reprint).

West, Thomas, *A Guide to the Lakes by the Author of The Antiquities of Furness*, Kendal and London, 1778.

Whitehead, Maurice, *Peter Newby, Eighteenth Century Lancashire Recusant Poet*, Lancaster, 1980.

Whittle, P., *History of the Borough of Preston*, Preston, 1837.

Willan, T. S., *The English Coasting Trade 1600–1750*, Manchester, 1938;

——, *River Navigation in England 1600–1750*, 1964.

Willey, Basil, *The Eighteenth Century Background*, 1946.

Wilson, C., *England's Apprenticeship 1603–1763*, 1965.

Young, Arthur, *A Six Months' Tour Through The North of England*, 1771 (1967 reprint).

Index

NB. The footnotes are not indexed separately from the main body of the text (i.e. the form '15n' is not employed).

INDEX OF PEOPLE

Maiden names and qualifying information are given in square brackets. Diminutives are in round brackets.

INDEX OF PLACES

INDEX OF SUBJECTS